PRAISE FOR *STONE BLIND*

Long-listed for the Women's Prize for Fiction 2023

"Reframes the familiar myth of Perseus and Medusa. . . . Brilliant."

—*The Guardian*

"Beautiful and moving."

—Neil Gaiman

"Witty, gripping, ruthless."

—Margaret Atwood

"A fierce feminist exploration of female rage, written with wit and empathy. Haynes makes the classics brutally relevant."

—*Glamour* (UK)

PRAISE FOR *PANDORA'S JAR*

New York Times Bestseller
A Waterstone's Best Book of the Year

"Funny, sharp explications of what these sometimes not-very-nice women were up to."
—Margaret Atwood, author of *The Handmaid's Tale*

"Natalie Haynes is both a witty and an erudite guide. She wears her extensive learning lightly and deftly drags the classics into the modern world. I loved it."
—Kate Atkinson, author of *Life After Life*

"Natalie Haynes is beyond brilliant. Pandora's Jar is a treasure box of classical delights. Never has ancient misogyny been presented with so much wit and style."
—Amanda Foreman, author of *The World Made by Women*

"Natalie Haynes is [Britain's] muse."
—Adam Rutherford, author of *How to Argue With a Racist*

"With references to Beyoncé, Star Trek, Ray Harryhausen . . . the most enjoyable book about Greek myths you will ever read, absolutely brimming with subversive enthusiasm."
—Mark Haddon, author of *The Porpoise* and *The Curious Incident of the Dog in the Night-Time*

"Witty, erudite, and subversive, this takes the women of Greek myth— the women who are sidelined, vilified, misunderstood, or ignored— and puts them center stage."
—Samantha Ellis, author of *How to Be a Heroine* and *Take Courage*

DIVINE MIGHT

DIVINE MIGHT

GODDESSES IN GREEK MYTH

NATALIE HAYNES

HARPER ● PERENNIAL

NEW YORK • LONDON • TORONTO • SYDNEY • NEW DELHI • AUCKLAND

HARPER ⬤ PERENNIAL

Originally published in Great Britain in 2023 by Mantle, an imprint of Pan Macmillan.

FIRST U.S. EDITION

Designed by Jen Overstreet
Title page artwork © Happy Art/Shutterstock

Library of Congress Cataloging-in-Publication Data has been applied for.

ISBN 978-0-06-331467-2 (pbk.)
ISBN 978-0-06-337709-7 (library ed.)

23 24 25 26 27 LBC 5 4 3 2 1

*For my mum, who would give Demeter a run for her money;
and my dad, who always let me bring the thunder.*

CONTENTS

DIVINE MIGHT

INTRODUCTION

IF OXEN and lions and horses had hands like men, and could draw and make works of art, horses would draw gods like horses, and oxen like oxen, and each would draw pictures of the gods as if they had bodies like their own.

The philosopher Xenophanes wrote these words in the late sixth or early fifth century BCE, and I have been turning them about in my mind since I first read them as a student. At first, I was most interested in the rebuttal of the idea that God made man in his image. Here was someone pointing out what seemed to me a much more plausible scenario: we create gods that reflect us and the way we see ourselves. This is a reasonably uncontroversial view if you read Homer, as an educated Greek like Xenophanes certainly had. Homeric gods are petty, aggressive, and routinely obnoxious. They are immortal, hugely powerful, and have the emotional range and sense of proportion we might expect to find in a toddler deprived of a favourite toy. The smallest slight or setback meets with coruscating rage; gods don't hesitate to unleash violence on mortals and other gods alike. Not only did the ancient Greeks seem to have modelled gods in their mortal image, but they apparently chose their worst selves as the template.

It can be rather bracing for twenty-first-century readers to discover just how badly behaved ancient gods were: raping, murdering, demanding child sacrifice, and more. I'm often asked to explain why and how people would worship such immoral (or even amoral) deities. Why – if we create gods in our own image – didn't the Greeks design nicer ones? My answers to this question vary, but in essence I think that Greek gods are capricious and destructive because they are connected with the natural world, which can often be the same – more so in prescientific times than now. When a bolt of lightning or an earthquake could destroy homes and families in an instant, when a famine or plague could devastate your agriculture and your livestock, you might struggle to believe in a benevolent deity. Trying to make sense of the world you inhabit would force you – wouldn't it? – to assume that sometimes a god was choosing to punish you, exacting revenge on your people or your land. If your crops failed, you needed something to explain it, someone you could try to appease. Artemis and Apollo were connected with the sudden – otherwise inexplicable – deaths of young girls and boys respectively. Child mortality was high in the ancient world; no wonder people sought an explanation. Of course men had a god of war and of course women had a goddess of childbirth. Just because a lot of people died young doesn't mean anyone wanted to.

We also need to remember that worshipping a god doesn't necessarily require approval of that god. People might experience love or devotion as they made their offerings of wine and animals. But – at least for some worshippers – they may have been simply acknowledging a figure who had power over them, in the same way that one might pay taxes to a despot or tithes to a corrupt church, because of fear or social obligation rather than approval or love.

And these aren't questions that I am imposing on the past, of how we respond to stories of gods and goddesses behaving badly. There is a dialogue by Plato called *Euthyphro*, in which Socrates – Plato's mentor and inspiration – is in conversation with a man named Euthyphro, who prides himself on his understanding of what is godly or pious. Socrates – at the age of seventy – is about to stand trial for the crime of *asebeia*, impiety. So he is keen to solicit advice from someone who professes expertise in these matters. But Socrates is soon astonished to discover the reason for Euthyphro's trip to Athens is that he is bringing a murder charge against his own father. The Athenians didn't have a civic prosecution service, so crimes had to be charged by individuals. Needless to say, for a man to prosecute his own parent was vanishingly rare.

Socrates is even more puzzled when he hears that Euthyphro is charging his father with murder, and the murder victim isn't someone to whom Euthyphro is related. Here – though Plato couldn't have known it – we see a remarkable example of moral relativism in action. Socrates might be shocked by Euthyphro's lack of filial piety, but we probably aren't. As Euthyphro points out, it doesn't matter whether he's related to the victim or not; murder is murder. This is surely a position that we would share: one life isn't worth more than another because you're family.

And the more the story unfolds, the more sympathetic Euthyphro seems: a man working on his land got into a drunken altercation with another man and stabbed him. Euthyphro's father tied the drunk man by his hands and feet and threw him into a ditch. The man died of exposure. This makes Euthyphro even more unpopular with his family: his father had only killed a drunk murderer, and anyway, he didn't even kill him on purpose (just ignored him until he died of thirst or the cold). To Euthyphro's family – and apparently to Socrates – Euthyphro is the impious one, charging his father for a crime he barely even committed. But to a modern audience, I suspect Euthyphro's position looks like the ethical one.

When challenged by Socrates on his notions of piety and impiety, Euthyphro claims no less an authority than Zeus as his inspiration. Zeus is considered the *ariston kai dikaiotaton* – the best and most just – of the gods, he says. And they think that even though Zeus put his own father (who deserved it, by the way) in chains. Other Greeks might see filial devotion as the most ethical behaviour, but Euthyphro has drawn a very different lesson.

The subject only grows more unclear as the two men discuss things further. This is often the case when Socrates is involved. But the questions he asks are ones we might also struggle to answer: if you have multiple gods who disagree, how do you know what is right? Two equally powerful deities could make equally strong cases for opposing actions. So we might find ourselves at a loss for what the most pious or godly behaviour is, even before Xenophanes confuses us further by telling us we're responsible for creating such chaotic deities.

Xenophanes elaborates on his argument that gods are culturally specific (though his work survives to us only in frustratingly short fragments). He moves from the animal kingdom to the human one to refine his point: Ethiopians say their gods have black skin; Thracians say theirs have red hair. This is quite a radical view for someone writing two and a half millennia ago; a few decades later, the philosopher Protagoras apparently had his work burned in the agora (marketplace) because he claimed that it wasn't possible to know whether or not gods exist. But while Xenophanes doesn't stray into such inflammatory agnosticism – he doesn't question the existence of gods – he does still observe that the way we depict or perceive gods might reflect our own appearances and values more than the gods we claim to define.

When I read these fragments now, I'm equally intrigued by a second point. Xenophanes asks us to imagine what would happen if those animals had hands and could draw, if they could make works of art like people do. But he doesn't use the word *anthrōpos* – which means 'man', in the sense of mankind: humans rather than gods or animals. He uses the word *andres*. And this word means 'men', as opposed to 'women'. The Greeks loved to divide things into binaries: mortal and immortal, enslaved and free. So Xenophanes is considering not the way that humans in general depict gods, but the way that specifically men do.

As I said, his work is fragmentary, and I am not claiming Xenophanes as a radical proto-feminist. But I have found myself coming back to this line and wondering what it might mean if men – and only men – made images of the gods – and goddesses – they worshipped. Would it make a difference? A quick glance at art history and its abundant supply of naked and desirable (to men) female bodies suggests that it might. But would it change the nature of the characters depicted, or just their physical appearance? And – most interestingly to me – would male and female characters be created in different ways?

Let's look at what happened when a new set of gods was created in the mid-twentieth century. Superman appeared in 1938 on the cover of the first issue of Action Comics. He wears an all-in-one blue bodysuit, with the signature yellow panel on the chest and a large *S* in the middle. He has red boots, trunks, and cloak. He is highly muscled, and even if we didn't notice that, we can see how strong he is because he is holding a car above his head.[1] The following year, Detective Comics introduced us to The Batman.[2] This hero (whose superpower is having a vast fortune) swings on a rope, his large bat wings fanning out behind him. His face is covered by a mask with two pointed ears, and his bodysuit is grey, with black boots and trunks. We can only just see the bat insignia on his chest, because he has scooped up a villain by the throat: the man's hat is falling past his shoe as they swoop through the sky. Again, we are witnessing a powerful figure exhibiting his strength. Two seedy-looking men in the foreground – one holding a gun ineffectually in his right hand – are watching the scene in astonishment.

These superheroes were so popular that they swiftly inspired many more. In the autumn of 1941, All Star Comics gave us Wonder Woman. But you'd have to buy the issue to find out, because she isn't on the cover.[3] Inside, we discover her wearing the famous red bustier and blue flared miniskirt covered in white stars. She looks strong and regal, wearing mid-calf boots, a small jewelled diadem and a pair of indestructible bracelets. And so she should – she is an Amazon, after all.

But as the years pass and the cast of characters increases, the slightly skewed reality of comic books – with their predominantly male writers and artists – produces some strange quirks. Batman is always a tough guy, as we'd expect from a man who puts on a disguise to fight and prevent crime. And – in general – male superheroes are strong: Superman comes from another planet and is virtually invulnerable, Wolverine has retractable claws of adamantium and can heal super-fast, the Hulk is incredible in both size and strength. To be a male superhero means to be powerful in brute physical strength, or to approximate that with your Batmobile. Even Spider-Man – a plucky young hero – derives super strength from his encounter with a radioactive spider, though his speed and agility are probably more important.

Heroes need villains, though Greek gods were often capable of being both at once: supporter of one mortal and destroyer of another. The villains Batman meets are often as iconic as he is: the Joker, the Penguin, and the unforgettable Catwoman. Batman's male adversaries can be physically imposing, like Bane. But the more predominant theme is one of insanity. The Joker is the most notorious, but Arkham Asylum – the facility where many of Batman's crazed enemies end up – has literally dozens of inhabitants. I suppose we might wonder just why mental illness has so often been connected with villainy. Facial disfigurement is also used in the comic-book world as a shorthand for being evil, and a character like the Joker handily combines both.

But Batman's female opponents – who also occupy a fine line when it comes to sanity – are usually presented as sexy first and foremost, even when their professional qualifications are impressive. Poison Ivy – botanist and biochemist – uses her plant-controlling skills to make any man fall in love with her. Harley Quinn – psychiatrist – presents as a cheerleader gone bad: candy-coloured hair in adorable pigtails, tiny shorts, tight T-shirt, baseball bat. As for Catwoman, it is hard to imagine any other character in the history of cinema who has been played by so many super-sexy women, from Eartha Kitt to Michelle Pfeiffer. And that is before we remember her skin-tight black latex suit with its cute little cat ears.

Male characters – in the hypermasculine world of superheroes – convey power first; the rest comes later. We might also have the hots for Wolverine or Aquaman (just to pick two names at random while staring at the internet), but desirability is a secondary characteristic for these heroes and villains. Female characters, though, are always presented through the prism of sexiness: Wonder Woman was as strong as Superman, but she also needed to have – in the words of her creator – the allure of a beautiful woman.[4] William Moulton Marston created Wonder Woman with a conscious nod to Greek myth and wrote knowledgeably about the Homeric tradition in superhero narratives. He wanted a female hero who was superior to men in strength, but who also excelled in feminine attraction. Boys reading about an alluring woman stronger than themselves will 'be *proud* to become her willing slaves!' Marston later wrote, of his pitch to publishers. Desirability (at least in the mind of her creator) was integral to the character from the outset.

So – to return to Xenophanes – if lions had hands like men and could draw, their gods would look like lions. But what would the goddess-lionesses look like? Would they conform to male ideals of femaleness, as female characters so often do in human art? And if those lions were still drawing their gods in the twentieth century, I wonder whether their comic books would follow the same pattern as ours have. Perhaps lions too would create hypermasculine characters with super-leonine strength, alongside sexy lionesses with skimpy fur? I suppose we'll never know. Although I can't help remembering that in 1994's *The Lion King*, the hero, his father, his evil uncle, his two fun pals, and his adviser are all male. The female characters are: his girlfriend, her mother, and one hyena.

I still like comic books, incidentally. I like Catwoman and Wonder Woman, even if they were created as male fantasy figures. Batman is a male fantasy figure too – even if it's his gadgets and his wealth that are the dream, more than his muscles. The same is true for James Bond, of course: it's his lifestyle that is desirable, rather than his body (although you are free to desire that too). My point isn't that men create deficient art, it's that if we only have art created by men, we might want to bear that in mind when we respond to it. James Bond shows us who Ian Fleming (and, by extension, at least some of his readers) wanted to be; Pussy Galore just shows us who he wanted to bang.

The solution to filling in the missing areas of this partial picture is simple. Women can now make art, and we require no one's permission. We can create our own stories of all those gods and monsters and – if we choose – make them in our image.

There is no finer example than that of Lizzo and Cardi B, in the video for 'Rumors': two women at the peak of their success, hitting back at those who spread lies and cruel jibes about them online. They quote some of the more outlandish claims and agree – deadpan – that all this nonsense is true. They also reject the endless critique of their bodies and behaviour: for being too fat, too slutty, too outspoken. And they do this dressed as Greek goddesses. Lizzo strides across her set – a computer-generated space filled with giant vases, their paintings animated and cheeky – in a draped gold lamé dress. It's cinched at the waist with a gold belt, and she wears gold boots, gold jewellery, and a glittering gold manicure. Her backing dancers, also clad in gold, appear on top of Ionic columns. Lizzo gives us a cheeky wink as she dances among them. The subtextual message of these empowering images against the lyrics, which detail just a few of the hurtful comments directed at her, seems clear. If you don't acknowledge Lizzo as a modern-day Greek goddess, you should probably look again.

The camera cuts to Cardi B, perched on a throne, reading a scroll. She wears a white slashed skirt and a gold bikini top, slender gold chains draping across her pregnant body. Golden sandals are laced up her calves. A sculpted snake curls up the back of her seat. In case you missed the Freudian subtext here, she is also wearing a pair of gigantic gold aubergine earrings. (For those of you who haven't been dating during the emoji era, this cartoon image of an aubergine has become symbolic of male genitalia. Take this knowledge and use it wisely.)

The women now appear together in all their glory: Lizzo has changed into a white bodysuit with a magnificent headdress that creates gold vase handles on either side of her head. She is not just a goddess, she is a work of art. Cardi B has an equally spectacular headdress: an Ionic capital – the top of a column – made in sparkling gold. Those haters can tell her she has fake boobs if they want to: she is architecture, she doesn't require their approval. Whenever I am asked if Classics is irrecoverably elitist – male, pale, and stale, as the accusation goes – I am going to refer the questioner to this video.

And I'll watch it again myself for good measure. That way, when I return to poetry, paintings, and sculpture made by male geniuses for millennia, I'll have another view in my mind as well. So this is my answer to that question prompted by Xenophanes. When women make art like men do, their goddesses look divine.

THE MUSES

WE ARE in a museum which is packed with exhibits but empty of visitors. Has it closed for the day, or are we here early? As we pick our way past sculptures of Athene and other gods and goddesses, daylight streams through a roundel in the roof of a gallery ahead of us. The darkness that surrounds us is banished from this bright column. It illuminates a single vase, a huge piece of black-figure terra-cotta. This shows one of the most popular scenes in Greek mythology: Hercules (Heracles, to give him his Greek name) in battle with the Nemean lion. The lion rears up on its back legs. Its jaws are open and one forepaw reaches out to claw at Hercules. The hero looks unconcerned, and his right arm is drawn back, ready to strike. His left hand reaches forward, mirroring the lion. Perhaps he is about to grab at the thick mane.

Above this image is a geometric black border, and above that, on the neck of the jar, is a second figurative image. Five Muses all wear similar but subtly different white robes, draping down from the shoulders, belted at the waist. Each has finely dressed hair: piled in curls atop her head, flowing in waves down her back, tied into a topknot. Five is an unusual number for Muses – according to the second-century geographer Pausanias, the earliest writers (now lost) claimed three Muses, then four. By the time of Hesiod in the eighth or perhaps seventh century BCE – and our earliest source – there were nine.

The Muses face us. We don't know it yet, but later we'll realize that they are Calliope, Muse of epic poetry; Clio, Muse of history; Thalia, Muse of comedy; Terpsichore, Muse of dance; Melpomene, Muse of tragedy. Clio holds a scroll to represent history, and Melpomene carries a tragedy mask. They may not be the first thing we see when we look at the vase, but they're soon the only thing. Perhaps it's a little reminder that the word *museum* means 'home of the Muses'. They own this space, and we are their audience.

This is the opening sequence of Disney's 1997 movie *Hercules*. The music begins to play, and the Muses do what has come naturally to them for millennia: they sing, and they dance. They act as the chorus of a comic play: they react to the plot as it occurs – most brilliantly as the backing singers in 'I Won't Say (I'm in Love)', midway through the film. They also provide us with some backstory at the start. In this instance, it is the story of the Titanomachy: the war between the Olympian gods, led by Zeus, and the Titans, an earlier race of gods who rose up against them. Although Zeus proved triumphant, we soon discover that the Titans are waiting to be released from their subterranean prison to try again. Hades – god of the Underworld – is ready to orchestrate this attack, but a puny mortal stands in his way.

And so the stage is set for a hugely witty and sophisticated version of the Heracles story. Not only that, but the Muses have continued in a tradition which began in Hesiod's poem the *Theogony*. This introduces us to the idea of a set of beautiful goddesses who tell us in song about the earliest gods. The Disney Muses do just the same thing: our story actually begins long before Hercules, many aeons ago, says Calliope, as they warm up that opening number. She's about to tell us a pretty outlandish story. So can we take their word for it? Well, Hesiod certainly does in his poem. And we should too. Even if these Muses weren't singing a gospel number, we would surely know they can be relied upon from the title of the song: 'The Gospel Truth'.

The *Theogony* tells the origin story of the gods, the very beginning of Greek myth. Hesiod details the creation of the earliest powers – Chaos, Heaven, Earth – and then the gradual arrival of more familiar divinities: nymphs, giants, Titans. Gaia and Ouranos—Earth and Heaven – produce many children, including Kronos, who will be father to Hestia, Demeter, Hera, Hades, Poseidon, and Zeus. Their mother, the goddess Rhea, helps Zeus to overthrow Kronos, just as the latter had overcome Ouranos.

But before Hesiod can tell us about any of these internecine battles among gods and goddesses, he has to begin at the beginning. This is – for Hesiod and for us – quite a knotty ontological question. Does he start with the first divine power – with Chaos (or Chasm, to give a more accurate translation)? That's quite a challenge, when it's a gaping void that our minds can barely comprehend. And besides, who is he to be telling this story? Why should we trust him? This isn't just about the unknowability of the primordial gods; it's about the reliability of our narrator. Hesiod needs to begin his poem with something his audience can understand, and he needs to prove he is the man for the job. And what better way to establish your credentials than by appealing to the Muses?

The first word of the poem is *mousaōn* – Muses are part of this story from the outset. And because Hesiod is keen to emphasize his close connection with them, he starts by telling us a little about them and where they live. They are the Muses of Mount Helicon,[1] he explains, in Boeotia, in central Greece. It is a large and sacred mountain, according to Hesiod (who lives nearby), and the Muses dance around a flower-bright stream and an altar to Kronos. They bathe in one of several rivers, then dance their fine dances on the high reaches of Helicon. Hesiod mentions their soft skin twice: when he describes them bathing, and specifically their feet when they dance. Expectations of feminine corporeal softness have existed for as long as women have been in stories, it seems: do not imagine these barefoot dancing Muses have rough skin anywhere, even on their heels. I half expect them to start advertising moisturizer at this point. But don't be misled into thinking all this soft skin means they aren't tough. Hesiod also notes that they dance with strong feet.[2] There is also something withheld about these Muses: from the high slopes of Helicon, they go by night, veiled in mist. It is only now, when they are effectively invisible, that they begin their song.

So what do the Muses sing about, within the poem Hesiod has created? The good news for him is that they sing about Zeus, and Hera,

Athene, Apollo, and Artemis, and the whole deathless race of gods.[3] In other words, the Muses cover the same kind of material that Hesiod is planning to, with the same cast of characters. Perhaps another poet might feel a bit intimidated by this, but not Hesiod. Because the Muses themselves taught him *kalēn aoidēn* – fine song. Until his meeting with these goddesses, Hesiod was no poet, no singer. Rather, he was a shepherd, tending to his flock at the foot of the sacred Mount Helicon.

This lovely poetic device offers validation in two ways. Firstly, we must accept that Hesiod really knows what he's talking about when he describes the Muses dancing or being swathed in mist and moving through the dark night. He was an eyewitness: he literally saw and heard this for himself. Equally, if you were having any qualms about Hesiod's qualifications to describe what is to come – the creation of the very first gods, to which he definitely was not a witness – worry no more. Because Hesiod has been in direct contact with the most authoritative source there could be: the divine Muses. And on the off chance you might consider the sharing of this story to be a bit self-important, Hesiod is about to deliver one of literature's earliest humblebrags. Because when he does meet the Muses, they don't congratulate him on his potential to be a great poet. They don't admire his sheep. In fact, they criticize him: shepherds, they claim, are awful, just bellies. Lucky these Muses will never need woolly socks.

But then they reveal something that is genuinely troubling, for those who might seek certainty in Hesiod's account of how the world begins. We know how to tell lies as though they were true, the Muses explain. And we also know, when we want to, how to sing the truth.[4] But how is Hesiod meant to know the difference? And, by extension, how are we? One story of the Muses told by mythographer Pseudo-Apollodorus[5] has them giving the Sphinx her famous riddle (solved by Oedipus before he meets and marries Jocasta), so perhaps they enjoy being an enigma.

The more times I read this opening to the *Theogony*, the more I like it, from the mock humility to the assurance of authenticity. And I think this might be my favourite part of it. We just won't know, according to Hesiod's Muses, if they're telling us the truth or not. It'll sound the same to us, and they've just confessed that they sometimes lie. They have removed certainty from this account while appearing to bestow it, and they have admitted it right at the start. I find myself wondering whether if all ancient texts on the origins of gods had come with the same disclaimer, we might have had to work a bit harder to find things to fight wars over.

The Muses then give Hesiod a laurel walking stick, and they breathe a godlike voice into him. All traces of humility are gone now: the Muses are making Hesiod their favourite with gifts and talent alike. A variation on this scene was painted by the French artist Gustave Moreau in 1891. *Hesiod and the Muse* is now held in the Musée d'Orsay. This Hesiod is no empty belly, though, nor does he look like an ordinary shepherd. This version of the poet is young, androgynous, beautiful. He is naked, his finely muscled body draped only with a narrow swag of rich, jewel-coloured fabric across the hip. He stands with his weight on his right leg; his left foot is flexed and leg bent. There are flowers trampled beneath him, narcissi perhaps. In his arms is not the laurel staff we might expect from the *Theogony*, but rather a lyre, highly ornate and painted bright red, white, and green. The strings are gold. His slender fingers hold it against his naked torso. His expression is quite sombre, his lips slightly pursed as he gazes down at the instrument. All his focus is on the lyre: this young man is dedicated to his newfound art.

Nestling into his back is a Muse. Her golden hair is tied back in a complicated bun, and she too is gazing at the lyre. Perhaps that's why she is pressed up against this naked young man (for what it's worth, I have to think of him as being a whole other Hesiod from the one who wrote the poems, as I cannot square the appearance of this beautiful naked man with the verse of the other. I often wonder if I had seen this painting when I was younger whether I might have done better in my Greek poetry translation classes). She wears a draped red dress over a white tunic, and her gold lyre is slung behind her so she can more easily teach Hesiod how to play his.

And she is doing this with great care. Her outstretched right arm – resting on Hesiod's wrist to help him with his fingering – is as finely toned as his. She holds golden laurel leaves in her left hand, and Hesiod wears a wreath of green laurel. It's almost invisible, because the leaves echo the feathers of her beautiful dark teal-coloured wings, which are spread behind them both. In the distance, above the arc of the wings, we see a bright star illuminating a temple that stands atop a dizzyingly steep rock. Music is not just a gift from goddess to mortal; it is also a way to celebrate the divine, another kind of temple. The scene is intimate and sexy, a reminder that art – and, in particular, creating art – can be a deeply arousing experience.

In the *Theogony*, Hesiod's Muses tell him that he must sing of what is to come and of what has already been. His subject – never in doubt – must be the blessed race of immortal beings. But first thing and last, he must sing of the Muses themselves. Hesiod adds that they sing for their father, Zeus, and these are the subjects they celebrate: the beginning of the gods, then of Zeus, then of men and giants.

But Hesiod has told us that he's going to sing about the Muses first – rather than about what they sing about – so he does. They were born in Pieria, northern Greece, to Mnemosyne, Memory.[6] This is the moment to remember that the earliest Greek poetry was composed rather than written (Hesiod himself was composing his verse: the texts we have of his work are from a later period). So memory was a crucial skill for a poet like Hesiod or Homer, who would perform his work rather than publish it.

The ability to remember was recognized as crucial in the fourth century BCE by no less a writer than Plato, in his dialogue *Phaedrus*.[7] Socrates attributes the invention of writing to an Egyptian god, named Theuth (his name looks impossibly pleasing in Greek, like a shelf with chubby bookends: Θευθ). But though Theuth makes his case for writing, claiming it will improve memory and wisdom, he can't find any takers. King Thamus, who is judging the usefulness of Theuth's many inventions, is wildly unimpressed by these claims. Actually, he says, the opposite is true. People will come to depend on writing, which is external, and stop using memory, which is internal. In fact, writing will make us forgetful. It is typical of Plato – using the character of his tricksy mentor, Socrates – to construct a written argument dismissing the value of writing. However reactionary we might tend to find Plato, he does seem to have a point here: great feats of memory do ebb once writing becomes commonplace. Certainly now we would consider it an astonishing thing if someone could memorize huge chunks of the *Iliad* or *Odyssey*. And yet rhapsodes (performers of epic poetry) used to do this for a living. Reading might open our minds, but it doesn't do much for our memories.

And so Hesiod reveals the intimate, maternal relationship between memory and any form of creativity. The Muses are descended from two powerful deities: Zeus, the king of the Olympian gods, and Mnemosyne, a Titan from the generation of gods before him. Mnemosyne gives birth to her nine daughters on Mount Olympus, so the Muses can also claim two lofty sacred homes: Olympus, where they were born, and Helicon, where they showed themselves to Hesiod. They are – from the day of their birth – *homophronas*,[8] of one mind.

And then, after a bit more on their dancing and singing and general loveliness, Hesiod gives us their names, the earliest time they are recorded in any surviving source. Homer has an earlier mention of nine Muses, but he doesn't name them, though he mentions an individual Muse and plural Muses on several occasions – most memorably, in the first line of the *Odyssey*, which begins, 'Tell me of the man, Muse, who was turned every which way'. Homer is not relating the story of the shipwrecked Odysseus on his own; he needs the assistance of a Muse. If she doesn't tell him the story first, he can't share it with us, his audience. So although this line may sound rather peremptory, there is real concern underpinning it. Poets need Muses or they can't compose anything. As Homer says in the *Iliad*,[9] these goddesses are always present and know everything. No poet could hope to have witnessed all these events that span across vast reaches of time and space, mortal and immortal worlds. So if the Muses don't share things with him, he won't have a story at all.

In the final book of the *Odyssey*, Homer says that all nine Muses sang at the funeral of Achilles.[10] Agamemnon – speaking from beyond the grave – tells Achilles what happened in the aftermath of his dying. It is characteristic of their relationship that even after both men have died, Agamemnon still feels that Achilles has all the luck. You were blessed, Agamemnon declares, to die at Troy, far from Argos. I feel sure you can guess where Agamemnon died, because his grudge-bearing is barely subtextual. It's right there on the surface for all to see. Why might Agamemnon be so resentful? Well, according to his account here, he died at the hands of his wife's murderous boyfriend, Aegisthus. There is no mention of his funeral, and we can assume it was perfunctory at best. Whereas Achilles – as Agamemnon relates at some length – had a grand send-off, attended by divinities including the sea nymphs and the Muses. All nine of whom sang lamentations for him. So this is what it means to be the son of a goddess and die a hero's death: the Muses themselves will sing at your funeral.

But we don't know the names of these Muses until Hesiod tells us in a great list.[11] Clio and Euterpe and Thalia and Melpomene and Terpsichore and Erato and Polymnia and Ourania and Calliope, who is the most important: she accompanies kings, he adds. In this list, the Muses have not yet been allotted their specialisms – something that doesn't happen until later accounts – but eventually they will come to cover everything from history writing to sacred hymns, dance to epic poetry. So Terpsichore is not yet the Muse of dance, and Polymnia (also called Polyhymnia) isn't yet in charge of sacred songs. They all share responsibility for making men persuasive, calming, and skilful in their speech. Literally, Hesiod says, they pour sweet dew onto tongues.[12] This is the Muses' divine gift to men, since it eases grieving hearts. For anyone who has ever soothed a broken heart by playing a sad song (or even a happy one, though I can't imagine who would do such a thing), we know that in this at least, Hesiod is bang on.

It's here we finally get a real sense of the Muses' power. Hesiod has already described them as charming and beautiful and soft-skinned, always dancing. But would Homer really need to begin the *Odyssey* by appealing to a lovely, dancing goddess? What he needs – just as Hesiod does – is talent, charm, persuasiveness, the ability to make things better in the hearts of his listeners with only the power of his words, his song. And these goddesses have that power, if they choose to share it. No wonder poets throughout history have petitioned them.

Hesiod concludes this brief section on the Muses by begging them to share their divine gift with him. He wants to compose his great poem about the gods, and he needs their help to do so. Tell me this story from the beginning, he begs. Tell me which of the gods came first. And so, after he opens his poem with an appeal to them as local goddesses of Mount Helicon, after his reverent description – as a local boy made good – of their dancing and homes, after his listing of their names, his praise of their talents and generosity and finally his impassioned plea for assistance, how can they refuse?

It is a quirk of the Muses' generosity that we only hear about them if they grant a poet's wish. You or I might beg them for divine inspiration and they might refuse us. They can't say yes to everyone, after all. But then, of course, we wouldn't find the words or ideas to compose our epic poem (or history, tragedy, etc.), so the work would never be created. In other words, no one can claim to have produced any work without their help: the very fact that it exists proves they smiled on us. If they don't accede to our request, there is nothing to bear witness to the refusal. Just a blank page, an empty stage, a silent lyre. Poets and artists throughout history have begged the Muses for assistance because the alternative is divinely bestowed writer's block.

This is what happens in a story from Book Two of the *Iliad*.[13] Describing a place – Dorion – in the Peloponnese, Homer remarks that this is where the Muses stopped the song – *pausan aoidēs* – of Thamyris the Thracian. Thamyris (also called Thamyras in different sources) makes an astonishingly stupid boast. Convinced of his prowess at singing, he claims he would beat the Muses in a music competition. No good ever comes of mortals boasting that they can beat the gods at anything. But poor Thamyris has not learned this basic lesson, and the payback is instant. Angered, Homer tells us, they paralysed him, took away his sweet-sounding song, and made him forget how to play the cithara (a stringed instrument, like a lyre).

The same story is told by Pseudo-Apollodorus in his *Bibliotheca*, but here the stakes are even higher, and the penalty for failure is correspondingly more terrible. In this version, the beautiful Thamyris again challenges the Muses to a musical contest. The Greek phrase describing this shows just what a dismal idea it is – *mousikēs ērise mousais*.[14] Obviously music belongs to the Muses – the words are as close in Greek as in English. And only the verb – meaning to challenge or wrangle or cause strife – separates them. This cannot end well.

Contests in Greek myth – and to an extent, in Greek history – are often fought for glory rather than material gain. There are exceptions, of course: the entire plot of Sophocles's *Ajax* is centred on the shame experienced by Ajax when he loses a contest to win the armour of the late Achilles. Odysseus bests him in a battle of bodies and wits and Ajax turns on his comrades, and then himself. But theatrical and sporting contests – from the Dionysia to the Olympics – were rarely rewarded with gold or other treasures. The most popular playwright might win a laurel wreath, say. Or Pindar (the early fifth-century BCE lyric poet from Thebes) might write an ode centred on a victorious athlete's tremendous sporting prowess.

But there are some interesting exceptions – in particular, contests for the prize of marrying a desirable woman. Penelope sets up just such a contest in Book Twenty-one of the *Odyssey*. Keen to avoid remarriage, she suggests that she will only wed a man who can string Odysseus's bow and shoot an arrow through twelve axes.[15] She explicitly refers to marriage with her, the queen of Ithaca (by which a man might acquire the status of Ithaca's king, we may suppose), as the *aethlon*–prize. The suitors all prove too feeble or unskilled to string the bow, enabling the disguised Odysseus to do so, and then to kill the men who have been pestering his wife.

Thamyris, however, has set his sights both higher and lower than marriage with the ideal wife of the *Odyssey*. The prize he chooses to be at stake in his contest with the Muses is the opportunity to have sex with all nine of them. I tend to like a man with ambition, but there are limits, and poor Thamyris has exceeded them. Apparently blind to the risk he is taking, he accepts their terms: yes, if he proves the better musician, he can have sex with them all (the Greek doesn't specify whether this would happen singly or collectively). But if he turns out to be less good than they are, they can deprive him of whatever they choose. There is no suspense at all in this narrative: how could there be? Thamyris has exhibited archetypal hubris, believing himself superior to goddesses. The Muses are better musicians, Pseudo-Apollodorus continues, and they take his eyes and his capacity for lyre-playing. Muses are not to be messed with.

Sophocles wrote a play based on this story, although only some fragments survive. *Thamyris* is probably the same play as one referred to in a couple of ancient sources as *The Muses*. Sadly, we don't know whether the Muses were individual characters or formed the chorus (although choruses usually had twelve or fifteen members, and there are never more than nine Muses). But we do know that Sophocles himself appeared in the first production, playing the cithara. According to one ancient biography of the playwright,[16] this is why his portrait on the Stoa Poikilē – a colonnade, or porch, built in the fifth century BCE on the north side of the agora or marketplace – showed him holding a lyre. You can still see the ruins of the Painted Stoa in Athens today, although Sophocles's portrait is long gone.

It's easy for us to forget that large parts of tragedies and all the poetry by Hesiod and Homer were not just performed but sung. So the Muses influence the creators on multiple counts: it isn't enough to be able to compose beautiful verses; you also need their help with your musical performance. And this Sophoclean version of Thamyris's story – even though the fragments we have are so few – is a perfect illustration of this. These poets depicting the Muses in their work are relying on those same Muses for their writing skill and their performing ability, and the loss of either would be disastrous. Is losing his eyes a much worse fate for Thamyris than losing his ability to play the lyre? How would it work? Would you forget how to play, and that you had ever been able to? Or would you simply lose the genius and keep the memory of it? Become Salieri to your own former Mozart? It's a brutal fate either way.

Comparatively few stories of the Muses survive from the ancient world, and they often show similar examples of instant and terrible revenge for hubristic bets and contests. The Sirens – who are the high watermark of destructively powerful song for us: *siren song* is a rare phrase that has leapt into regular language from myth – lose the very feathers from their wings when they propose and then fall short in a contest with the Muses.[17] Not only do the Muses take the Sirens' feathers, but they decorate themselves with them: a casual, ornamental triumphalism.

But the Muses might have a good reason to be so defensive. In Book Five of Ovid's *Metamorphoses*, his vast compendium of transformations in Greek myth, Minerva (the Roman name for Athene) visits the Muses on Mount Helicon. She's keen to see the spring which formed at the spot where Pegasus – the winged-horse offspring of Medusa and Poseidon – kicked the ground with his hoof. The Muses are delighted to show off their new water feature, and one of them pays Minerva a compliment: she could join the Muses if she chose, because she has placed a high value on the arts. And the Muses' life would be fully delightful if, this unnamed Muse says, they were completely safe.[18] But everything terrifies their virgin minds, she continues. The awful face of Pyreneus still appears before her eyes, and her mind has not yet recovered. Now, we might try to diminish this experience as an exaggeration for poetic effect, but it's hard to see why. The Muse is very clear in describing what sounds a lot like post-traumatic stress: constant anxiety and repeatedly seeing the face of a man who has obviously scared her.

She continues with the story. The Muses were going to their temple on Mount Parnassus, which meant travelling through land Pyreneus controlled. He approaches them *fallaci . . . vultu* – literally with a false face. He addresses them as the daughters of Memory. He knew who we were, she adds. He begs them to stay with him, because it's raining. Gods have visited lesser homes than his, he says. The Muses are moved by his words and the weather, and they go inside. When the wind changes and the rain stops, the Muses try to leave. But Pyreneus locks them in and *vimque parat*[19] – prepares to use force, i.e., to attempt rape. The Muses use their wings to escape him. Pyreneus follows them, climbing to the top of a high tower. Whichever way you go, he says, I'll take the same path.

Both his language and his behaviour make him seem somewhat deranged at this point, like a villain in a melodramatic thriller. And the

Muse describes him as *vecors* – mad. He obviously cannot pursue nine winged goddesses, separately or together. He falls on his face, quite literally and from a great height, smashing his bones. He hits the ground and, as he dies, stains it with his wicked blood.

The Muses have clearly been scarred by this encounter. Their superiority to their assailant is never in question, as they tell the story: they are immortal, they can fly, they outnumber him. But his attempted assault on them has proved no less distressing because of this. Even at this unspecified time after the event, the memory of it keeps the Muses from having a wholly blessed existence. Instead, they live with a constant fear that they might be unsafe, or become so. The consequences of an attempted attack can be felt in many ways, even for a goddess.

At this point, the Muse is interrupted by the sound of flying wings and chattering voices. In the trees above them nine magpies have perched. Minerva is perplexed for a moment, because the voices sound so human. But the Muse explains to her that these magpies are new-comers.[20] They were mortal women, daughters of the wealthy landowner Pierus and his wife, Euippe. And they have found themselves in this birdish predicament because they – like so many others – lost a contest with the Muses. This crowd of stupid sisters (the Muses never promised you an unbiased account) travelled to Parnassus and declared war on the goddesses. The phrase she uses is *committit proelia* – join battle. And you can see what she means when one of the daughters of Pierus starts talking. Stop deceiving the uncultured mob with your empty sweetness, she says. If you trust your talent, you'll compete against us. We won't be beaten in voice or in skill. And we number nine, just like you. If you lose, you give us two sacred springs. And if we lose, we'll give up our home and our lands. The nymphs can judge the competition.

Now, where I come from – and Birmingham has very little in common with Mount Parnassus in other regards – this is fighting talk. What is it about the Muses that make men and women alike think they can compete with them, conquer them? They are both appreciated (by poets in their opening lines) and underestimated (by musicians, Sirens, sisters, and more). They are not the only goddesses to be treated in this hubristic way: Niobe compares herself to Leto, Arachne compares herself to Athene. We'll see more of these stories of unwise mortals and their attempts to be superior to the gods in later chapters. But it does seem to happen to the Muses with uncommon frequency. I wonder if it is because their qualities are almost designed to lull us into a false sense of safety: they're pretty, they dance, they sing. These characteristics are all possessed by other goddesses or even mortals in more threatening ways: we're often told that Aphrodite and her favourite half-mortal woman Helen of Sparta (later, Helen of Troy) have a destructive quality to their beauty, or at least inspire a destructive (or self-destructive) quality in the men who desire them. The Maenads, or Bacchae – the women possessed by a religious frenzy for the god Dionysus – have a destructive quality too, when they dance. They rampage through the wild forests and mountains, and any man with sense keeps his distance, because the alternative is very likely to be death, torn limb from limb by these super-strong, divinely inspired women. Meanwhile, the Sirens are so lethal to sailors that only one man – Odysseus – hears their song and lives to tell the tale. And that is only because he has followed the advice of the witch-goddess Circe and ordered his men to tie him to the mast of his ship so he physically cannot throw himself into the sea when he feels the overpowering urge to do so.

The Muses don't come across as dangerously beautiful, but rather – as Hesiod presents them – as beautifully pretty, part of a gorgeous bucolic landscape. Their song doesn't make men drown trying to hear more; it inspires them to create poetry of their own, to play and sing and compose. Their dancing doesn't even make their feet rough, let alone result in any limb-tearing. Though the Muses referred to by Pindar are *ioplokamōn*,[21] they have hair the colour of violets, which does at least give them a pleasingly Gothic vibe.

So if we were trying to describe the Muses in contrast to these other characters, we might think of them as constructively beautiful, rather than destructively so. They make us better by their existence. Because they have songs and dancing and musical talent, so might we if we ask them very politely at the beginning of our creative endeavour. But some people cannot see such generosity without wanting to possess it like Thamyris, defile it like Pyreneus, or overthrow it like the daughters of Pierus. And it is when threatened – in either their bodily integrity or their reputation – that the Muses snap and take their revenge.

The Muses don't want to compete with the daughters of Pierus; they consider it *turpe* – shameful[22] – to have this contest, but more shameful to surrender. The nymphs agree to be the adjudicators and promise on their rivers (the nymph equivalent of swearing on a sacred book) that they will judge fairly. The first Pierid steps up to sing and delivers the story of the Gigantomachy, the war between gods and giants. In her version – contrary to the received version the Muses might be familiar with – the giants are victorious over the gods. Again, it is hard not to see this as an early salvo in a war you cannot hope to win. Not only are they taking on the Muses in their own backyard, but they're singing songs about immortal gods and goddesses being losers.

In response to this performance, Calliope steps up to deliver her divine riposte. She begins by reminding her audience that one giant – she names Typhon, though other sources say Encelados – is imprisoned beneath Mount Etna in Sicily. His subterranean writhing and fuming are what cause Etna's sporadic eruptions. She then goes on to describe the abduction of Proserpina – Persephone, to give her her Greek name – by Pluto, or Dis or Hades. This is a well-worn tale, in which a god is a sexual predator and a goddess – Proserpina's mother Ceres, or Demeter – is a tireless heroine: we'll look at it in more depth in Demeter's chapter below.

One of the qualities a good performer must have is to know her audience, and Calliope includes a whole section on how the nymph Cyane tries to prevent Pluto's kidnap of Proserpina. Cyane stands up to him and tells him off, reminding him he should have sought Proserpina's consent and her mother Ceres's permission. The nymph then refuses to let him pass. Pluto uses divine force to blast a new route through to Hades. Cyane is so distressed by his behaviour that she melts into the water in which she lives.

Now, it hardly needs saying that if your song is being judged by nymphs, it is no bad thing to include a tragic section on a brave nymph who tried to help save the life of an innocent goddess from the sexual predations of her uncle. Cyane behaves in a sisterly way to Proserpina, so perhaps the nymphs judging this contest will extend the same courtesy to Calliope. The Muse then continues with her theme of female solidarity.

Ceres begins searching for her stolen daughter and – who could have predicted it? – another nymph, Arethusa, offers help. She saw the frightened Proserpina being taken down to the Underworld to become its queen. With this information, Ceres can approach Jupiter, the king of the gods, and demand the return of her daughter. Jupiter is no help, preferring to define Pluto's sustained sexual assault on Proserpina as an act of love.[23] But Ceres refuses to give up, even when all seems lost. The compromise which Jupiter settles on – that Proserpina can return for only part of the year, which is why we have cold, dark months without her in winter – is the grudging response of male deities having to accommodate a goddess who will not give up.

Meanwhile, Calliope is still not done. She returns to the subject of nymphs and has Arethusa recount her own story of trying to avoid sexual assault, at the hands of the river god Alpheus. She – like Cyane – transformed into water to elude rape at the hands of this god, who was much stronger than she. Calliope then tells one last story of the duplicitous king Lyncus – who tries to kill a young man, Triptolemus, whom Ceres protects – and her song is finally over.

After this virtuoso performance of musical storytelling, coinciden-tally featuring heroic and tragic nymphs, the result of the contest is never in doubt. The daughters of Pierus have been almost entirely forgotten by this point – we have been so caught up in the tale within the tale. But the unnamed Muse is still talking to Minerva about Calliope and the con-test, and she explains that the nymphs unanimously awarded victory to the Muses. The Pierids do not accept defeat lying down[24] but start taunt-ing the Muses (and presumably also the nymphs). Our narrator explains that she now spoke out, telling off the Pierids for adding insults to their preexisting crime. Our patience has run out, she says, and we'll punish you as our anger demands. The women laugh at this Muse and scorn her threatening words. And as they laugh, their skin grows feathers, their faces form beaks, and their arms become wings. There's nothing to stop you picking a fight with the Muses, but you may find yourself changed into a magpie if you do.

If you want to show the Muses proper respect, it's pretty clear that you shouldn't challenge them to any sort of musical duel. The more ap-propriate thing to do is address a poem to them, as poets throughout the ages, from Homer to Byron, have done. But what if you admire the Muses yet don't aspire to poetic creativity yourself? Then you might choose instead to do the same as the owner of the Villa Moregine. In 1959, a motorway was being built to connect Naples and Salerno. Six hundred metres south of the Stabian Gate of Pompeii, a villa was dis-covered. It featured a large courtyard, with at least five triclinia – dining rooms. On the walls of these formal dining spaces were breathtaking frescoes. Their perilous location near the roadworks led to the frescoes being moved into the large palaestra (exercise ground) in Pompeii, where they are now displayed. The space known as Triclinium A showed the Muses alongside Apollo.

The background is a dark rich red, known as Pompeian red – these rooms would have been an intense dining space. The Muses wear pale,

floaty dresses and laurel wreaths. Some stand at the top of ornately decorated green and gold columns, while others simply float in the air. By
the time these frescoes were painted – the middle of the first century CE,
certainly before the year 79 – the Muses were well established in their
different specialist fields. They have props to make this clear to the casual diner: Clio is holding a scroll to represent history, Terpsichore has
a lyre in her hands, Erato strums a cithara. Thalia holds a grotesque
comedy mask and Calliope bites on the end of her stylus, a writing tablet
open in her left hand – even the great Muse of epic poetry needs a moment to think of the right word occasionally, perhaps. Euterpe has a pair
of flutes, one in each hand; Melpomene gazes upward, a tragedy mask in
her left hand. Ourania holds a beautiful glowing sphere to represent the
heavens. Polymnia has sadly not survived to the present day.

These gorgeous frescoes raise an interesting question, however:
where is the Muse for painting? We're accustomed to seeing references
to the Muses in work which they directly inspire: poetry, plays, song.
The Muses sing, so Hesiod sings. But while these paintings are inspired
by the Muses – their appearance, their beauty – the artist did not need to
appeal to a specific Muse to help him with his creation. Unlike the Sophocles play about the Muses' powerful revenge on Thamyris, this is not a
work that proves its own divine assistance by existing at all. The painter
could, presumably, have painted similar portraits of nymphs or Graces
without running the risk of offending his own inspirational deity.

A second point to note is that the Muses – for all their focus on
the arts – are also involved in scientific endeavours. If you want to be
a successful astronomer, it will be Ourania to whom you must appeal.
The Muses have chosen to inspire scientists as well as artists. We're so
accustomed to a dialogue which pits these two areas of study against
one another – utility versus beauty – and yet the Muses wouldn't recognize this division. Why wouldn't you want your scientific pursuits to be
beautiful? And why wouldn't you apply forensic accuracy to your dance

or song? The distinction that only sciences are useful and only arts are spirit-enhancing is a nonsensical one. I couldn't write as much without scientists having designed my computer. And some of those scientists must want to read about Greek mythology after a long day at work. These Muses always remind me that scientists and artists should disregard the idiotic attempts to separate us. We are all nerds, in the end.

These frescoes are also a magnificent reminder of who is the real talent when it comes to creating an artistic or scientific performance. The Muses are the original creative force, and the artist must appeal to them for help: that is the attitude taken by Hesiod, by Homer. As we've seen, Hesiod spends the whole opening section of his poem explaining how he is able to talk about the gods at all: it is the Muses who inspire him, who give him his gift. Before then, it was all just sheep for this shepherd. And as for Homer, he doesn't even pretend he is the one in control. 'Sing, goddess,' he pleads. 'Tell me, Muse.' His best bet as a mortal rhapsode, it seems, is to try to capture something of their divine magic. Compare his opening lines with that of his great imitator, Virgil, in the *Aeneid*. *Arma virumque cano* – I sing of arms and the man. By the time Virgil is composing his epic, in the late first century BCE (Virgil died with the poem unfinished in the year 19), he is assuming responsibility for the words and the Muses have taken a small step back. Virgil still needs and wants divine encouragement, but he is the creator.

Gradually, the request to the Muses to smile on our creative endeavours becomes less a prayer and more a formality, a way of explaining to your audience that you are composing a certain type of poem, or perhaps taking yourself a certain kind of seriously. It becomes a mechanism to show your readers or audience that we should pay attention now. Perhaps it always was, but Muses shed some authority along the way.

By the twentieth century, Muses have had their creativity clipped away altogether. Poets, artists, and musicians still have muses, but the role is largely to be pretty and make a man creative. There are occasional

male muses who inspire both male and female artists (Leigh Bowery and
Lucian Freud, Aaron Taylor-Johnson and Sam Taylor-Johnson), but the
trope tends to be a male genius, such as Picasso, inspired by his tormented
muse, one of whom was Dora Maar. Maar was the inspiration for Picasso's *Weeping Woman*, one of many of his portraits to depict her in a state
of distress. Picasso described women as 'machines for suffering', so it's
perhaps not a surprise that he seemed happy to contribute so fully to their
unhappiness.[25] Their relationship was always troubled and marginalized,
and Maar's skills as both photographer and painter were largely overlooked
until recent exhibitions allowed her to be rediscovered as something more
than a man's inspiration. In Grace Nichols's excellent poetry collection, *Picasso, I Want My Face Back*, she gives voice to her imagined version of
Maar, who is a 'battered muse / my private grief made public,'[26] and describes herself as 'an accomplice to her own uprooting.'

It is a glorious rebuttal of the archetype of a modern muse: she is
the object of the male gaze, and her own perspective is wholly or mostly
disregarded. But this Maar wants her face back, 'the unbroken photog-
raphy of it'. However much we may admire the work of Picasso, why
must it entail ignoring the work of Maar? Nichols reminds us of Maar's
own chosen art form (she was taking photographs on a film set when she
first saw Picasso) at the same moment she rails about her role as a muse.
There are mutually creative partnerships in many art forms (Sylvia Plath
and Ted Hughes, to pick just one of the more renowned), but we tend not
to consider these in the muse category. Plath certainly inspired Hughes
and vice versa, but the very fact that both are celebrated artists in the
same field seems to prevent us from thinking of either as a muse. Muses
are socially subservient in this modern setting, their only role to be seen
or heard as the predominantly male artists see and hear them; they are
bodies and names, hymned for their beauty and their love. And yet, creativity in response to creativity is closer to the relationship Homer and
Hesiod have with their Muses.

So let us return to the subject of these goddesses from ancient myth, rather than their modern namesakes with no power and terrible taste in men. When they leave Mount Helicon, where do Muses end up? In 1980, the answer is Los Angeles, where they find themselves painted onto the wall of an otherwise unremarkable building near the seafront. How they have become trapped there is anyone's guess, because these are certainly not just images, but real three-dimensional goddesses caught in this mural. In a moment of sudden animation (conveyed – as was the medium of the time – by means of bright cartoon light outlining their individual forms, which inevitably makes people my age want to congratulate them on their breakfast choices), they come to life and begin dancing in the small alley in front of their mural. Suddenly, the light overpowers the dance, and they shoot one by one into the sky, like comets. Except for one, who diverts her trajectory to stop right in front of a young painter, Sonny Malone (Michael Beck). She kisses him, then disappears. He is instantly smitten, as anyone kissed by Olivia Newton-John must be.

The film *Xanadu* was not a box office hit, in spite of this arresting opening sequence. This was probably more surprising in 1980 than it now seems: Newton-John was hugely popular after starring in *Grease* two years earlier. Her songs from the soundtrack album of *Xanadu* topped music charts in multiple countries, so audiences liked the star and they liked the music. In other words, the film should have had all the ingredients to be a great success, but it was hamstrung by several unfortunate factors.

Firstly, the plot of *Xanadu* is pretty thin. This is by no means enough to sink a musical: *Cats* has no discernible plot at all, yet it played on stages around the world for decades, generating billions of dollars. Audiences lapped up the song and dance numbers and didn't concern themselves with the lack of narrative drive. But *Xanadu* does try to tell a story – it just doesn't do it terribly well. Kira (Newton-John) has been sent by Zeus to help open a roller disco in an abandoned old music venue, then she falls in love with Sonny and is allowed to stay on Earth to be with him. Even for a time as enthusiastic about roller-skating as the early eighties, this is a fairly minor motivation for a ninety-six-minute musical. And the premise is a bit shaky: if roller discos are so great, why would anyone need a Muse's help to open one? They could just whack up a sign with a pair of skates on it next to a wooden floor and rake in the money. Also, why would Zeus and Kira feel so strongly that LA – a roller-skating paradise in cinema and television at that time – was in need of their assistance? If someone needed help to open one in, say, Alaska and couldn't work out how to keep the skaters from colliding with bears, divine intervention would make more sense.

Then there is the problem that the plot offers no real setbacks for the characters to overcome, which robs the movie of any sense of drama: no evil billionaire owns the venue they want to convert and is refusing to sell, no officious town mayor has staked his reelection campaign on opposing roller discos, no baffled classicist arrives to ask why a Greek Muse wants to name a club after a celebrated location in Samuel Taylor Coleridge's poem *Kubla Khan* (which is not set in ancient Greece, but rather in China in perhaps the thirteenth century). No jeopardy ever threatens the enterprise: they build Xanadu in the first venue Kira shows Sonny, the builders are delightful, the process is painless, and the club opens. The end. There is a brief frisson of worry when Kira has to ask her father, Zeus, if she can stay on Earth, but luckily he agrees to her request after the mildest and briefest opposition, long before your heart rate might have increased.

Additionally, the film is off-balance because neither of its stars plays the lead: Newton-John's name appears before the credits, but she doesn't have much to do except for her songs. You might think that introducing nine Muses at the beginning of the movie would give plenty of scope for both music and wit – we only had five in Disney's *Hercules*, and they created a glorious all-singing, all-dancing, all-plot-recapping chorus. But 1980 was a bleak time for women in cinema, so Kira doesn't share any dialogue with her sisters, just a couple of dance numbers. Indeed, the movie is so uninterested in the idea of women playing actual named characters that Kira is the only Muse named in the credits. The others are given numbers: Muse #1, Muse #2, and so on. I hesitate to wish divine vengeance on anyone, but if challenging the Muses to a contest will provoke them to convert you into magpies, we can only assume that the trees of LA were riddled with corvids after this insult.

And even then cinemagoers might have forgiven the sidelining of Newton-John had the producers placed Gene Kelly in the lead. He was, after all, Gene Kelly. In this, his final film role, Kelly – pushing seventy but looking fifty – plays Danny, a former big-band clarinettist and zillionaire property developer who wants to open a new club. Kelly has such an effortless charisma that he can't help but upstage Sonny as he both roller-skates and tap-dances like *Singin' in the Rain* happened five minutes ago.

There is a subplot between Danny and Kira that is alluded to in an early duet: that she appeared to him in the forties and inspired his clarinet-playing. Perhaps this is what made him so successful that he could live in a mansion and buy a huge nightclub (impoverished clarinettists, please take note). But any hint of an intergenerational love triangle is quickly crushed by the film's relentless focus on Sonny, by far the least interesting of its characters. He is a mildly tortured genius who just wants to paint, but it's hard for the audience to invest in his artistic career. It is one of the strange quirks of cinema that you can only ever ascertain the relative quality of artworks in a film from how the characters react to them, and *Xanadu* is no different: Sonny's colleagues admire him as a genius, but his paintings look identical in quality to theirs. They all paint giant versions of album covers onto canvas, for reasons largely unclear (though they have a bad-tempered boss who demands his album-cover paintings ever sooner, allowing Sonny no time to wander the streets of LA looking for Olivia Newton-John).

The script and production problems of *Xanadu* wrap around and reinforce one another. Sonny coincidentally finds an image of Kira on an album cover, bumps into her in the street, and encounters no real opposition to their relationship: there's no jealous ex or raging god in the background. And because he has so few choices to make, he can't reveal much personality. Sonny even quashes our chance to know for sure which Muse Kira is. When she tries to tell him her real name, she begins 'T—' but he kisses her before she can say, 'Terpsichore,' the Muse of dance.

We have no idea why Kira would be interested in Sonny as a visual artist when she is – at least in this iteration – the Muse of roller discos and not the Muse of eighties album art. Did he paint the mural which celebrated the nine Muses at the start of the film, and to which he will later return to find Kira? Are they rewarding him for this by making him rich and successful as a nightclub owner? If only the film's producers had cared.

I was too young to see this film when it was released, or at least that is what my parents now claim. They in turn were too young to see the Rita Hayworth movie with which *Xanadu* shares what little of a plot it has. *Down to Earth* was released in 1947, and stars Hayworth as Terpsichore, a high-minded goddess living on Mount Parnassus. She is appalled to discover a decidedly lowbrow show is in rehearsals on Broadway, featuring all nine Muses as a bunch of boy-crazy gals. She takes particular exception to the depiction of herself as the one who puts the ants in the dancers' pants, which is very much not how she perceives her role. Terpsichore does a deal with the heavenly world's head administrator (even goddesses are subject to the whims of men in suits in this universe) and heads down to earth to improve the theatrical offering. Inevitably, she takes the lead role, after pushing herself into the rehearsal of a dance number and effortlessly upstaging every other performer. The scene is both comic and serious – we're marvelling at Terpsichore's ghastly behaviour while being seduced by Hayworth's inescapable charm.

This conflict is mirrored on the screen: her female costars are annoyed and confused by the inexplicable arrival of this shameless woman. The men watching from the auditorium are as smitten as we are. In particular, the show's writer and male lead, Danny (Larry Parks), who gives her the female lead role while she is still trying to work out what to call herself. Since she is now playing the role of Terpsichore in his show, she needs a new name and decides on Kitty as her alias. The couple fall in love, and Kitty uses her influence on Danny to make the show less racy and more balletic, in spite of the reservations of other members of the cast. As the company discovers at the first preview, she has accidentally pushed Danny towards creating a huge theatrical flop: the audience are falling asleep in their seats. Kitty is full of remorse when she discovers what she has done, not least because she has otherworldly information that Danny's show must be a success because his life is on the line. He owes money to a gangster-cum-theatrical-angel who will cash out if the show doesn't fly (this movie has more than enough plot to fill its running time, incidentally).

Luckily, Danny is able to explain to the Muse of dance what a successful Broadway show should look like and salvage the production. If this sounds like a terrible example of mortalsplaining, I should say that it is a delightful film, not least because it knows who its star is. The camera is scarcely off Hayworth, and we fall as fully in love with her as Danny does. And although Kitty isn't given divine dispensation to remain on earth, she is given a glimpse of the future, when she and Danny are reunited.

Watching these two cinematic treatments of the Muses made just over thirty years apart provides a neat illustration for what happens in Hollywood to female characters over that time. In *Down to Earth*, Terpsichore might be pompous and not very sisterly (she almost tramples on the woman playing her in the Broadway show in her eagerness to take the spotlight), but she is at least the focal character in the story. By the time Olivia Newton-John takes on the role, the idea that a musical might focus on a female character is more fantastical than the plot.

And yet, as we saw above, you mistreat the Muses at your peril. Perhaps *Xanadu*'s box office return was their punishment.

There is one Muse we haven't yet discussed, and that is because she is a somewhat liminal figure, hovering in the space between historical and mythical. The notion that the lyric poet Sappho is the tenth Muse is one that dates back to ancient times. It's an observation attributed to Plato, though the provenance of the quotation has been questioned. It can be found in the work of Antipater of Sidon,[27] a second-century BCE writer, who confirms this trope that Sappho doesn't belong in the traditional list of nine lyric poets alongside Alcaeus, Stesichorus, Pindar, and more. Sappho isn't the ninth man, claims Antipater, but the tenth Muse.

Now, as so often with ostensibly flattering remarks about women, there are some rather dubious assumptions to be considered here. Sappho is like a Muse why, exactly? Because she is a glorious singer, composer, and performer, perhaps? Or is it just because she is female while doing those things and so were the Muses? The crucial point to note is that the eight other poets on the canonical list are all men. So is it a compliment that Sappho doesn't belong there, because she belongs with the Muses, or is it a way of removing her from the conversation about who makes great art? Great poets must be male, because there they all are, proving it. The great female poet can be disregarded because she is basically inhuman, a goddess, and so doesn't count. We don't see Pindar being scooped off the list and counted in with Apollo.

Sappho is and was a mysterious figure whose biography is almost entirely invented by whoever is reading the minuscule fragments of her work that survive to us (out of nine books of lyric poetry that she is believed to have composed, fewer than seven hundred lines survive, and many of the fragments we have are just one or two words long). Guesses have been made about her profession, her sexual preferences, her age, her marital status, and much more. The temptation to mythologize such a woman is understandable, even in the ancient world when more of her poetry was available to scrutinize. But the same mystery encircles Homer (one poet or many, blind or sighted, and so on) and yet no one suggests that he might be an extra deity. It's hard not to feel that Sappho is being praised and demoted at the same time: a goddess, but not really a poet, therefore.

And it's a liminal status that holds her. In Ovid's *Heroides* collection, he imagines the abandoned women of Greek myth and writes poetic letters from them to their absent menfolk. The final letter is from Sappho to a handsome boatman named Phaon. Again, we see the same praise/demotion in play. Sappho is moved from the historical realm to the mythical; she is placed alongside Helen, Penelope, and Medea. And yet, even as her talent renders her special, she is reduced to a pitiable older woman pining hopelessly for a handsome young man. None of her girl-crushes made her feel this way, she says, twisting the knife further. Where would women be without men to cure them of their dalliances with women and show them what real desire feels like?

Much as I admire Sappho, I would prefer to keep her on the mortal plane and keep the divine Muses numbering nine. They have spent more time than is reasonable having to defend themselves and their reputations against predatory kidnappers, boastful young women, and male musicians with an exceptional sense of confidence in their own sexual prowess. They shouldn't also have to worry about gaining or losing members of their elite gang. Sappho was a woman and a poet, a creator of beautiful verse that is as immortal as the Muses who inspired her. And just like her male contemporaries, this was enough to make her an artist, but not a god.

HERA

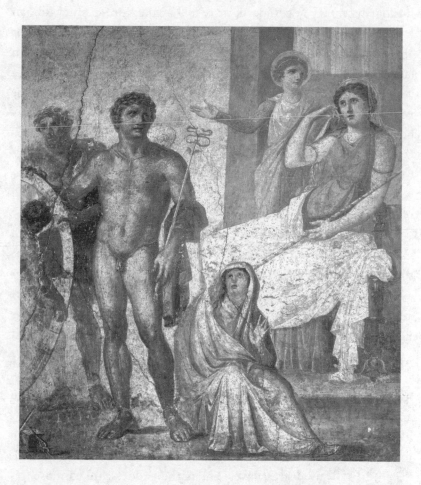

THE PEACOCK was a wildly exotic bird to the ancient Greeks: Alexander the Great is said to have been captivated by their beauty in India in the fourth century BCE. Indeed, we're told by the third-century Roman writer Aelian that Alexander threatened the weightiest punishment for anybody who killed one.[1] His tutor, Aristotle, wrote on their lifespan (about twenty-five years) and breeding habits (up to twelve eggs once a year).[2] And if you plan to raise peafowl, Aristotle has some advice for you: your best chance is to remove a couple of the eggs and let a regular hen sit on them. Peahens are not the problem here, in case you have them pegged as being rather flighty; they do their best to keep their eggs warm and safe. The problem is the peacock, which attacks a broody peahen and tries to crush her eggs. Because of this threat, wild peahens will often disappear and lay their eggs in secret.

The peacock, it seems, has dazzled us with his good looks and blinded us to his bad behaviour. There is something almost hilarious about the showiness of his beauty. In his 414 BCE play *The Birds*, Aristophanes has a bird walk onstage (it is – at the risk of telling you something you have already worked out – a man in a fancy bird costume). What's that? says Euelpides, an Athenian man. It's clearly a bird, but what kind is it? It isn't a peacock, is it?[3]

Beautiful, jealous, destructive, comical: the peacock was the perfect match for Hera, the goddess everyone loves to hate. Before we go any further, I should explain that I do not love to hate her. I genuinely like her, and I am not just saying that because I don't want her to turn me into a cow, or persecute me with snakes, or madden me with a gadfly until I kill my dearest loves. She is the goddess linked most frequently to spectacular and creatively unpleasant revenges (one woman is punished for collaboration with Hera's enemy by being turned into a weasel, of which more below. Hera's animus is so comprehensive that she doesn't even have to perform this transformation herself; she has hench-deities). When I said I was planning to write a book about goddesses, a classicist friend of mine said he couldn't wait to see how I rehabilitated Hera. Well, wait no more – I'm about to tell you that she has been misrepresented. Or, at the very least, that she was provoked.

But let's begin with the story of why peacocks were linked to Hera. As with so many stories about the queen of the gods, this one begins with her husband, Zeus, raping a woman. In this particular case, the woman is Io, daughter of the river god Inachus. This story appears in Book One of Ovid's *Metamorphoses*. Inachus is hiding in a cave, weeping because his daughter has gone missing. He doesn't even know if she is dead or alive.[4] We know – because Ovid tells us – that Io was returning through the woods to her father when she caught the eye of serial sexual predator Jupiter. The Romans' version of Zeus was Jupiter or Jove, and they knew Hera as Juno. He greets her as *virgo Iove digna*[5] – a virgin worthy of Jove. These are words to strike fear into the heart of any girl who doesn't wish to be assaulted by the king of the gods. And Io is just such a young woman. Jupiter has barely started trying to impress her with his promises to keep her safe from wild animals and his boasts about sending lightning hither and thither. Like all the most seductive speeches, this one finishes with the words 'Don't run away from me.' Because, as Ovid drily remarks, she was running. Jupiter responds by cloaking the wide earth in darkness, so he can rape her in secret.[6] Even Ovid – who was a man of his time when it came to issues of consent – doesn't try to make this scene less upsetting than it is: *occuluit tenuitque fugam rapuitque pudorem*. Every word contains a *u* sound, which makes the whole line feel sorrowful and oppressive. There are three active verbs: Jupiter conceals, and holds and rapes. He has all the power in this sentence. Io is literally caught mid-escape, as the word *fugam* – flight or escape – is trapped between two of Jupiter's verbs. The last word of the line, *pudorem*, means 'shame' or 'modesty'. Jupiter has trapped her, raped her, and taken her virginity. And yet, Io is the one who experiences shame. Although she'll barely have a chance to feel it.

Meanwhile, Ovid says, knowing exactly how to build suspense, Juno has noticed the sudden darkness spreading across the fields. She dismisses natural causes: not caused by the river, not because the earth is damp. Her third idea is the right one. She looks around to see where her husband might be. She's caught him so often before, Ovid remarks.[7] She has a quick check round the heavens and can't see him anywhere. Either I'm making a mistake, she says, or he's injuring me. This is not Juno's first rodeo; she knows what the odds are. She orders the fog to make itself scarce.

But this isn't Jupiter's first rodeo either. Guessing that Juno will be looking for him and the girl he has attacked, he turns Io into a snow-white cow. In one of my favourite lines in this entire fifteen-book poem, Ovid adds, '*Bos quoque formosa est*'[8] – she was cute as a cow too. Juno isn't fooled, of course: we know that she and her husband have performed this same dance many times before. Nice cow, she remarks. Where's it from? And when Jupiter gives an unconvincing reply, she asks him to give the cow to her as a gift. Her husband is torn, wanting to keep the cow for himself but not wanting to raise his wife's doubts further. He reluctantly hands over bovine Io to his wife, but Juno is no less suspicious for it. She sets the monster Argus to watch over Io; he has a hundred eyes in his head, Ovid explains,[9] which rest two at a time. If this seems like overkill – a ninety-eight-eyed panopticon to check that one cow doesn't get up to much – then Juno's escalating responses to Jupiter's continuing infidelities are going to perplex you further.

Argus does indeed watch Io like forty-nine hawks. She experiences what must feel like a clawing nightmare. She is trapped in a pen at night. She can't reach out and plead with Argus to release her, because she no longer has arms. She tries to speak, but her voice is unrecognizable and the sound she makes – of a lowing cow – frightens her. It is a constant theme in the *Metamorphoses* that someone who loses their voice loses their power. Io goes to the banks of the river Inachus, where she often used to play.[10] But she catches sight of her horned reflection, and that terrifies her too. The pathos only builds when the naiads – her sisters – and the river – the god of which, remember, is also her father – don't recognize her. Robbed of any alternative, Io follows her father and her sisters around. Even though her father doesn't know her, he offers her some fresh grass. She licks his hand as she eats the grass, and cannot hold back her tears. She may not be able to speak, but she does have a conveniently short name. So she scratches the two letters into the ground. The word Io in Greek is an exclamation of sorrow, so she is bemoaning her fate at the same moment she reveals it.

Inachus now understands that this friendly cow is the daughter he believed dead. But there is no relief in the discovery that she is still alive: unable to communicate with Io in any meaningful way, Inachus wishes for death to release him from his great sorrow. Her guardian Argus separates them, moving Io to a different pasture. He never takes his gaze from her.

Finally Zeus decides to god up and put Io out of this misery. He sends Mercury (Hermes, to the Greeks) to kill Argus and free her from her awful imprisonment. Mercury – always cunning – plays the pipes to try to lull Argus to sleep. It half works: some of the hundred eyes close, but others stay alert. Argus asks what this fancy new instrument is, and Mercury explains the invention of the pan pipes (by the god Pan, unsurprisingly, while he is pursuing a wood nymph named Syrinx, who is doing her utmost to avoid him. There really is nothing like Greek myth for reminding us that the countryside is rarely the blissful idyll for young women that it is for young men and gods. More frequently it is the source of sexual threat and constant anxiety. Although we'll discuss the counterexample of Actaeon and Artemis later on).

The lengthy tale of Syrinx and Pan is enough to put the hundred-eyed

monster into a sound slumber. And Mercury is quick to seize his opportunity. Stabbing Argus in the neck, he then lobs him off a cliff. The light
that had shone in his hundred eyes is extinguished, Ovid says, and night
fills them all at once.[11] And the daughter of Saturn – a poetic variation on
Juno – plucks out these eyes and places them like glittering gemstones in
the tail feathers of her bird.

Raging doubly at the loss of her guardian and at Io, the original
target of her wrath, Juno persecutes the traumatized cow by sending a
horrifying Fury to pursue her. The cow flees in terror across the entire
world, eventually finding herself on the bank of the Nile. Only now does
Jupiter step up and grant her prayers, pleading with Juno to persecute Io
no more, promising she will cause Juno no further pain. The goddess is
lenita – soothed or calmed – and Jupiter turns Io back into a beautiful
nymph. She is still too afraid to speak at first, in case she only makes
the lowing sound she made as a cow. Again, voicelessness means power-
lessness, and regaining human form is not enough to give her back any
sense of power; it takes time for her to learn to speak again. No wonder,
after everything she's been through.

This, then, is the story that connects Juno or Hera to her sacred bird,
the peacock. And it is a connection that operates in both myth and reality: according to the comic playwright Antiphanes – who wrote a huge
number of plays in the fourth century BCE before his somewhat unlikely
death, having been hit by a pear[12] – her temple at Samos was populated
by golden peacocks, admired by all who saw them.[13] But however beautiful these birds are, the eye-catching tail is a reminder of her failed attempts to keep her eyes – at one remove – on her husband and one of
the many young women he desires and accosts. It is also the archetypal
story about Hera: pathologically jealous wife (with good cause) taking
vicious and extended revenge on a goddess, nymph, or mortal woman
who is in no way responsible for the behaviour which has aggravated
Hera's temper. Perhaps it's time to take a few steps back and look at how

Hera and Zeus ended up in this toxic relationship – and why the problem is so frequently deemed to be Hera, with her disproportionate rage
and cruel revenge, rather than Zeus.

The alliance of Zeus and Hera is an early example of someone marrying the girl next door. Or slightly closer than that: Zeus and Hera are
both children of Rhea and Kronos, but the latter is so neurotic about a
prophecy predicting he'll be overthrown by his own son that he swallows his children whole when they are born. Rhea wearies of losing one
child after another to Kronos's insatiable paranoia, so when she gives
birth again, she tricks him, persuading him to swallow a stone rather
than the newborn Zeus. Then Zeus – with help from the goddess Metis –
forces Kronos to vomit up the stone and the siblings. Perhaps you might
not see this as the ideal way to meet your current sister and future wife,
but we have to allow that ancient deities don't always observe the same
niceties we might.

Hera doesn't seem to grow up alongside her siblings. Several ancient
authors – Homer, Ovid, Pseudo-Hyginus[14] – describe her as the foster
daughter of Oceanus and Tethys, both Titans and parents to multiple
river gods. Hera seems to be quite a dutiful daughter, visiting these parents and asking them for help. One might legitimately suppose that she
didn't feel a huge affinity for her actual parents, since one of them had
swallowed her whole at birth. Certainly she has an affectionate and re-
spectful relationship with Tethys: in the *Iliad* Hera describes the goddess taking her from Rhea and raising her well. The tenderness in her
words when she talks about Tethys is rather startling in context. We are
so accustomed to viewing Hera through the lens of shrewish wife and
implacable enemy. But here she seems young and vulnerable, thinking
of Tethys, who took care of her when she was in need. An abusive father,
a passive mother, a kindly foster mother and a seemingly less present
foster father: it's not wildly surprising that this woman might end up
in an abusive marriage of her own. Pausanias, incidentally, suggests the

Horai, or Seasons, as Hera's joint foster mothers.[15] But given the lack of sisterly affection Hera shows towards most goddesses, this idea is rather harder to get behind.

The courtship of Zeus and Hera features another bird, which is then depicted alongside Hera on statues. Again, we turn to Pausanias, tirelessly travelling around Greece to bring us these stories from every corner. He is writing about Mycenae, which was and is a place with a magnificent dual identity. It is both a historic location (where you can follow in Pausanias's footsteps) and a mythic one (where you can stand in the footsteps of Clytemnestra as she waits for her perfidious husband Agamemnon to return from the Trojan War). Pausanias takes us to the Argive Heraion – temple of Hera – a couple of miles outside Mycenae. As he follows a stream towards the temple, he mentions another possible set of foster carers for Hera. This time the daughters of the river Asterion – Euboia, Prosymna and Akraia – are given credit for nursing the queen of the gods. As so often with these seemingly contradictory narratives about goddesses, gods, and heroes and their locations and family connections, Pausanias mentions this quite casually. It surely reveals that the people of this area – like many others – wanted to lay a claim to the goddess. Building a temple is not enough; they want to entwine her in their topography, include her alongside their local mythological characters.

The ruins of this temple remain today, but Pausanias – writing in the second century CE – could see a lot more than we can. He can name its architect (Eupolemos) and describe the narrative themes of its decorations (the birth of Zeus, the Gigantomachy – or battle between gods and giants – and the Trojan War). But most interestingly for us, he could also see the statue of Hera that formed the focal point of this place of worship.[16] It is seated on a throne, he says, and is huge, made of gold and ivory. It was crafted by the sculptor Polykleitos, and this Hera wears a crown decorated with the Graces and the Seasons. As so often with

Greek myth, these abstracts are personified as beautiful young women. In one hand Hera has a pomegranate; in the other she holds a sceptre. Pausanias won't tell us any more about the pomegranate because it is forbidden (due to its connection to the Eleusinian Mysteries, we must presume. These highly secret religious rituals focused on Demeter and Persephone, who was notoriously force-fed pomegranate seeds by her uncle, kidnapper, and then husband, Hades. The pomegranate was often therefore associated with Persephone, and with the dead more generally. The sacred rites of this cult were not to be discussed outside their practice, and Pausanias is scrupulous about observing this silence. Which is rather a pity, because I long to know more about the pomegranate in general, as well as the meaning it held in this particular depiction of Hera).

But there is also the sceptre in Hera's other hand to consider. And sitting on it, Pausanias continues, is a *kokkux,* or cuckoo. Because, they say, when he loved the virgin Hera, Zeus changed into this bird and she chased him to have as a toy or pet. And then, having already inserted a chunk of narrative distance with 'they say', Pausanias adds that he isn't writing this stuff about the gods because he believes it, he's just writing it. It seems that his desire not to blaspheme the Eleusinian Mysteries is quite a bit stronger than his belief in a god turning into a cuckoo to seduce a goddess who wants a pet bird.

I have some sympathy with Pausanias here, since I too have been perplexed by Zeus's habit of converting himself into a bird for the purposes of impressing or beguiling women. Having dismissed the notion of a seductive swan many times before (the guise in which he impregnates Leda, mother of Helen of Sparta), I would now like to add my suspicion that I would find this lascivious cuckoo no more alluring than the swan lothario. But perhaps that is because I am no longer an impressionable *parthenos,* or virginal girl, as Hera is when Zeus pulls off this feathery switch. I instinctively feel that teenage me would have been, if anything, more scornful of the whole idea, but I suppose it's impossible to know for sure.

This statue was widely admired in antiquity, as was the sculptor Polykleitos – some Argive coins showed miniature representations of it. What is perhaps most interesting about it is the way it shows multiple facets of Hera. The sceptre depicts her as powerful, which she is: queen of the Olympian gods, no less. But the pomegranate connects her to other goddesses: Demeter and Persephone at least, and perhaps earlier iterations of female deities too. And then there is the cuckoo, resting on the sceptre. Even at her most powerful and queenly, we are reminded of Hera as a young girl, chasing after a cuckoo, not realizing that her little bird is the vastly powerful Zeus engaging in precisely the kind of animal transformation that he will later employ to seduce one young woman after another.

But at this point, Zeus is employing all his seductive zeal in the pursuit of Hera. She is not his first choice of partner, as Hesiod explains in the *Theogony*. First, the king of the gods sets his sights on Metis, mother of Athene.[17] Then he marries Themis (the names are so similar, I always assume he chooses these wives for the increased chance of bluffing his way past saying the wrong name at a crucial moment); she gives birth to multiple children, including the Fates. Zeus fathers the Graces with Eurynome, then goes to the bed of Demeter, who gives birth to Persephone. And then, as seen in the previous chapter, he fathers the gold-crowned Muses with their mother Mnemosyne. Still short of a full set of Olympian gods, he impregnates Leto, who gives birth to Apollo and Artemis. And very last of all, notes Hesiod,[18] he makes Hera his wife, and she produces Hebe (the goddess of youth), Ares (the god of war), and Eileithyia (a goddess of childbirth). No wonder Hera displays so many signs of jealousy and insecurity. She is often blamed for her venom in punishing the multiple nymphs and women Zeus rapes or seduces. Surely this – her late arrival in the bed of Zeus – might begin to explain why her animus is so strong. Perhaps she recognized that she was never first in his mind, just one in a series of conquests to create mothers of his divine offspring. Yet she is the goddess who takes on the status of queen of the Olympians, and his previous partners are lower profile, or forgotten altogether. That huge Argive temple to Hera is not unusual: the Heraion on Samos was nearly three times the size of the Parthenon in Athens. Hera is celebrated across the Greek world, and the worship is on a grand scale. And it was also an old religion, even then. Pausanias describes a most ancient statue of Hera in the city of Argos[19] – made from pearwood, not large, and she is seated, he says. The earliest depictions of gods tend to be made from wood, and very simple. So an old, plain wooden statue has as much grandeur as a later, more ornate version.

Still, it is one thing for Hera to have reasons to feel content and secure, but it is another for her to believe them. And so much of her vindictive behaviour seems to stem from a place of deep insecurity. Every goddess who precedes her in Zeus's affections produces divine offspring. And almost every mortal woman he subsequently pursues then produces a demigod or a fully fledged god (Semele, a human woman, is mother to Dionysus). Perhaps Hera's aggression stems from a very real fear that she could be replaced at any moment as queen of the gods. What does she have that this succession of women who come before and after her do not?

Well, firstly, she has a wedding. However much we may deplore a patriarchal tradition that allows a woman to be passed from the control of a father to the control of a husband, it was one of the few ways women could achieve any kind of secure status in the ancient world. And Hera obviously does not pass from her father to her husband, because her husband is also her brother and he has – at the very least – overthrown their father and, according to most sources, imprisoned him as well. Zeus saves Hera and their other siblings from Kronos's crazed consumption, and then – after a separation of uncertain duration during which she grows up with foster parents – wants to marry her. It is just about possible to impose a romantic rescue narrative here if one omits virtually all salient details. But it is hard to imagine anyone looking at their family dynamics and imagining a happy marriage ahead.

Nonetheless, they do marry, and we can conclude from one source at least that this is what Hera wants. After Zeus tricks her with his cuckoo impersonation, we're told by the scholiast (an ancient literary commentator) on the third-century BCE poet Theocritus's *Idylls*[20] that when Zeus returns to his usual godlike appearance he promises to marry Hera. She has been refusing sex with him because of their mother, i.e., because they have the same mother. But marriage would render this situation less problematic (for Hera, if not for us). Homer also implies an illicit early relationship (and a fun one), as he claims they shook the bed, in secret from their dear parents.[21] The word *philous* – loving, dear – is doing quite a bit of work in that sentence, at least as far as their father is concerned. But both these stories suggest a consensual physical attraction kept either at bay or secret because of their mother. So the issue seems to be one of formalizing the relationship rather than avoiding one because of its incestuous element. Hera is given the promise of marriage, and that ends all scruples.

The wedding is suitably grand, and their wedding gifts from Gaia – the goddess of the earth – are some of the most notorious objects in Greek myth: golden apples. These mythic fruits (are they apples, pomegranates, or something even more exotic?) provide the narrative twist in multiple stories and myth cycles. Atalanta is waylaid by Hippomenes (also called Melanion) because she cannot resist picking up golden apples when she sees them. Hera, Athene, and Aphrodite compete for the golden apple dropped at the wedding of Thetis and Peleus (who would go on to become parents of Achilles). This apple is inscribed with the words *tēi kallistēi* – 'for the most beautiful', which is what causes so much bother. And Heracles is sent to collect some of these golden apples from the garden of the Hesperides, where the apple tree is kept safe for Hera. So secrecy, adventure, and discord are gifted into this relationship right at its commencement.

And so is desire. According to the poet Callimachus, Zeus experiences a hunger or desire for Hera that lasts three hundred years.[22] And in the *Iliad*, when Hera wants to distract Zeus from the battlefield, it is Aphrodite she approaches for help. Aphrodite agrees to lend her a magic garment, worn between the breasts. But this isn't enough for Hera to be sure she can carry out her plans uninterrupted. So she then offers one of the Graces as a wife to Hypnos, the god of sleep, if he will overwhelm Zeus after this seduction. Hera also promises Hypnos that her son Hephaestus will make him a beautiful throne, and she has to line up a whole set of deities to get what she wants, which is for Zeus to fall asleep for a while so she can advance the Greek cause on the battlefield and work against the Trojans. Aphrodite's special bra has the expected effect on a god already known for his tendency to succumb to temptation; Hera seduces him and then Hypnos knocks him out. Hera gets her own way, in other words, by exploiting the sexual desire of a god who so often exploits others.

But even when she is at her most seductive, there is a sliver of ice in the heart of this relationship between husband and wife. Homer shows us a version of Hera who uses deception to get what she wants from everyone. The word in Greek is *dolophroneousa*[23] – to have a mind full of tricks. The same word is used to describe Hera whether she is approaching Aphrodite for assistance or her husband for sex. Homer gives us a long description of Hera preparing herself for the encounter with Zeus: bathing, beautifying, dressing in her finery. And she does all of it (we are given to understand) with an ulterior motive. Of course, we may choose to see this as an early example of the tired old trope that men want sex and women trade on that desire to get what they want. But this isn't a sitcom, and Hera's desires are epic in scale. She isn't putting out for a new conservatory, she is using the undeniable power of sex with her to advance the cause of the Greeks in the greatest conflict of the time – one of the greatest literary conflicts of all time. What is so interesting about them as a couple is that they manage to create discord even when none is needed: Zeus already knows the outcome of the Trojan War will favour the Greeks. The Fates have spoken. And yet he chooses to delay the victory, encouraging the Trojans as a favour to Thetis (who wants the Greeks to suffer for disrespecting her son Achilles). Zeus's own son Sarpedon (not Hera's son, naturally) fights and dies for the Trojan cause. It wouldn't require an ego as big as Hera's temples to wonder whether Zeus chooses to do this – at least in part – just to antagonize her. No wonder she needs so many tricks and allies to get her own way. She is performing a sort of divine diplomacy, forging alliances to ensure that the Greeks do indeed win the war they are fated to win.

We sometimes overlook this, focusing instead on her unquenchable animus against the Trojans. Homer implies she feels this way because Paris awarded the golden apple 'for the most beautiful' to Aphrodite rather than to Hera.[24] And it is brutal to witness: even after Hector's death – and the desecration of his body by Achilles – Hera is still arguing that the gods should not intervene, not even to return his body to the Trojans so they can bury their great hero.[25] Here, she presents her argument openly, not with a mind full of tricks. So Homer calls her *leukōlenos* – Hera of the white arms – rather than using an epithet which focuses on her deceit.

And the argument she makes is that Hector isn't divine; he isn't even semidivine, like Achilles. Thetis, the mother of Achilles, is a powerful goddess in her own right, and Hera takes a moment to remind Zeus that she (Hera) raised Thetis herself. She has an almost grandmotherly relationship to Achilles. Hera is so often associated with the persecution of women and children embroiled in her husband's desires, we almost overlook that she can be maternal even with children who aren't her own, so long as her jealousy isn't roused. A beneficiary of loving foster parents herself, Hera has played that role for Thetis.

She continues: Hector is just mortal. So why would the gods concern themselves with his fate so closely? Zeus begins his reply by asking her not to be angry, before doing what he intended to do all along: allowing the body of Hector to be taken back to Troy. He summons Thetis, knowing that he must separate her from Achilles if he wants the latter to agree to hand over Hector to his father, Priam. And Hera, acting against her own wishes, tries to make things easier for Thetis: she gives her a golden cup to drink from; she speaks to her kindly.[26] Hera can be kind and placatory on occasion, even when she has failed to get what she wants.

So perhaps her cruelty really does stem from insecurity. Her persecution of the Trojans is unreasonable, but it isn't irrational: Paris, a prince of Troy, insulted and undermined her. So she punishes the whole city of which he is a prince. It isn't proportionate, admittedly, but the gods are rarely measured in any of their responses to provocation. And while we might wonder if she could just get over the minor mortal insults, we see that Zeus himself enjoys reminding her of all the times when he has preferred someone else. Let's go back to that seduction scene in Book Fourteen.

Hera arrives at the peak of Mount Ida, near Troy, wearing all her finery, primped for action. Her efforts pay off instantly. I have never wanted anyone more, says Zeus. Not a goddess, nor a woman.[27] So far, so charming. Not the wife of Ixion, he continues, who gave birth to my son Perithoös. Not Danaë, who bore Perseus. Nor the daughter of Phoenix, who gave me a couple more sons. Not Semele (mother of Dionysus) or Alcmene (mother of Heracles). Not Demeter (mother of Persephone), nor Leto (mother of Artemis and Apollo). I didn't want any of them as much as I want you.

I would hesitate to offer anyone relationship advice, but just in case you need it: this is an absolutely catastrophic way to compliment anyone and I urge you never to do it, even if it sounds fine in your head. It is not fine. No wonder Hera's wrath is triggered by the loss of a golden apple when Paris decides Aphrodite is prettier. How many times can one woman be made to feel like she has come second in a man's estimation?

It must be made worse by the fact that Hera's appearance seems to echo (or foreshadow) that of the women Zeus uses to betray her. Another of Homer's epithets for her is *bōopis* – cow-eyed. We might rather compare a brown-eyed person to a doe, but the comparison to a cow is particularly relevant in light of the Io story. Hera has beautiful big brown eyes, like a cow, so Zeus makes Io even more like one. Whatever the desirable quality, Hera always seems to fall short by a fraction.

The one area in which that is not true is in the sheer quantity of spite she can direct at an individual, a family, or an entire population. Other gods and goddesses certainly try to compete with her in this field (special mentions must go to Athene, Poseidon, Aphrodite, and more). But it is hard to think of a character who so consistently behaves so cruelly across so many different stories. Hera is villainous in multiple narratives, most famously that of Heracles, which we'll come to shortly. Often it is provoked by her considerable sexual jealousy, but not always: in one version of Teiresias's story, she curses the prophet for his answer to a question about proportionate sexual pleasure.[28] At this point in his life, Teiresias has lived as both a man and a woman: his male-to-female change occurs after he sees snakes mating near Mount Cyllene. At a later date, Teiresias catches sight of another pair of snakes going at it, and this turns him back into a man. Unexpected snake sex obviously has hormonal effects that science has yet to uncover. These encounters make the seer uniquely qualified to settle a dispute between Zeus and Hera about who enjoys sex more, men or women. Teiresias says women have nine-tenths of the pleasure, and men enjoy – if that's the word for it – a measly tenth. Hera is so vexed by this truth coming out (I mean, opinion being offered) that she promptly takes away his sight.

But Hera is more frequently angered by personal slights, and she is especially antagonized by Zeus's habit of having children without her. She produces a son, Hephaestus, in retaliation for Zeus's sudden (and apparently motherless) creation of Athene. This account of her revenge procreation dates back at least as far as Hesiod.[29] Hera is right – as usual – to suspect Zeus of dubious behaviour here: although Athene is born from his head, fully formed, she is not as motherless as all that. Zeus had impregnated and then swallowed the pregnant Metis so she wouldn't produce a son who might overthrow him. These things obviously do run in families, or at least in this particular one. So we might well feel sympathy for Hera up to a point: she has been betrayed again, and this time Zeus has raped or seduced one of his previous wives. Rather than persecute Athene, as we might expect, Hera tries a different tactic: doing to her husband exactly what he has done to her. But when she sees her son Hephaestus and realizes he is lame, she is furious. According to Pausanias,[30] she hurls him from Olympus when he is born. Her temper is no sweeter when faced with a defenceless newborn god, it seems, even when he is her own. But Hephaestus is not defenceless after all: he vengefully (*mnēsikakōn* in Greek: it even looks malevolent) sends his mother a gift, a golden throne. But his craftsman's skill is superhuman, of course, and the throne is rigged. Hephaestus has attached invisible bindings to it, so that anyone who sits in the chair is tied to it. Dionysus (who better?) has to get the vengeful blacksmith drunk before he can be prevailed upon to release her. An interesting question posed by this anecdote (though not asked by Pausanias) is, if Hera is as awful as the stories all show, why do any of the gods want her free?

And at least Hephaestus is a god when Hera chucks him off a mountain. This is not the case for Heracles when Hera discovers her husband has had yet another child with a mortal woman. She doesn't throw him from the lofty peaks of Olympus. But, according to the second-century mythographer Pseudo-Apollodorus, she does send two giant snakes to his bed to kill him when he is eight months old. Her plan is foiled when Heracles strangles the snakes instead: he is truly his father's son. This anecdote is often presented as an archetypal example of Hera's limitless malevolence. So it's worth noting that Pseudo-Apollodorus offers a quick alternative. In one version of the story, he says, it isn't Hera who sends the snakes. It's Amphitryon, Heracles's stepfather. I wonder if this caveat hints at why the other gods might have pleaded with Hephaestus to free the foul-tempered goddess. If Hera is at large, you can behave as badly as you like, and someone will probably blame her instead.

One of the things that is most awful about Hera, once you have her ill will directed at you, is that she never seems to tire of vengeance. Io is tormented above and beyond what anyone could deem proportionate, even if she had been a willing party in Zeus's assault on her, which she was not. The comprehensive list of persecutions is a long one: Callisto, whom Hera turns into a bear and then persuades Artemis to shoot;[31] the pregnant Leto, whom Hera pursues to the ends of the earth so she cannot give birth;[32] Semele, whom she tricks into asking to see Zeus in his real form. Semele promptly dies of fright from the thunderbolt which appears before her.[33] Hera attacks women, babies, gods, and men with a cheerless indifference to the merits of each case. She afflicts Dionysus and others with madness;[34] she persecutes nearly everyone with giant serpents.

And no one receives a more sustained campaign of Hera's rage than the son of Alcmene and infant scourge of snakes, Heracles. Indeed, she begins this persecution before he is even born, as Ovid relates the story.[35] Desperate to punish Alcmene for her pregnancy, Hera prevents her from giving birth at her due time (she charges a goddess of childbirth, Eileithyia – Lucina to the Romans – to intervene). This plan works very well for several days, resulting in agony for Alcmene and no baby. But then a slave woman, Galanthis, realizes that the obstacle to a safe birth is divine in origin, so she plays a trick. Rushing out of Alcmene's rooms, she notices Lucina and declares that the baby has been born and that congratulations are in order. Lucina is so distracted by this that she leaps up and unclasps her hands. This loosening of her body loosens Alcmene's, and the baby is safely delivered. In revenge, Lucina turns Galanthis into a weasel.

So Heracles survives Hera's early attempts on his life. Her name forming the beginning of his is not a coincidence, by the way: he is named 'Glory of Hera', presumably in an attempt to win over the furious goddess. Needless to say, it is wholly ineffective. In the most notorious version of the myth, as told by Pseudo-Apollodorus,[36] Hera drives Heracles mad, so much so that he murders his wife Megara and their children (I can't apologize enough if you only know this character from the Disney movie and I have just broken your heart. It kills me too, for what it's worth). His penance for this killing in unsound mind is to serve a ruler named Eurystheus for twelve years and perform the labours that are asked of him.

Heracles is told by a priestess of Apollo that after completing these labours he will become immortal. This raises an interesting conundrum, given that we are looking at a society and a myth culture which prizes immortality and immortal fame above all things for a hero. By maddening Heracles, engineering the deaths of Megara and their children, and causing Heracles terrible guilt and grief before a lengthy period of servitude, Hera has certainly achieved her goal of punishing the illegitimate son of Zeus. But she has also inadvertently helped to create his mythic status. Heracles was – and is – one of the most well-known heroes in Greek myth. His image was painted on countless pots and wine cups; he is instantly recognizable thanks to the club he carries and the lion skin he wears. The labours are one of the most enduring stories of any Greek hero, and none of them would have happened if Hera hadn't loathed him so utterly. So, while she achieves her goal, Hera has to live with the knowledge that she has helped to create this demigod herself. 'Glory of Hera' is a more appropriate name than it first appeared. But even after his labours are completed, Hera's rage is not spent. As Heracles sails away from Troy (which he sacked a generation before the more celebrated war that finishes the city for good), Hera sends vicious storms to endanger him.

Perhaps you have been wondering where Zeus is in this story. Why does he not intervene to protect his son from his wife's rage? Perhaps he too wants Heracles to become immortal, and sees that surviving the machinations and complications of Hera's wrath is the way to do it. But these storms push him over the edge. His anger is finally roused and he hangs Hera in chains from Mount Olympus as a punishment.

This is clearly intended both to injure and to humiliate. Even the gods can feel pain: Aphrodite receives an injury from the Greek warrior Diomedes during the Trojan War, for example. Perhaps hanging from chains wouldn't cause Hera long-term damage, but it is nonetheless likely to be a very uncomfortable experience. And chaining her up is intrinsically degrading – this is the kind of punishment that might be meted out to a slave, a criminal. Hera is queen of the gods, and she finds herself being treated in this way for her attitude to a mortal man. It is reminiscent of the punishment of Prometheus, who is chained to a rock to have his liver pecked out each day by an eagle, Zeus's favoured bird. He too won't die of this experience – his liver regenerates each night so he can be tormented anew the following day. Prometheus is tortured for going behind Zeus's back to help mortal men by giving them fire. Hera is punished for cruelty towards a mortal man, but one suspects that going behind Zeus's back is again the real crime. No wonder Homer gave her a mind full of tricks and guile.

It is Hephaestus, incidentally, who comes to Hera's rescue, or at least tries to. But in the version of the story told by Pseudo-Apollodorus,[37] he is cast down to earth by Zeus. This story is also referenced in the *Iliad*,[38] where Hephaestus tells his mother that they cannot hope to cross Zeus and remain unhurt in the process, reminding her of the time he was hurled from the heavens to Lemnos, an island in the northern Aegean Sea. This, then, is a different telling of a god throwing Hephaestus out of Olympus. Earlier, we saw that Hera hurled him out in a fit of pique, but here Zeus is the cruel one, punishing his wife's son for trying to defend her. Again, we see that whenever anything unpleasant happens, Hera can always take the blame.

The more time you spend examining these stories of Hera's bad behaviour, the more reasons you tend to be able to find for why she might be behaving unreasonably, or why someone else is the guilty party but blaming Hera is so convenient. It is a misogynist narrative as old as time itself, and never out of fashion: the real problem in any bad family dynamic isn't the irascible, lecherous patriarch, but his patience-sapped wife. So it makes perfect sense to say that it's Hera who sends the snakes to kill baby Heracles, because that's exactly the kind of thing she would do. Sure, sometimes it's Amphitryon who tries to kill the baby. But a wicked stepfather is a much less potent archetype than the cruel stepmother, so the version which prevails is that Hera is the villain.

We like to be able to separate heroes, villains, and victims. It's convenient for a simple narrative, but it isn't always reflective of the truth. Again, in Book One of the *Iliad*, Hera tries to find out what Zeus is planning with Thetis (to favour the Trojans and kill many Greeks, to punish the latter for their treatment of Achilles). She begins by being direct, asking who he has been conspiring with now. The word Homer uses to describe Hera's tone is *kertomioisi*.[39] This is usually translated as taunting or mocking, but literally it contains the idea of cutting. That is why Hera's words sting (which might be a better translation): because she can cut right to the heart of her listener. But also, isn't there a suggestion that her own heart might be damaged by her husband plotting with Thetis? Thetis has gone straight to Zeus and bypassed Hera altogether, even though theoretically the two goddesses both root for the Greeks.

We cheer Thetis on because it's the first book of the poem and we want the plot to advance. But her successful pleading with Zeus ensures more Greeks will die to gratify her son's wounded pride. That is what Hera is trying to prevent. For all the descriptions of Hera as resentful and jealous, she isn't actually wrong in this case. Zeus is plotting against her beloved Greeks to reward one man's ego.

Zeus tells her to mind her own business, and Hera responds by pointing out that she has done, until now. But now she suspects him of endangering the Greeks. Zeus the cloud-gatherer replies,[40] says Homer. This has always seemed like the perfect double meaning to me. It's a grand epithet for the god who conjures thunderbolts and lightning, but it's also the ideal description for the aggressive bluster he now employs. Largely, it must be said, to intimidate his wife from pursuing her wholly accurate suspicions any further. You're always suspicious, nothing ever gets past you. But you can't do anything about it except be further from my heart and that will be worse for you. Shut up, sit down, and obey me, because none of the gods on Olympus can help you if I lay my invincible hands on you.

This is an explicit threat of violence, which we know is not an idle one: Hephaestus will remind us in a few lines of the previous occasion Zeus laid hands on Hera. Her justified suspicions are belittled and she herself is silenced and threatened. If this were happening now, we would call it abuse. So he spoke, concludes Homer, and Hera was afraid. She sat down in silence, her heart twisted. And through the halls of Zeus's palace, the gods were angered.[41] So not only does Homer invite us to consider Hera the injured party in this conversation, if we choose to see it, he also shows us that the other Olympian gods are angered by this scene. Zeus's bullying of his wife doesn't seem any more reasonable to the gods who witness it than it seems to me, reading about it now.

The undeniable truth about the marriage of Zeus and Hera is that it is neither a match of equals nor a meeting of minds. Ultimately, Zeus is more powerful and nothing Hera does can change that. She resorts to trickery and seduction to get her own way because she is not strong enough to oppose him outright, and they both know it. Her other option is to accept that she can never disagree with him, or at least that she will always lose. And who would agree to a marriage like that, even if she did find herself queen of the Olympians?

There is a fresco in Pompeii in the House of the Vettii. This large house probably belonged to two freedmen (ex-slaves who had purchased their freedom or been manumitted, often in an ex-master's will), who evidently had a great passion for both art and mythology. The walls are covered in magnificent paintings, not least of which is the *Punishment of Ixion*. This scene shows the fate of Ixion, which we can find in more narrative detail in Pindar's second *Pythian Ode*, a poem written to celebrate a victor in a chariot race at Delphi. Ixion has a history of appalling behaviour: he has already needed purification for the murder of his father-in-law. And Zeus – in a rare moment of generosity – extends this moral cleansing by inviting the wrongdoer to dine with him on Mount Olympus. Ixion has offended the rules of *xenia* – guest-friendship – by inviting a man to his house and murdering him. But he is then offered the highest form of *xenia* from the king of the gods himself.

And Ixion now offends the rules again: as a guest of the king of the Olympians, he nonetheless develops an interest in the queen. He desired Hera, says Pseudo-Apollodorus, so he tried to take her by force.[42] Pindar considers this an act of hubris – shameful pride.[43] Hera tells her husband that Ixion has assaulted her and Zeus decides he should test the truth of her words. Now, of course, someone might argue that Hera deserves to come under suspicion, given how frequently she employs deceit in her dealings with Zeus. But this story must come relatively early in their relationship, and it is hard to imagine a worse response a husband could give to his assaulted wife than to suggest he needs to check whether a murderer is also capable of being a rapist, or whether she's just making it up. Zeus's tactic is to fashion a woman from cloud and make her identical to Hera – a beautiful calamity for Ixion, as Pindar puts it.[44] Ixion does indeed accost the cloud, which produces a child to prove it. And so Zeus finally believes his wife and punishes Ixion by having Hephaestus bind him to a wheel which will be forever in motion. Ixion's wheel, incidentally, is one of the torments that comes to a halt when Orpheus plays his music in the Underworld in his vain bid to restore his wife, Eurydice, to the world of the living.

And this is the scene which we can see on the fresco in the House of the Vettii. On the left-hand side of the fresco, Ixion has been fastened to the wheel. Its weight rests on the hand of Hephaestus, his expression somewhat haunted, as though he doesn't want to start it moving in the knowledge that it will never stop. Hermes stands naked in the centre of the scene, his gaze pointedly directed the opposite way; he will escort miscreants to their punishment, it seems, but he doesn't really want to watch. Kneeling at his feet is a rather melodramatic female figure (perhaps Nephele, Hera's cloud twin). Her left hand is raised, fingers splayed, and she looks up at Hermes in distress. Is she worried that she too will be bound to an unending torture? Or perhaps she feels guilty for her part in the trap.

And on the right-hand side of the painting, Hera sits on a golden throne, a sceptre in her left hand, bangles wrapped round both upper arms. She wears a small crown, from which a veil drops over her hair. Her right arm is bent, fingers crooked, as she adjusts her veil, or perhaps the top of her cloak – no torture, however severe, disturbs her very much. Her large brown eyes gaze blankly at Ixion, and her small bow of a mouth is slightly open. Every ounce of her posture and expression seems to declare her utter contempt for this obnoxious, presumptuous man. Ixion gets what he deserves, in other words. But Hera doesn't seem satisfied.

When I first saw this fresco, I was about nineteen, I think. I didn't

know the story of Ixion and his attempted rape. I'm not even sure I noticed the man on the wheel, particularly. All my attention was drawn to
Hermes and Hera and the tension between them: he seems to be trying
to make eye contact but her gaze is directed a little too high. What I
saw – still see – is Hera's weariness, her boredom with the whole thing.
She refuses to engage with Iris (the rainbow goddess who stands behind
her, gesturing to the wheel), Hermes, or Nephele. She barely seems to
register that they are there; she is numb. Yes, Ixion is punished, but she
has had to deal with the experience of being attacked and then the additional trauma of not being believed when she told her husband what
happened. I always get the strong impression that Hera's mood would
improve considerably if Zeus were being tied to a wheel as well. At least
then the old lech would have to keep his hands to himself.

As we have already seen, temples to Hera were vast in size and scope.
This surely conveys a sense of profound respect and affection for her,
as well as reverence. All the gods inspired reverence, after all. But they
didn't all get giant temples, three times the size of the Parthenon. Focus
on the raft of ancient myths which tell us of her villainy and cruelty
and we might wonder at this seeming contradiction – because the material evidence that survives to us today implies a much more beloved
goddess than we find in the majority of stories told by Ovid or Pseudo-
Apollodorus. The temples seem to speak to the grand, epic Hera we see
in Homer. Even when she is petty and bickering with her fellow deities,
she does so in pursuit of a great goal, and one her Greek audience would
appreciate: Greek victory in the Trojan War.

And this Hera – the one planning her battle strategy and always
focused on any small advantage she can accrue – does occasionally still
flash into view. In the 1963 film *Jason and the Argonauts*, directed by
Don Chaffey and brought to glorious stop-motion life by Ray Harryhausen, we see a version of Hera who is every inch the hero's divine
helper, with no hint of marital jealousies or anything else so banal. The

screenplay was sufficiently close to the ancient epic poem, the *Argonautica*, that the third-century BCE poet Apollonius of Rhodes gets a rare credit on the Internet Movie Database. And the version of the gods it presents is very much in the spirit of ancient epic: Apollonius was taking his inspiration from Homer and other poets who had come before him. Zeus, Hera, and the rest of the Olympians exist in a semidetached enclave from which they look down on the mortal world as a game, an illogical chessboard. They involve themselves in mortal affairs, but only within certain boundaries. In this version of the myth, it is Zeus who largely dictates who can help or punish whom, though we may remember that in Homer, even Zeus is partly constrained by what the Fates allow.

Hera involves herself in Jason's life at its outset, much as we have seen in the Heracles story, but with a more benign intent. As Thessaly falls under attack from the villainous Pelias, a young woman named Briseis (daughter of the usurped king Aristo) rushes terrified through the burning streets. She is carrying a wailing baby, trying to console him as she goes. When she arrives at a sanctuary, it is a cool, dark temple – not just her sanctuary, it transpires, but that of the goddess Hera. There is a mighty seated statue of the queen of the gods. It owes something to those descriptions of the Heraion at Argos that we read in Pausanias. Briseis prays before the statue and begs that her prayers be heard. Her sister is already dead. She is desperate for the goddess to protect not her, but the baby, Jason.

In the shadows beneath the statue, a robed figure appears. We would assume she was a priestess until we hear her voice. We know her at once: Hera has taken on an embodied form in her temple. When Pelias races in through the doors looking to kill any descendants of the rightful king, the shadowy figure tells him to be silent, but – failing to recognize her – he asks if Briseis's prayers have been heard. Hera tells him they have, but he kills the young woman anyway. It is the will of

Zeus, he declares. It is not the will of Zeus, Hera replies sharply. And she tells him the gods have abandoned him. He does not dare kill the baby, which evidently has the protection of a far greater power than he does.

Hera reappears on Mount Olympus, fuming about the profaning of her temple. Killing or harming suppliants in sacred spaces is always a shocking moment in Greek myth: Priam, king of Troy, is killed in similar circumstances when his city is destroyed. His daughter Cassandra is raped as she holds on to a statue of the goddess in the temple of Athene. The violence done to her is so great that the statue itself is damaged.

It is interesting therefore that Hera – so often presumed to be the most spiteful and vengeful of goddesses – does not take her revenge on Pelias for his profanation of her sacred space. Not only does she not do this in the film, she doesn't do it in the *Argonautica* either. Hera has the power to persecute the wrongful king to the ends of the earth and back again, but she prefers to do things in a more roundabout way, by helping Jason. Pelias is destined to die at the hands of a one-sandaled man, and (though he doesn't know it yet) this will be Jason.

Zeus allows Hera to help Jason five times: this is his final word on the matter. And we cut to twenty years later, since to the gods that is no time at all. Jason is now a grown man, who leaps into water to rescue a drowning stranger. The stranger is Pelias, of course, and his near-death experience is caused by Hera, who knocks him off his feet and holds him underwater. In the act of saving Pelias, Jason loses a sandal, so the prophecy is fulfilled. Pelias sees the danger and sends the young man on an impossible quest to try and find the Golden Fleece.

The god Hermes spirits Jason up to Mount Olympus, where he is dwarfed by the giant deities. Hera introduces herself to him and explains that she will be his protector on his quest to the far-off land of Colchis. When returned to the mortal world, Jason starts to recruit his Argonauts. His ship – the *Argo* – has a beautiful figurehead of Hera which faces in towards the ship rather than out towards the sea. This handy arrangement allows Jason to consult Hera when he needs her advice. She directs them to an island when they have run out of water, then tells Jason how to attack the bronze giant, Talos, who is determined to kill the Argonauts. His wrath is incurred by Hercules, who disobeys Hera's instruction to take nothing from the island. This scene – which is not in the *Argonautica*, where Medea fights Talos instead – has echoes of the *Odyssey*, where Odysseus's men disobey his direct instructions to harm nothing on an island where they land for safety. They meet a terrible punishment for ignoring this advice when they kill and eat sheep sacred to the sun god.

Hera's five favours are used up before Jason arrives in Colchis. Medea, a priestess of Hecate, becomes his helper there instead. When Hera sees them kiss, she looks decidedly peeved. But is she worried for Jason, because she has seen that this woman will cause him terrible grief in his future? Or is she jealous because she would like to be kissing the young hero herself? Either way, she doesn't interfere but allows the two lovers their happy-ever-after moment, after Jason finally gets the girl and the fleece.

So the version of Hera we meet here is far from the raging goddess we so often see. She is irritable on occasion, and petty too, as are all the gods. But she is kind to Jason and patient in taking her revenge on Pelias. This is not a version of her who arbitrarily punishes women, even ones who kiss men she likes. In fact, Zeus seems far more vengeful than Hera in this telling of their story: he is the one persecuting a man named Phineus by sending harpies to steal his food every day. The Argonauts intervene to save him from perpetual hunger by trapping the monstrous bird-women. Hera, meanwhile, has the perfect opportunity to squish Hercules and claim that Talos did it, but she maturely resists the temptation.

There is a similar reading of Hera in Rick Riordan's books, particularly Percy Jackson and the Olympians, Book 4, *The Battle of the*

Labyrinth. Our plucky boy hero finds the goddess in the strange and terrifying underground labyrinth, built by Daedalus but somehow stretching across the world. This Hera is rather tetchy when Percy mentions his friend Thalia,[45] one of Zeus's illicit love children. But she doesn't smash him to smithereens, nor has she turned Thalia into a cow, or a bear (Thalia does still get turned into a tree, but no one can be a winner every day, and she is restored to a more mobile form thanks to the Golden Fleece). When asked what she wants by Percy's fellow quester Annabeth, Hera explains that her goal is to keep the Olympians – squabbling as much as ever in this iteration – together. Hera isn't given the chance to interfere very often, she explains, but once every quarter-century or so, Zeus allows her to help a hero if she cares very deeply. So again, it is Zeus who decrees how much Hera can or cannot do to help a young hero. But it is the intensity of Hera's desire to help that decides who gets the divine intervention.

These Heras – perversely, given the film is thousands of years later than the poems which provide its source material, and the novel is almost fifty years later still – seem to me quite convincing depictions of a goddess men and women might worship as well as fear. Surely this is the aspect of Hera that a society would build a massive temple to revere: a helper, a saviour, loyal to the last. Perhaps it's because I saw the Harryhausen film so many times as a child, so Hera seemed both magical and quasi maternal, like a fairy godmother but in a more exciting (to me) world of shimmering golden fleeces and skeleton warriors rather than one of handsome princes and missing shoes. Watching it now, I still feel echoes of that response: Hera can't or doesn't save Briseis, but she does grant the young woman's prayer, and once she has committed to a cause or a person, she is as unswerving in her devotion as she is when her anger is roused. You would want Hera to defend you, and you would want your enemies to be hers.

If all we had was the Hera who persecutes Io, Callisto, and the rest in

Ovid's *Metamorphoses*, we might think she hates women. Yet Hera is – perhaps more than any other goddess or god in the Olympian pantheon – a representative of her constituency: married women. She can be petty, yes, but that is hardly a gender-specific trait and is perhaps not even confined to those who are married. She exists in a highly patriarchal society, and it shows: she has no control over Zeus's dubious shenanigans. Her status – powerful in some ways, utterly powerless in terms of her husband's violence and infidelity – entirely reflects that of the women who made their sacrifices to her. If you could be divorced at the whim of your husband, and could never initiate divorce yourself (as was true of women in fifth-century BCE Athens, for example, and in many societies since), if he could have sex with anyone he chose but you could only wait at home, your behaviour curtailed by society's expectations and your husband's superior physical strength and potential for violence, you might also be spiteful to the women he desired. What if they displaced you; what if their offspring displaced yours? These were real fears for women in the Greco-Roman world. No wonder Hera, and her Roman counterpart, Juno, held such sway. They represented the role of married women in societies which offered women little alternative. It could be the route to great happiness, but as Euripides's Medea famously declared: If her husband is happy in the marriage, a woman's life is enviable. If not, it's better to die.[46]

But what if you can't die? However melodramatic Medea's sentiments may be, she does have that option available to her (and the other, even more violent ones she eventually chooses). She considers suicide at various points in the play – a dreadful solution to what she perceives as her intolerable situation. But Hera is stuck with Zeus for eternity, unless he boots her out and replaces her with a younger model. And then where would she be? A footnote in mythography, like her predecessors? Her status depends on her husband – whose wandering eye is of literally mythical proportions – retaining his interest in her. No wonder she's intolerant. I'm starting to feel insecure just writing about her, and I don't even have a husband.

When I began this chapter, I wondered why there are relatively few examples of Hera in modern culture, certainly with regard to Aphrodite, Gaia, Persephone, and many of her divine contemporaries. As I've written it, I've realized that almost the opposite is true. There are countless examples of women frustrated by their unbreakable bond to an unfaithful husband. But they all tend to be in comedy. The idea of the bossy, suspicious wife trying to manipulate her irascible, unreasonable husband becomes a wildly popular comic trope found everywhere from Ovid to *Fawlty Towers* (it has always pleased me that Sybil Fawlty shares her name with the ethereal priestesses who spoke in riddles, when Prunella Scales played her as such an entirely unethereal presence). So Hera loses her epic grandeur and becomes a punch line. And we lose track of the interests of such a woman, because she wouldn't be as funny if she were a fully rounded person. So we forget about Hera's passion to help heroes, to defend Greeks at all costs during a conflict, and to protect married women. We forget that her daughter Eileithyia is a goddess of childbirth. These two goddesses would hold the greatest sway over the lives of adult women living around the ancient Mediterranean. You wanted a decent husband, and you wanted to survive giving birth. These aspects of Hera's power are far from being a joke.

Perhaps the most poignant modern version of Hera or Juno isn't on-screen, onstage, or in the pages of an adventure story. Rather, it lifted off from Cape Canaveral in Florida on the fifth of August, 2011. The *Juno* spacecraft spent five years flying to – of course – the mysterious planet Jupiter, to try and discover more about it. In their press release, NASA made the connection explicit: 'The god Jupiter drew a veil of clouds around himself to hide his mischief, and his wife, the goddess Juno, was able to peer through the clouds and reveal Jupiter's true nature.'[47] Appropriately enough, as she journeyed through space, *Juno* caught sight of Io and Europa, moons named after two of the many young women Jupiter assaulted.

So even in her most distant, futuristic iteration, Juno is forever in pursuit of Jupiter, still searching for his infidelities, still finding them. A small Lego figure of both Jupiter and Juno formed part of the spacecraft's crew (there was also a Lego Galileo).[48] In 2016, when her voyage of discovery was completed, Juno was deorbited into Jupiter.

Together forever, once more.

APHRODITE

LIGHTS SPARKLE off a spinning disco ball, and the music begins to pulse. The camera pans down to reveal a woman with enormous back-combed hair, arms stretched up in a pose that is both triumphant and supplicatory – she might have just completed a flawless gymnastic routine, or she might be about to appeal to a goddess. Perhaps it is both. Anything seems possible in this world out of time. Her expression is unreadable: her eyes are hidden behind large, dark, circular glasses.

The pose is initially the most surprising element. The image which inspired this moment of performance art is rather different. Botticelli's *Birth of Venus* is one of the most recognizable paintings in the world. Almost three metres wide, and close to two metres tall, it hangs in the Uffizi, in Florence.[1] Venus stands in the centre of the canvas, almost the same size as the gallery visitors looking at her flawless pale skin, her flowing golden hair. It is tied back in the loosest ponytail, but it's blown to one side, thanks to the god, Zephyr, hovering to her right, who puffs his cheeks to send a breeze in the direction of this fresh-born goddess. He wraps his left arm around another goddess or nymph, both of them naked but for their billowing cloaks. She embraces him jealously: not just both her arms wrapped round him, but one leg too. And her hands are clasped tightly, fingers interlocked. She is taking no chances that he might let her go and disappear with the beautiful stranger who stands before them, her toes resting on a giant, creamy shell. And yet, she can't tear her gaze away from Venus either. Pink flowers rain down around them onto the pale green sea. To Venus's left is a much more respectably dressed goddess, perhaps one of the Graces. She has neatly plaited hair, and even the loose curls over her ear are in tidy rows, though she must be caught in Zephyr's breeze too. She wears a long-sleeved white dress covered with sprigs of delicate blue flowers. She stands calmly, unsurprised by the arrival of the goddess. She seems to have been waiting, in fact: she holds a dusky pink robe, patterned with leaves and flowers, ready to clothe Venus's naked body.

But it is Venus's posture that is so intriguing. Her weight is on her left foot; her hip curves because of it. Her right hand covers her breasts with what might best be described as tremendous ineffectiveness. Her right breast is partially concealed, but the left one is fully visible. Her left hand holds the ends of her long blond locks and presses them into her thigh. No wonder Zephyr is blowing hard enough to puff out his cheeks. We cannot see her pubic hair, because her ponytail obscures it. But we can hardly help thinking of what is hidden beneath. In covering her body – Venus's expression is completely serene; there is no subtext of shame here, even in fifteenth-century Italy – the goddess draws our attention to it more fully. And she is already virtually life-size, naked, and in the very centre of the canvas. She had our attention.

This is a pose of Venus – and before her, Aphrodite – that dates back to antiquity. The Aphrodite of Knidos was sculpted by the great artist of the fourth century BCE, Praxiteles. It doesn't survive to us today, but once stood in the temple of Aphrodite at Knidos, in Asia Minor (modern-day Turkey). In fact, according to Pliny the Elder, Praxiteles carved two sculptures of Aphrodite, one clothed and one naked.[2] The people of Kos, who had commissioned him, preferred the one wearing clothes. So the people of Knidos took the naked version – one of the earliest nude images of the female body. The Knidians found themselves in possession of a huge tourist attraction as people flocked to see the goddess. The statue was famously beautiful from every angle, and it was displayed in a shrine that was open on all sides. One man is said to have been so besotted with her that he hid in the temple at night and masturbated over her, staining the marble of her thigh. I suppose art lovers come in all shapes and sizes.

On a slightly more savoury note, in a collection of epigrams called the *Greek Anthology*, there is a reference to this statue, attributed to

Plato.[3] Aphrodite travels across the sea to Knidos, wanting to see this celebrated representation of herself. When she finally sets eyes on it, she asks, 'When did Praxiteles see me naked?' There can be few greater compliments for an artist than that.

This statue of Aphrodite may not survive, but copies of it do, including one in the Ludovisi collection at the National Roman Museum. She has the same pose: weight on one foot, hips curving to the side. She has serried curls rather than the tumbling locks that Botticelli gives her. And she makes no attempt to conceal her breasts: she is lifting a robe in her left hand, about to cover herself. Aphrodite is often presented to us wet – fresh from the sea, or from bathing – which means she is usually naked. Her right hand is held in the characteristic pose, in front of her pubic triangle. This pose has been called the *Venus Pudica*, which tends to be translated as 'Modest Venus'. But the word *pudica* means something rather uglier than 'modest', with connotations of shame or disgrace. It is a source of ongoing irritation to me that the words we use to describe female genitalia become more misogynistic the more apparently neutral they are: *pudenda*, something to be ashamed of; *vagina*, a sheath for holding a sword. It makes me long for some brisk monosyllables.

A further variation on this pose can be seen in the British Museum, which holds the Lely Venus on loan from the Royal Collection. This is a second-century Roman copy of a Greek statue, and it shows a crouching Venus, left arm resting on left thigh, right arm raised to cover her breasts. As with the Botticelli, only one breast is partially concealed, and the other is all the more noticeable because of it. Again, this Venus was designed to be seen from all angles; a curator at the museum once told me that her buttocks had been groped by so many visitors they became discoloured and had to be cleaned.

It is the standing version of Aphrodite or Venus that has been most copied, however, perhaps because the Botticelli painting is so well-known. I can't now remember if I had seen it before I first saw Terry Gilliam's *The Adventures of Baron Munchausen*, released in cinemas in 1988, which offers an homage to the image, starring a teenaged Uma Thurman as the naked Venus who is born from a shell while the baron and his comrades watch. There are many things that might trouble us now about this moment, not least a seventeen-year-old actress appearing nude from within a giant shell, long hair in her left hand, pressed against her body like the Botticelli Venus, her right arm held in front of her breasts. This divine appearance is witnessed by Oliver Reed (playing Venus's husband, Vulcan), John Neville (playing the baron), and Eric Idle (playing his companion Berthold), all of whom were old enough to be Thurman's father. Grandfather, in Neville's case. But Gilliam knows the art to which he pays homage, and the otherworldly beauty of Thurman's serene face (to which she carefully matches an expressionless voice) is a perfect echo of the painting.

And so let us return to the disco ball, spinning above the triumphant Aphrodite, or Venus – she is about to use both names. This one does not stand in a giant shell, nor is she naked. Rather, she is wearing shells in the form of a sequined bikini, with a gauzy skirt attached. Her expression and voice are as affectless as Thurman's: she may be singing about Venus, but she isn't roused – at least in this moment – by desire or any other emotion. Her backing singers march around her, repeating the crucial word, 'Venus'. Supporting Lady Gaga is, perhaps, the most disciplined performance the Muppets have ever given.[4] Even Animal plays the drums with more precision than usual in this Thanksgiving special, which aired in 2013.

There is a more dramatic (though perhaps less celebratory, and missing critiques of her performance from Statler and Waldorf, which is a deal-breaker for me) music video attached to the Lady Gaga song 'Venus'. *G.U.Y. (An ARTPOP Film)* was shot in Hearst Castle at San Simeon, California, a location with preexisting classical cinema connections: it featured in Stanley Kubrick's Roman epic, *Spartacus*. Its palm trees, light-filled colonnades, and statue-dotted staircases convey the grandeur of a semidivine palace, with an early twentieth-century twist. The shadows are long, and dancers dressed in increasingly outlandish outfits – bikinis, fetish gear – parade across the courtyards. Their almost robotic precision is what the Muppets so successfully pastiche in their version of the song. Here, Gaga is an injured Eros or angel, perhaps, carried by her followers to the swimming pool, where a healing ritual is performed before the camera pans to the Real Housewives of Beverly Hills, reality TV stars, all wearing bubblegum pink as they appear to play cello, tambourine, and harp.

As so often with Gaga, the layers of allusion are multiple and complex. Is she Eros – winged and wounded by an arrow shot by another Eros? – or Aphrodite? The song begins with a reference to the planet Venus (and goes on to include references to several more planets), but repeatedly describes her as the goddess of love. The healing ritual recalls a baptism, the location and costumes might have leapt from a surrealist painting, and the artificiality of nonmusicians miming the playing of instruments all add to the dreamlike sense that we are everywhere and nowhere, on earth, in space, in the past (several pasts) and the future.

Our confusion, and the accompanying feeling that we might as well simply lie back and let it wash over us, are familiar emotions to experience in the realm of this goddess. The sense of being overwhelmed by desire is not unique to human beings, either. Birds do it. Bees do it. And – at least according to the *Homeric Hymn to Aphrodite* – so do wolves, lions, leopards, and bears.[5] High up on Mount Ida, near the fabled city of Troy, they gambol and fawn at Aphrodite when she goes past, as surely we all would. The goddess is delighted by this attention and rewards the animals with a jolt of desire. They couple up, withdrawing into dark recesses *sunduo* – two by two – which already implies more fun than they had on Noah's ark. The *Homeric Hymn* makes no mention of any fleas, less still educated ones. But, if they are also present, we can safely assume they are at it too.

This bucolic scene reveals something we might already know about Aphrodite, but that is not immediately obvious in Botticelli's rendition of the goddess: her tremendous power. We know that love and desire can play havoc with our lives, but we are human and complicated. Afflict us with unrequited love and our responses vary from suicide attempts to poetry. But this pack of predators is rendered instantly kittenish by her presence. Did they want to experience this powerful urge for sex? Did they feel its lack before? They have no say in the matter. Anyone who has experienced the dizzying sensation of falling in love at first sight may well know how they feel.

Human propensity to be helpless in the face of desire is widely attested, and largely unchanged through time: love poetry is one of the oldest literary forms there is. But the way we view the causes of lust has changed. Now, if we experience raging lust or desire for someone we may not even know – an actor, a pop star – we would probably call it a crush. If it is for someone we barely know – a new colleague, the man with glorious red hair who works at the bakery – we might glamorize it as love at first sight. We might think of the love as having its origins in our hearts and minds. Or we might think it emanates from the object of our affection. But we would be unlikely to consider that our feelings have been bestowed on us by a third party altogether.

For the Greeks (and the Romans), Aphrodite – like Eros with his bow and sharp-pointed arrows – applies desire to us externally. If those wolves happened to be behind a tree at the precise moment when she lobs (and this is the verb in the *Homeric Hymn* – *bal* – to throw) desire in their direction, there might be a lot fewer wolf cubs around in a few weeks. And perhaps if we'd just happened to duck at the crucial moment, our broken hearts could have been avoided. But then we would also never have experienced the thrill of sudden and overwhelming desire.

In this *Homeric Hymn*, Aphrodite is travelling through the woods as she makes her way from Cyprus to Troy.[6] She is a goddess with a long history in the east, as the successor to Ishtar, Inanna, and Astarte, great goddesses who arose in what we would now call the Middle East – Babylon and Nineveh were thronging places of worship – and who were all linked in earlier times to the planet we know as Venus. But if these goddesses can be traced back to the Middle East, we might be wondering exactly where Aphrodite comes from. Botticelli's enduring image of her appearing from a large shell clearly places her in the sea, but which one? Aphrodite is linked to two locations in particular, as Hesiod tells us in his *Theogony*. And although Homer offers us an Aphrodite who is the daughter of Dione and Zeus[7] (Dione is a Titan – one of those early goddesses who predate the Olympians. We'll return to her occasional walk-on role as Aphrodite's mother shortly), most sources give her a rather more violent entry into the world.

For Hesiod, Aphrodite doesn't have a mother, and her father is accidental. As you may remember, Kronos is born to Gaia – the earth goddess – and Ouranos – the heavens. But Ouranos fears his children will overthrow him, so he keeps them hidden away in a recess in the earth, refusing to let them out into the world. Gaia is pained and exhausted by the endless weight of holding her offspring within. She creates a sharp sickle and gives it to Kronos, who gladly takes on the responsibility of unmanning his father. The precise topography of their encounter is not made explicit by Hesiod, but Kronos is presumably still inside Gaia's womb when he takes the blade to Ouranos's genitals. Having castrated his father, Kronos throws the disembodied parts into the sea. They are carried by the surging waves for a long time, Hesiod remarks.[8]

The spume coalesces around the sperm (sometimes I write these sentences just to see if my editor still has a red pen), and Aphrodite forms from this frothing white aftermath of violence. This is why men call her Aphrodite, Hesiod adds: because she is *aphrogenea*,[9] born from the foam. Created in this white sea-foam, Aphrodite first approaches Cythera, he says. Cythera lies off the southern coast of the Peloponnese, the fingers of which almost point to this little island. And from there she heads to Cyprus, a long way east across the Mediterranean. Both these islands give epithets to Aphrodite: she is often called Cytherea, or Cyprian. He adds an unexpected etymological pun. Aphrodite is also called *philommēdea* – laughter-loving – because she was created from *mēdeōn* – genitals. I sometimes wonder if this story could be more unsettling to the average male reader; I think this final touch probably ensures the answer is no.

Before he moves on to discuss the origins of his next chosen deities, Hesiod makes one final observation about Aphrodite's *moira* – her allotted area of expertise, among mortals and deathless gods. No one is immune to her power, in other words: the gods themselves are as much at risk of falling in love as the rest of us. And then he describes her *moira* in more detail. It is, he explains, the conversations of girls, and smiles, and deceits, delight, sweet love, and softness. It's hard to decode the precise role of the male gaze here: Are the girls' conversations about the boys they can't stop thinking about? Are they the lovers, whispering about their beloveds? Or is it that the girls' conversations make them desirable to men, to Hesiod? Are they merely the objects of affection? The all-powerful influence of Aphrodite implies that it is probably both.

If you visit Paphos, on Cyprus, you can go to Aphrodite's rock, the exact place where the goddess is believed to have stepped out of the Mediterranean Sea. It's a wildly popular destination: I visited once in mid-November, and it was still full of visitors determined to make their offerings to the goddess, and perhaps improve their chances in love. On my way to this numinous place (like so much of Cyprus, it seems to occupy a space between divine and mortal), I spent the afternoon at the Hambis Printmaking Museum nearby. The celebrated Cypriot artist and printmaker Hambis Tsangaris has created a vibrant and witty series of prints of the birthplace of Aphrodite, using a repeated heart motif to illustrate the power of this goddess and her close links to Paphos. In one glorious image, her rock is made of huge yellow and orange hearts, almost melting into crags and fissures. Smaller green hearts tipped onto their sides create the illusion of the rock's vegetation. In the foreground, a naked pink couple embrace: she has tiny green hearts for her hair; his hair and beard are depicted with blue ones. Around them, multicoloured hearts spring from the grass like flowers. I have had this print on my wall for a year or so now, and I have long since accepted that not only does it make me happy every single day, it is somehow also as accurate a record of that place as any of the photographs I took.

This heart-studded depiction of Paphos – and of the influence Aphrodite has on those of us she happens to fix with her attention – is far more familiar to us than the violence of her origin, of severed genitalia landing in a roiling sea. But in many ancient sources, Aphrodite is presented as not only a goddess who can fill us with pleasure, but one who can also torture us with pain. Love poets have a love-hate relationship with their patron goddess, just as they tend to with the objects of their affection.

And none more so than Sappho. One of the longest pieces of her poetry to survive to us is addressed to *poikilophrōn athanat'* – cunning immortal – Aphrodite.[10] *Poikilophrōn* is usually translated as 'sly' or 'wily', but it literally means to have a mind that is multicoloured or spotted, which I think suggests beautifully the somewhat arbitrary nature of Aphrodite's favours. Sappho is pleading with the goddess for help. Aphrodite reminds her that she has heard the poet's prayers and come to her aid before. They have a long-standing relationship, in which Aphrodite hears her voice, and acts – poets obviously get a better response from goddesses than the rest of us, but I suppose they probably sing a better prayer. For Sappho, when Aphrodite intervenes in the mortal realm, it involves leaving her father's golden house – this father is presumably Zeus, so Sappho seems to be in the same tradition as Homer, rather than Hesiod.

Aphrodite travels in a chariot pulled by (what must be a large number of) sparrows. When she reaches Sappho, she smiles and asks Sappho why she is praying again. What is going on in Sappho's mad heart: the word *mainolai* shares the same root as our word mania. But then she cuts to the chase: Who do you want back? she asks. So this, obviously, is Sappho's problem. She doesn't need help in finding love, she needs help in keeping it. Aphrodite's answer comes in a verse which should fill every reader with recognition, hope, and fear in equal parts. This, I think, is the emotional backbone for every yearning love song written since.

If she now runs away from you, Aphrodite promises, she'll soon be chasing you. If she now refuses your gifts, she'll soon be giving you presents. And if she doesn't love you, she will, soonest. And then the real kicker: *kōuk etheloisa* – even if she doesn't want to. Sappho welcomes her response, and the final line of the poem sums up her position neatly – *summakhos esso*, she says. Be my ally.

Summakhos means 'a person who fights alongside you': Aphrodite isn't a metaphorical ally, she's a literal one. Which is lucky, because when you're in love, you're at war. This is a metaphor which will extend throughout ancient love poetry: the great Latin love poets like Catullus and Ovid routinely present themselves as warriors in the service of love. Sappho here offers an early version of this theme, the notion that love can be fatal, that a beloved can be your greatest enemy.

I find my response to the poem has changed a great deal over time. I first encountered Sappho as a teenager, and then (I am sorry to tell you, but it's bound to come out sooner or later) I could see nothing wrong at all with her approach. If I'd believed Aphrodite would steer her sparrow-drawn chariot to 1990s Birmingham, I would have prayed just the same way myself. Don't ask me why it seemed reasonable to me to want someone so much that you prayed for them to love you even against their will. I cannot give you an answer. Now this notion seems to me to come straight from the pages of *Jessica Jones*, where the super-hero's nemesis, Kilgrave, employs mind control over anyone he chooses. Adapted for television in 2015, the series focused on the horrifying cal-lousness with which Kilgrave (played by David Tennant) can demand affection from almost anyone but the person he most desires, Jessica herself (Krysten Ritter). The faces of those he exploits are never more tormented than when he casually insists they look happy to welcome him into their homes, or otherwise fulfil his desires. It's bad enough to be forced to act against your own wants and needs; it's somehow worse to be asked to appear delighted by it. Sappho's prayer – and Aphrodite's response – now seem to me to occupy similar territory. I suppose this is probably the time to issue a blanket apology to all those boys, but hopefully my fascination with them turned out to be character-building for everyone.

Let us return to Aphrodite in the *Homeric Hymn*, travelling across Mount Ida and bewitching its wolves and lions as she goes. She is en route to Troy, which is still thriving – we are several decades before the war that will cause its destruction. As we have seen above, Aphrodite is usually the goddess dispensing desire as she pleases. But on this oc-casion she is the one experiencing ungovernable longing, and it is Zeus who has done this to her. Irritated by Aphrodite's apparent immunity to lust for a human being, Zeus has implanted sweet desire for a mortal man into her heart.[11] And so, Aphrodite finds herself in pursuit of An-chises, who is (somewhat confusingly, but the Trojans make a habit of this kind of thing) both a prince of Troy and a cowherd. So dazzled is the goddess by the sight of this mere man that she heads to Paphos to get ready for what we might euphemistically describe as a date night. The Graces bathe her and perfume her and dress her in all her finest clothes and jewellery. Now she is laughter-loving and arrayed in gold.[12]

Aphrodite returns to Mount Ida from Cyprus and heads straight to where she last saw Anchises, whom the hymn describes as a hero with divine beauty.[13] After all her preparations, she now uses her magic powers to disguise herself. She appears to Anchises as a *parthenos* – a maiden – because she doesn't want to scare him.[14] But who is she kidding? Aphrodite is no mistress of disguise. The moment he lays eyes on her, Anchises tries to guess which goddess she might be: Artemis? Leto? Aphrodite? Themis, Athene, a Grace, a nymph? Credit where it's due, he obviously realizes it's better to cover all his bases rather than risk offending her by guessing the wrong name.

Aphrodite's first response is a paper-thin denial: I am not a god, she says,[15] in the way that no one except a god would ever need to. I'm mortal, my parents are mortal (my dad is a renowned king, maybe that's why you're mistaking me for a god). And how come I can speak Trojan as well as my parents' language? Certainly not because I'm any kind of deity. It's because I had a nurse who came from here. So she taught me. Great, glad we've cleared that up. The god Hermes, who I certainly don't know because we both live on Mount Olympus, said I should sleep with you. So, hi! Let's get married. My parents will love you and send you loads of gold.

It is no exaggeration to say that this may be my favourite proposition in all literature. Anchises, to his enormous credit, says he would cheerfully move in with Hades for just one night with this woman.[16] And he gets his desire, a mortal with a deathless goddess, albeit a mortal who doesn't know what he's doing or who he's really with.[17] They have sex, and she sends him to sleep. In ancient poems, divinely bestowed sleep is usually presented as a gift, although the modern reader may find this entire scene rather low on informed consent, and rather high on unrequested sedatives.

Now, many of us may know what it is like to wake up the next morning and be surprised to find who we spent the previous night with.

For Anchises, the experience is somewhat heightened, since Aphrodite has literally changed while he slept, reverting to her true goddess state. When he sees her, he promptly hides his face behind his cloak, and pleads with her not to leave him impotent.[18] Mortal men who have once shared a bed with a goddess have this problem, he says. Aphrodite comforts him by explaining that he is loved by the gods, so nothing bad will happen to him. He is about to become a single parent, however, as she will give birth to Aeneas, so called because of the terrible pain it causes her to have had sex with a mortal (Aeneas is linked here to *ainos*, a Greek word meaning painful or terrible). As mornings after nights before go, this one might best be described as quite invigorating for Anchises.

Aphrodite goes on to share the salutary story of Eos – Dawn – who falls for a mortal man named Tithonus and asks for him to be granted eternal life. Sadly, she forgets to ask for eternal youth, so poor Tithonus gets older and smaller and more crunchy until he eventually becomes a cicada. But if Anchises thinks he's got things tough, imagine how it is for Aphrodite – she'll be mortified for her whole endless life because she had sex with him.[19] She makes one final stipulation: she'll return in a few years with their son Aeneas, who will be raised by nymphs in the meantime. And if anyone then asks Anchises who his child's mother is, he needs to say it's a nymph. Mention Aphrodite's name and he'll be on the receiving end of one of Zeus's thunderbolts. As I said, it's an invigorating start to the man's day.

This poem is a wonderful celebration of the ruthless qualities Aphrodite possesses, even on this rare occasion when she herself is not in control of desire. Anchises – however we might blanch at her deceit – has been treated remarkably well, by the standards of ancient myth: it is a great deal more fun being seduced by Aphrodite than abducted by Zeus (which she herself tells us when she reminds Anchises of his ancestor Ganymede, who was spirited off to Mount Olympus by Zeus, losing contact with his grief-stricken father and everyone else he knew). Anchises will have a son to show for it, and Aeneas will be so devoted to his father that Virgil will call him *pius* – dutiful – Aeneas. But if ever we needed reminding that desire is amoral and wholly devoid of sentiment, Aphrodite's behaviour towards Anchises is highly illustrative. Give the goddess what she wants, and she'll leave you with a lovely unharmed child and a promise that you won't get hurt. If I were looking to draw a parallel here, she probably reminds me most of the mafia.

All of this raises an interesting question, incidentally. Which is this: If you had been seduced by the goddess of beauty, love, and sexual desire herself and then instructed to tell no one about it, would you keep it quiet? Just casually carry on with your life, parenting your child, batting away enquiries by saying you'd had sex with a hot nymph? Would that be such a challenge, if the alternative were to be struck by actual lightning, sent by the king of the gods himself? I feel sure you have already guessed that the answer to this question is: yes, yes it would.

The circumstances of Anchises blurting out his sexual history are lost in the mists of time, but we can see the result of it in the second book of Virgil's *Aeneid*. Aeneas departs Troy on the night the city is sacked: his destiny is not to die there, like so many of his peers, but to set sail with a party of survivors and found a new Troy, eventually, in Italy. As he makes his way through the burning city, Aeneas takes his son and his father with him, famously neglecting to keep track of his wife, Creusa, who is left behind and appears only as a ghost wishing him well with any future relationships. But Aeneas has to carry Anchises on his back, because his father is too old and infirm to walk himself (he will die of old age in Book Three). We can confirm the diagnosis in a fragment of a lost play by Sophocles. Dionysius of Halicarnassus quotes the line in his history and says that Anchises has a wound on his back from the lightning strike.[20] So perhaps the moral of this story is that if a goddess tells you to keep your mouth shut on pain of meteorological revenge, you should.

In spite of her physical distance from Aeneas – handing him over to the nymphs to nurse, and then to his father to raise – Aphrodite is deeply invested in his well-being. In Book Five of the *Iliad*, Homer shows Aeneas on the battlefield up against Diomedes at the precise moment the Greek warrior is having a particularly brutal run of success. Aeneas is no slouch himself; Homer has just compared him to a lion.[21] But Diomedes chucks a huge rock at him, which catches him on the hip and sends him crashing to the ground. Aeneas would have died where he fell, Homer says, had his mother, Aphrodite, daughter of Zeus, not been keeping a close eye on him. She wraps her arms around him, to keep him from being hit by a spear, and then carries him from the battlefield. But Diomedes is not ready to give up his quarry, and he is not afraid of the goddess. He chases after her with his bronze spear, recognizing that she is no warrior.[22] He catches up with her and injures her hand with his spear, slicing through her robe, which was made for her by the Graces. Ichor – the substance gods have instead of blood – flows from Aphrodite's hand. She screams and pushes Aeneas aside. But Apollo is there beside her to look after her son.

Even now, having injured one of the great Olympian gods, Diomedes shows no remorse. Instead he taunts her, telling her she shouldn't get involved in war – she cajoles women (and not men, seems to be his point. And even if she does, she certainly doesn't fight them). Aphrodite borrows horses from her brother Ares, who does belong on the battlefield, and escapes to her mother, Dione, who heals her wounded hand and takes away the pain. No wonder Homer gives his Aphrodite a mother: we all want someone who will kiss it better when we are hurt.

In case you're wondering how things work out for Diomedes after this extraordinary attack on the gods, he survives the war and thrives in its aftermath. But in the field of love and sex, things don't go quite as well. We hear from various sources such as Pseudo-Apollodorus that his wife Aegialia betrays him with a man named Cometes.[23] Perhaps he should have been a little less hasty to injure and insult a goddess who cajoles women.

Aphrodite, meanwhile, after Athene complains to Zeus that she should be nowhere near a battlefield, is ordered by the king of the gods to avoid it in future. But her son certainly lives to the end of the war and beyond it, to fulfil his destiny to found a new city, a second Troy. So Aphrodite's refusal to stick to her *moira*, her allotted expertise – however much it aggravates Diomedes and his patron goddess, Athene – shapes the aftermath of the war. And, according to Virgil, connects the Romans to her directly. So she may become a goddess who shuns war, but her bellicose descendants won't let that put them off.

There is another story about Aphrodite in Homer, but this one appears in the *Odyssey*. When Odysseus lands at Scheria (also known as Phaeacia), the final diversion on his much-delayed return to Ithaca, he hears a bard performing at dinner. Demodocus sings about the affair between Aphrodite (who is married to Hephaestus, the blacksmith god) and Ares, the god of war.[24] Not only do they have sex, but they do so secretly, in Hephaestus's bed. No one can keep a secret from Helios, of course: the sun god sees everything. He doesn't keep quiet, either, but promptly takes the bad news to Hephaestus. The blacksmith heads straight to his forge to hammer out chains that are both invisibly fine and unbreakably strong. Raging at Ares, he sets his trap, hanging the threadlike chains from the ceiling and wrapping them round the bed. Not even the immortal gods could see them, Demodocus explains.

Having set his trap, Hephaestus withdraws to a safe distance and waits. Ares – keeping watch for another opportunity to seduce Aphrodite – heads straight into their house and suggests a further liaison, since Hephaestus is away. Aphrodite happily agrees. The two gods head to bed and are almost immediately caught in the trap: they can neither move nor get out of the bed. Hephaestus makes a swift return, Helios again supplying him with the crucial information.[25] Hephaestus yells to Zeus and all the other gods, demanding they witness this scene which, he allows, may seem funny to them, but is infuriating to him. Look at Aphrodite, he demands, always dishonouring me. She loves destructive Ares, because he is handsome and strong-footed. This may seem like an odd feature to mention, but it is clearly a painful point of contrast to Hephaestus, with his damaged foot, that Ares is gorgeous and his feet are perfect, so of course he would be the one Aphrodite prefers. And hidden in there is a second layer of hurt and anger: Ares can only destroy; that is what war is about. Hephaestus doesn't need to make the contrast any plainer. We already know he is creative, a maker of beautiful and wondrous objects, not least because his wife and her lover are trapped in some of them as he speaks.

Hephaestus invites the other gods to come and look at the couple in bed, at the sight that grieves him so terribly. Aphrodite is beautiful, he concedes, but she has no self-control. He calls her *kunōpidos* – dog-faced – an insult which Helen of Sparta has thrown at herself in Homer's *Iliad*.

We might well wonder what the specific meaning of this insult is, since it is used of the most beautiful woman and the most beautiful goddess in these poems. It obviously cannot contain connotations of ugliness, at least not physical ugliness, which we would probably mean if we used a similar insult today. And the character of a dog in modern culture is usually presented positively: loyal, devoted, and so on. Again, this is clearly not what is intended in Homeric language, although the *Odyssey* contains one of literature's most loyal dogs, Argus, who waits for his master to return for twenty years before dying of old age and shock when he finally recognizes Odysseus on the hero's return to Ithaca. But for Hephaestus, his wife is shameless, like a dog. It seems to imply that he considers her sexually promiscuous or undiscerning, even though he himself has already remarked on Ares's good looks.

Poseidon, Hermes, and Apollo all come to his house, as requested. The goddesses, Demodocus says, stay modestly at home. The gods laugh at the scene, as Hephaestus had predicted, and share helpful platitudes: no good comes from bad deeds. They agree that Hephaestus should be given back the bride-price he paid to Zeus to marry Aphrodite (financial assessments of women's worth were common in the ancient world, and often dependent on their chastity), and they think that Ares should pay a fine. And then, as is so often the way with men who disapprove of women, they wonder if she might be interested in sex with them. Apollo asks Hermes if he would take his chance to have sex with golden Aphrodite, even if that meant he would be chained up like this. And Hermes replies, yes. In fact, he would run the risk of being bound three times as tightly to have sex with golden Aphrodite. I have sometimes wondered if the prospect of being tied up in golden chains actually adds to the appeal as far as Hermes is concerned: he seems so quick to reply and to raise the question of more and tighter restraints. But I accept this isn't a very scholarly response to the text.

The gods all laugh at their own sexual badinage, except for one. Poseidon doesn't laugh, Homer says, but rather begs Hephaestus to free Ares, promising him that Ares will pay the fine that Hephaestus has demanded. But Hephaestus isn't so easily bought: How would I bind you, he asks, if Ares gets away with it? Poseidon pledges to settle the debt himself if Ares doesn't pay. And at this point Hephaestus agrees, because he feels he has an obligation to Poseidon. He frees the trapped gods from the snare, and both withdraw from Olympus. Ares goes to Thrace, in northern Greece. And laughter-loving Aphrodite heads to Paphos, returning to her sanctuary on Cyprus. There she is bathed and oiled by the Graces who so often attend her and then dressed in beautiful clothes. She is, Demodocus says, *thauma idesthai* – a wonder to behold.[26]

This moment, I think, reveals the heart of Aphrodite's power. No matter what the situation, no matter how humiliated or shamed she is supposed to feel according to the men around her, she is restored to her usual smiling serene beauty in the blink of an eye. Even when she is physically injured by Diomedes, she is soon healed by her mother. And here, where male gods have gathered to laugh at the scene of her trapped in bed with her illicit lover, where she has been vilified and mocked by her husband and made the subject of salacious remarks by her siblings (according to Homeric genealogy, she is sister to Apollo and Hermes), she departs the scene as laughter-loving as ever. Her beauty, her perfection are unharmed by whatever happens to her.

Perhaps this is key to all these deities: they are unchanging, after all, because they are immortal. But there is something about Aphrodite that reminds me of women applying their lipstick in a war zone – you can't take away her game face. Or certainly not for long. Make her fall in love with a mortal man and she will disguise herself, seduce him, threaten him, and leave him. Make her your laughingstock and she will only make you want her more.

There is one recent example of Aphrodite being treated as the butt of a joke, and it is in Woody Allen's Oscar-winning 1995 movie, *Mighty Aphrodite*. The film stars Allen in his perennial role of a well-to-do New York guy, this time a sports writer named Lenny Weinrib. Lenny and his wife, Amanda (Helena Bonham Carter), adopt a baby, who – after being surrounded by positive attention and educational toys – turns out to be gifted, at least in his parents' estimation. Lenny decides he wants to know more about Max's genes and tracks down his birth mother, Linda.

Linda, played by Mira Sorvino (her voice a glorious high-pitched foghorn in homage to Judy Holliday in *Born Yesterday*), is a porn actress and prostitute. The joke – of course – is that she isn't very bright, and Lenny sets himself the task of turning her life around to something more respectable: a hairdresser, as it turns out. Lenny tries to fix Linda up with a boxer who is very stupid indeed, but he turns nasty and hits her when he finds out about her chequered past. Lenny is briefly abandoned by his wife, and he and Linda seek solace in one another's arms. Nine months later, she has Lenny's daughter, though he never finds out, because by this time Linda is married to Don, a helicopter pilot she meets by accident, an unashamed deus ex machina. A year or so later, Linda and Lenny bump into one another in a toy store. He is accompanied by her son, though she doesn't know it, and she is with his daughter, though he has no idea.

The presentation is self-consciously Greek-theatrical, with a chorus singing, dancing, and commenting on the action, as we might expect to find in an Aristophanes comedy. The chorus characters are largely Theban, including Laius and Jocasta, the birth parents of Oedipus. No wonder, since adoption is such a major theme of the movie. And Allen has tremendous fun playing with everything from the plots to the conceits of Greek tragedy. Achilles only had an Achilles' heel, Lenny whines to Linda when she asks for his help defending herself against a violent pimp; I have a whole Achilles' body. The pimp is bought off with basketball tickets – one of two plot points that rely on Allen's sportswriter job (the other is a rather sweet scene at the horse races, reminiscent of *My Fair Lady*, which was inspired by *Pygmalion*, as is this film. Linda is as loud and inappropriate at the races as Eliza Doolittle, but her conversation tends towards her history in pornography, rather than a mere expletive).

Mira Sorvino won the Academy Award for Best Supporting Actress for this role, and it is wholly deserved. The film has a few jarring elements: Allen is more than thirty years older than either Bonham Carter or Sorvino, which makes his marriage seem – if anything – less likely than his fling with Linda. But I can't pretend this was unusual when the film was released: enormous age gaps were quite common in nineties cinema (Allen was a repeat offender, but so was Jack Nicholson in *Wolf* and *As Good as It Gets*, Al Pacino in *Frankie and Johnny*, and Harrison Ford in *Six Days, Seven Nights*, although I tend to excuse Harrison Ford everything because I am morally weak on the subject of Dr Jones. It is

an ongoing source of disappointment in my life that while archaeolo-
gists have become more of a feature, very few of them look like a young
Harrison Ford).

More troubling is the fact that after Kevin – a semiprofessional
boxer and a giant of a man – has hit Linda in the face hard enough to
give her a black eye, Lenny still tries to persuade her he might be the
man for her. At the end of the film, we see everyone happily coupled up:
Lenny and Amanda, Linda and Don, Kevin and his nameless wife on a
farm somewhere. The unavoidable sense that this man might thump his
wife at any moment plays havoc with the cute everything-is-wrapped-
up-neatly ending, at least for me.

The film works on one level because Linda is dumb and yet her child
is a genius, and Lenny learns that nature might have less to do with
his child's abilities than nurture. But though Linda is inappropriate and
hilarious, she really isn't any less smart than anyone else. Actually, it
is Lenny who is the idiot, neglecting his wife to pursue his interest in
Linda; Amanda has to leave him before he realizes what is really important to him. None of his ideas to improve Linda's life have a positive
effect on her – when she decides to quit prostitution at his behest, her
pimp threatens her with violent assault, and she has to embarrass Lenny
at work before he will offer to help her. And the boyfriend he picks for
her is incredibly dim, and a wifebeater.

In fact, it is Linda who makes the choices that improve her life, as
when she slows down her car to pick up the guy in the broken helicopter
because she is kind and won't leave a man stranded. And it's Linda who
realizes that Lenny cannot continue to be in her life now she has met
her future husband: if either of their marriages is to succeed, they must
cease their friendship. When they meet in the toy shop, it is clear that
she is the one who has moved away from him, delighted though she is to
bump into him. She instinctively knows the truths he fumbles to find.

This is surely a further reference to *Born Yesterday*. Judy Holliday's

Billie Dawn is another variant on Eliza Doolittle, this time reworked as a gangster's moll learning about political life and engagement in Washington, DC. Her boyfriend and his crooked pals underestimate her because she has a high-pitched voice and apparently no attention span. William Holden plays Paul, a political journalist hired to educate Billie so she doesn't embarrass her boyfriend in their new social milieu. But – naturally – the two fall in love because he realizes almost immediately what every other man in Billie's life has missed (except her father, whom she has been too ashamed to contact for many years): Billie is a bright woman who just happens to sound like a ditz.

Sorvino's performance in *Mighty Aphrodite* imbues Linda with sincerity and emotional clarity, both of which are lacking in Lenny's world. Does she foolishly believe she could be a Broadway star when she is turning tricks and taking the occasional porn gig? She does, but there are plenty of very smart people who have thought the same thing. And when reminded that she could have another fulfilling life that she would enjoy – as a mother and a hairdresser – she grabs the opportunity to make the change. Lenny, meanwhile, loves having Max in his life but had to be forced into the adoption by his wife. He was less able than Linda to name what he wanted and chase it for himself. If Linda seems inappropriate, it is only because Lenny has taken her into a world she doesn't know. She isn't stupid, she's just new, like Eliza and Billie. The film is a rare example of an Aphrodite – in her metaphorical sense as a beautiful woman – who is both sexy and funny. Linda is laughter-loving, as Homer would describe it; she prides herself on her sense of humour. And – as with Hermes in the *Odyssey* – men desire her even as they mock her.

But there is another side to Aphrodite, one that has no laughter to it at all. If slighted, Aphrodite's revenge is both comprehensive and horrific. I have written elsewhere about her treatment of Hippolytus (who scorns her) and his stepmother Phaedra (who shows her every deference but is punished just the same with the agony of unrequited and illegitimate desire, followed by disgrace and death). So let's look here at a different example, folded into the story of Aphrodite's own great heartache: her love affair with the beautiful Adonis.

As so often, it is Ovid who tells a detailed version of this sad tale, in Book Ten of his *Metamorphoses*. Because he is Roman, he uses the goddess's Roman name. So this is the story of Venus and Adonis.[27] This beautiful young man should not even exist: his mother, Myrrha, developed an intense inappropriate sexual desire for her father. Cinyras was not incestuously inclined, but did like having sex in the dark with a young woman who said she was the same age as his daughter. Thus Myrrha conceives a baby. Because of her actions, Myrrha prays to be transformed. Still pregnant and weeping, she is turned into a tree. Her tears form the precious resin myrrh.

The tree is bent and groaning until Lucina, goddess of childbirth, takes pity on the baby and the tree and intercedes. Its bark cracks open and the baby is born. This is perhaps the only moment of extant Latin literature that foreshadows William Friedkin's tree-based cult horror movie from 1990, *The Guardian*. In the unlikely plot, Jenny Seagrove plays Camilla, a nanny who repeatedly inveigles her way into a family's trust before feeding their babies to a large tree in the nearby forest. Her dual life (as some kind of forest spirit) is only uncovered when one couple follow her into the woods and find a malevolent tree with babies apparently trapped beneath its bark. When they attempt to kill Camilla, she draws energy from the tree she has sustained with human lives. Only when the tree is attacked does Camilla start to lose her life force. In my memory, which I refuse to sully by rewatching the film now, the husband takes a chain saw to the tree, and when he lops off a large branch, Camilla loses an arm, or possibly a leg. I cannot in all conscience say this is a good film, but I would be lying to you if I said it hasn't occupied a fond leafy place in my memory for the best part of thirty years. Don't go in sober, is my advice.

Myrrha's baby survives the tree's wooden labour and is pronounced beautiful by all who see him. Even Envy would agree, says Orpheus, who is narrating this whole section of the *Metamorphoses*.[28] The years slip past and Adonis becomes an increasingly handsome man. Handsome enough to please even Venus, Orpheus adds, and avenge the fiery passion that destroyed his mother. And so before their affair can even begin, we've been reminded by the musician that love is often dreadful rather than delightful, something to be avenged rather than enjoyed.

Venus's passion begins with a simple accident: Cupid gives his mother a kiss while wearing his quiver, which is full of those passion-inducing arrows. He grazes her breast, and his injured mother pushes him away. She is more seriously injured than she appears, even though she doesn't realize it at first. *Capta viri formā* begins the next line of Orpheus's song – captured by the man's beauty.[29] She stops caring about the places she usually loves: the shores of Cythera, Paphos surrounded by the sea, Knidos rich in fish, Amathus rich in metals. She abandons the divine realm too. In three perfect words that summarize all obsessive love, Orpheus sings: *caelo praefertur Adonis* – she prefers Adonis to heaven.[30]

Venus's behaviour changes in other ways too. She has always tended to spend her time in the shade, indulging herself and intensifying her beauty. But now she's running through the woods and over the rocks so she can stay close to Adonis at all times. She's wearing a knee-length tunic, like Diana (or Artemis, if you prefer). In fact, she is engaged in full Diana cosplay, even hunting with dogs, though she avoids the more dangerous quarry – lions and bears and so on – and sticks to chasing rabbits and deer. She advises Adonis to do the same. Be brave when the animals are running away, she says. Take care of yourself for me and don't attack anything that nature has armed. Your youth and beauty shake me to my core, but they won't affect lions or wild boar. Especially avoid lions, huge, raging creatures. I loathe the whole breed. Adonis asks why she dislikes lions so much, and Venus says she will explain the cause of her old grievance. The couple settle in a shady spot (old habits die hard, it seems), and she tells him the story as they lie on the ground together, interrupting herself only to kiss him.

Maybe you've heard of a woman who outclassed men at running. This wasn't a story, a rumour; she really did beat them. You wouldn't be able to say whether her foot speed or her beauty was more exceptional. And she asked the god about a husband and the god replied, no need of a husband for you, Atalanta. Avoid the very idea of husbands![31] The Latin here reads *fuge coniugis usum* – flee the use of a husband – which I may yet have as a tattoo. Although I'd have to be sure to stop before the next line, where the oracle has bad news: though you won't escape, you'll keep your life but lose yourself. Atalanta withdraws into the woods to avoid the flock of suitors who want to marry her. She refuses to consider anyone who can't beat her in a race. And if he loses the race, he dies. Those are the rules. She is so beautiful that the suitors all agree to these terms.

Among the spectators of this high-stakes footrace is a young man named Hippomenes, who wonders why anyone would put himself in so much danger in his desire for a wife. But he changes his mind when he sees Atalanta for himself (she looks as good as me, says Venus immodestly. Or you, Adonis, if you were a woman), and decides to enter the contest.[32]

Having watched her beat all the other suitors, Hippomenes asks Atalanta to test her skills against him. Looking at him, Atalanta isn't sure if she'd rather win or lose. *Which god hates his beauty so much they want him to die?* she wonders. Although she claims she isn't moved by his good looks, it's his youth that weakens her resolve. But then she reasons with herself that he has seen the others fail and die and he still seems to want to take the risk. If she'd been the marrying kind, she concedes, she would have happily shared her bed with him.

Hippomenes now prays to Cytherea, a poetic name for Venus. Help me in my brave attempt, he begs. Encourage the passion you've given me. Venus hears his prayer at a moment when she happens to have her hands full of golden apples. She gives these to Hippomenes and instructs him in their use. And then the race begins. Atalanta is easily the better runner: Hippomenes is breathless and dry-mouthed, but she holds back, delaying when she could have passed him. Luckily, the time when women repress their abilities to avoid making a man feel bad about himself is long gone.

As they close in on the finish line, Hippomenes drops one of the golden apples, and Atalanta is consumed by desire for it. She runs off the track to pick it up. Hippomenes surges ahead, but Atalanta soon catches him and passes him once more. He drops the second apple, and she stops to collect it before racing past him again. He prays to Venus one more time. Then, in the final part of the race, he throws the third apple as far from the racing line as he can, to delay her for as long as possible. Atalanta almost leaves it, but she can't resist Venus's trinket and she goes off to fetch it. It's just enough time to allow Hippomenes to win.

But does he then thank Venus for helping him to victory? Does he burn incense in her honour? He does not. He forgets he owes his life and his bride to the goddess. Suddenly, says Venus, I was consumed with rage.[33] She decides to make an example of the pair. You will note that Atalanta wasn't involved in the prayers to Venus or in the knowing neglect of her, but she is about to be punished even so. They are passing by a shrine of the great mother goddess Cybele, and Venus hits Hippomenes with an urgent desire for sex with Atalanta. Cybele is predictably enraged that her temple has been profaned and turns the pair into lions. The mother goddess then tames them with a bridle between their teeth.

So avoid lions at all costs, Venus tells Adonis. Actually, avoid all creatures that like a fight. Don't let your bravery destroy us both. This is obviously a perfectly reasonable moral to draw from the tale, although

I have tended to prioritize the more subtextual moral (don't pretend to be less than you are to make a mediocre man feel better, as you will both regret it when you have tails).

This is a side to Venus that we have seen elsewhere and can never be overlooked: her favour is both conditional and temporary. And when it is withdrawn, the penalty can be devastating. Yes, Hippomenes is ungrateful, but surely a goddess isn't counting every swirl of burning incense. Aren't there enough lovers worshipping her across Greek myth for her to let this one go? Of course there aren't. And even if you are incredibly devout, like Phaedra – who literally builds Aphrodite a temple – you can still end up on her wrong side as she is nonetheless destroyed by her after two years of constant misery and pain.

Even Adonis, who certainly attracts her favour and reciprocates it, doesn't have long to enjoy it. Venus finishes her story and heads off in her chariot, which is now pulled by swans (perhaps Sappho's sparrows had grown tired). Adonis immediately attacks a boar, precisely the kind of animal his lover urged him to avoid. The boar spears him in return, burying its tusks in his groin. Even from the skies near Cyprus where she is heading, Venus hears his groans and steers her swans straight back in his direction. She sees him lying dead in a pool of blood. She tears at her dress and her hair in grief; she beats her breast. The serenity she has always displayed when faced with any setback – even being caught naked in bed with her lover by her husband – is nowhere to be seen. Now she grieves like the rest of us, raging at the Fates. Persephone was allowed to turn a girl into a plant, she says. Even in her grief, Aphrodite cannot help comparing herself to other goddesses, it seems. So she also creates a horticultural memorial, sprinkling the pooled blood with nectar. An hour later, a flower the same colour as Adonis's blood rises from the pool. It's the same colour as the pomegranate seed, Orpheus says. This fruit reminds us further of Persephone, and of poor, beautiful Adonis entering the realm of the dead. The flower has only a brief life: it is blown away by the winds. And so Aphrodite's great love is, in the end, no less transitory, no less cruel than those of her mortal subjects.

Cy Twombly produced a graphism – one of his scribbled writing pieces that he resisted calling graffiti – in Rome, in 1975, titled *Venus*. He lists various of the goddess's names or epithets: Aphrodite, Venus, Asteria, Nymphaea, Morpho (misspelled as *Mopho*). All the names are in grey pencil – graphite – except one, Venus, which is scrawled in oil paint, bright blood red. And beneath this is a scribbled red flower. So while Adonis's flower has only the shortest life in Orpheus's telling of the story, here at least, their love – and his life as commemorated by his goddess-lover – has its memorial. Venus is not just the beauty that we see in Botticelli, she is the broken-hearted lover that we read in Ovid. And it is that side of her that Twombly chooses to celebrate. Born from the white foam, Aphrodite's love is marked with the red flower.

ARTEMIS

'ITS STRUCTURAL perfection is matched only by its hostility,' says Ash, memorably played by Ian Holm. 'I admire its purity. A survivor . . . unclouded by conscience, remorse, or delusions of morality.' He is describing the ruthless predator which is picking off the crew of the *Nostromo* one by one in the 1979 film *Alien*. It's perhaps not the first thing to come to someone's mind when they see a statue of Artemis holding her bow, face impassive and arms relaxed even as she raises the weapon, her fingers extending towards the now-lost string, ready to let an arrow fly. But it was the first thing to come to my mind looking at a pair of statues in the Archaeological Museum in Heraklion. Artemis is about to shoot seven girls, while her brother Apollo slaughters their seven brothers. There is no hint of emotion on the face of this goddess, about to wreak unthinkable destruction on a family. She is indeed unclouded by conscience or remorse. All great hunters share this quality: Kyle Reese (Michael Biehn) describes the same phenomenon in 1984's *The Terminator*. 'It can't be bargained with. It can't be reasoned with. It doesn't feel pity, or remorse, or fear. And it absolutely will not stop . . . ever, until you are dead.' I didn't start this book expecting to compare Arnold Schwarzenegger to the goddess Artemis, but we are where we are.

The story of Niobe and the devastating punishment for her hubris illustrates one aspect of Artemis very well: the iciness with which she approaches most interactions with mortals. The Heraklion statue is not unusual. In the Louvre is a *krater* – a large, two-handled vase, used for mixing wine and water – depicting the death of the Niobids, or children of Niobe. It was decorated by the Niobid Painter and stands half a metre tall with huge black handles near its base. The vase depicts the terrible carnage of this scene: bodies lie collapsed on the ground, arrows protruding. Apollo takes aim at another hapless victim. Just behind him, Artemis holds her bow in her left hand, stretched out in front of her. Her right hand reaches over her shoulder, nimble fingers raising an arrow from her quiver. There is no expression on either of their faces. The Niobids must die, so these two expert archers will kill them without hesitation.

You may be wondering what possible wrong Niobe could have committed to warrant such a horrific punishment. Homer has Achilles remind Priam of the story in the final book of the *Iliad*. In this telling, Niobe has twelve children (later sources will agree on fourteen). Proud of her fecundity, Niobe describes herself as the equal of fair-cheeked Leto, goddess and mother of Apollo and Artemis.[1] And because of this vain and foolish boast, all her children are slaughtered by Leto's furious offspring. They lie unburied for nine days, Achilles adds. This coincides neatly with what has happened to Hector, the son of Priam, killed twelve days earlier by Achilles. Apollo has intervened to keep his body undamaged and untouched by scavengers. But Niobe doesn't have this consolation: her children lie unburied – and therefore, presumably, unable to cross into the Underworld for nine awful days. No one else can intervene to bury them, because Zeus has turned her compatriots to stone.[2] Only on the tenth day do the gods relent and bury the children themselves.

Niobe is a case study in grief, her mourning exemplifying a terrible exaggeration of what most mortals will ever suffer. Although none of the tragedies written on this subject survive, Niobe's story was told by Aeschylus, Sophocles, and Euripides. That these plays were popular and well-known might be deduced from the way Aristophanes references at least one and possibly more than one version. In 422 BCE, a character in his comedy *The Wasps* is acquitted, but only if he agrees to recite a monologue from *Niobe* (which version is unclear). And in 405 BCE, the opening of *The Frogs* parodies the Aeschylean version of *Niobe*. For a play – or a couple of plays on the same theme – to have resonance beyond their own performances is impressive. But Aristophanes was making these jokes seventeen years apart, and his latter play was produced around fifty years after Aeschylus had died. Perhaps we can conclude that the play continued to be performed in Athens for decades. But whether it was or not, the story of Niobe losing her children in a killing spree perpetrated by two Olympian gods seems to have exerted an enduring hold over comedian and audience alike.

There is no more difficult goddess to pin down than Artemis. Partly, this is because her name was attached to goddesses across the Greek world with whom she shared one or more characteristics. This sometimes led to a merging of the two deities, a process known as syncretism, meaning that the characteristics of multiple goddesses were folded into one character. This is true of all Greek deities, of course, as we saw with Aphrodite, who is gradually mapped onto earlier goddesses representing love and desire and femaleness. But with Artemis, aspects of her nature in different parts of Greece are so various as to be almost contradictory. She is the queen of wild animals, but she also hunts and kills them. She is the protector of young girls, but she sometimes demands them as sacrifices. She is the sister (often twin) to Apollo but sometimes they are born on completely different islands. She can heal mortals but she can also cause sudden, otherwise inexplicable deaths.

Artemis is linked to multiple locations where her name is twinned with local cult deities. These all tend to focus on a different characteristic: in southern Greece – the Peloponnese – she is Artemis Limnatis[3] and Artemis Orthia; in Attica she is sometimes Artemis Bendis;[4] Arcadian Artemis is a goddess of nymphs; Taurian Artemis had a taste for human sacrifice. Local cult beliefs are attached to Artemis's name whenever the Greeks decide to syncretize her with a local goddess they haven't met before. The Romans will call her Diana, and the Greeks will sometimes combine her with Selene, the moon goddess (her brother is similarly connected to the sun) or Eileithyia, a goddess of childbirth. Acquiring expertise in this field is no mean feat for a virgin.

In this chapter we will examine some of Artemis's contradictory characteristics, but I don't expect to be a lot closer to defining her at the end of it than I am now. For a long time, I assumed that if I just read more and thought harder, I would find the key to unlocking her. The truth, of course, is that she isn't a puzzle to be solved. And perhaps it is appropriate that she is so hard to capture: like any true hunter, she is a mistress of camouflage. But before we come back to this element of her nature – the young woman armed with bow and arrows, readying herself to shoot – let's consider some of her other aspects.

Artemis is one of the virgin goddesses of Olympus (alongside Athene and Hestia), and this is what connects her to girls and young women, who are so frequently her worshippers. There is plenty of archaeological evidence for the practice of giving childhood toys to Artemis (among other gods and goddesses, but she does seem to have been the most popular recipient). And the *Greek Anthology* tells us about these gifts, saying that girls give up their dolls to Limnatis (Artemis – one of her cult titles).[5] These might be quite sophisticated toys, too; ancient Egypt had already produced jointed figurines, and the Greek craftsmen followed them. The word *korē* – meaning 'maiden' or 'girl' – appears three times in this one line of the *Anthology*. Once it applies to the girls bearing gifts, then it describes the dolls they're carrying, and lastly it is a reference to Artemis herself, the unmarried goddess. The connection is quite explicit: girls are sacred to Artemis, and she is sacred to them. They dedicate their dolls to her when they reach an age to be married (a much younger age than we would probably want to imagine – early to midteens). They are leaving their childhood behind and embarking on adult life, and the dedication of the doll symbolizes this. Artemis occupies an interesting state: she is certainly not a child, but she rejects the traditional life of a Greek woman.

Pausanias comes across all kinds of different Artemis worship as he travels around Greece. In Patrai (on the northern coast of the

Peloponnese) he finds yet another variation of Artemis: Artemis Laphria. It is, he adds, a *xenikon onoma* – a foreign name.[6] This Artemis apparently took her name from a man named Laphrios, who set up her statue, which was *arkhaion* – ancient – but was still being honoured during Pausanias's visit, many centuries later. The statue showed Artemis in a customary pose, hunting. It was made of ivory and gold.

Worship of this particular Artemis comes across as a fiery festival of chaotic zoological shot put. It all starts in a reasonably formal way, with a procession that culminates with a priestess riding along in a chariot pulled by deer. The goddess herself is often shown in just such a vehicle, so we can easily imagine that the procession was an earthly echo of her divine progress, assuming the deer weren't distracted by nuts or berries or another deer. But the next day is the time for sacrificial offerings, and this is where things start to go downhill. First, says Pausanias, people throw live birds onto the altar, then deer and wild boar. Just to add to the image of a wooden altar seething with furious and terrified animals, they then chuck live wolves and bear cubs into the mix. If what you're thinking now is that this scene could only be improved if someone started lobbing fruit at the menagerie, then you have something in common with the citizens of ancient Patrai. It is only at this point that the priests set the huge wooden altar ablaze.

When Pausanias is visiting the area, he observes a bear and some other animals making a run for it, like creatures from a beleaguered ark trying to escape a pyromaniac Noah. But these animals do not live to fight another day: those who had thrown them onto the altar in the first place (and the Greek word *embalontes* does literally mean 'throw in or on') recapture them and chuck them back onto the fire. You don't have to have been a vegetarian for decades to find this scene both demented and traumatic. No one, Pausanias drily observes, can remember anyone being wounded by the animals.[7] For the record, I don't think anybody should be trying to throw a bear into a fire, but I find it almost impossible to imagine such a person would (or should) escape this attempt uninjured.

This scene of carnage seems hard to reconcile with the common artistic image of Artemis as a woodland goddess, riding through mountainous forests with her entourage of wild creatures. The chorus of Aeschylus's *Agamemnon* describe her love for lion cubs and the young of all wild beasts.[8] They certainly don't mention her taste for seeing these little creatures thrown onto a blazing pyre. It's easy for us to forget that animal sacrifices in ancient Greece were burned, so the stench would have been horrific, and the smoke – from the freshly chopped trees used to make this altar, as well as the animals – must have been chokingly thick.

But there are plenty of stories of Artemis revelling in the destruction of human and animal alike, even though she is so closely associated with wild creatures and their environment. As we saw above, Artemis and Apollo were quick to avenge their mother's thin skin and wipe out Niobe's many children. But sometimes her wrath is incurred without a word being spoken. Pausanias goes on to share a story which occurred at the shrine of yet another version of the goddess in the Patrai area, Triklarian Artemis.

This Artemis – like many of her iterations – is served by girls who are too young to marry. When they come of age, they are replaced by another girl. But one beautiful priestess, Komaitho, catches the eye of a very good-looking young man named Melanippos. He falls in love with her and she with him, but their parents will not let them marry. The young people do as young people will, and more than once. Not only that, but they do it in Artemis's sanctuary. In a rage at having her sacred space profaned by sex, Artemis visits every punishment on their people: crops fail, unknown and deadly illnesses afflict them.[9] The only way to appease her, according to the Delphic Oracle (and it should know, since it is sacred to her brother Apollo), is to sacrifice the most beautiful boy and girl to her every year henceforth. Human sacrifice of the pretty continues each year until a wildly convoluted solution is eventually found, after the Trojan War, involving a second oracle, a madman, and a mysterious box. This date – perhaps 1,400 years before Pausanias is writing – gives us an idea of the great antiquity of the tale he has uncovered here.

But Artemis was never a stranger to child sacrifice, as two of Euripides's plays illustrate all too well. *Iphigenia in Aulis* was probably the last play Euripides wrote – it was produced posthumously, around 405 BCE. It depicts the events which take place when the Greek forces mass at Aulis, planning to set sail from there to Troy. Achilles is already known to be the greatest warrior among them, but Agamemnon is the commander of the Greek war effort. They are, after all, planning a campaign to retrieve his absent sister-in-law, Helen. In the buildup to the events dramatized in the play, we discover that the Greeks have been unable to set sail. They are, as Agamemnon describes it to an old man, *aploiai khrōmenoi* – without the possibility of sailing. The cause is eventually deemed to be some kind of offence given to Artemis.

The exact nature of this offence varies depending on our source. Perhaps Atreus, father of Agamemnon and Menelaus, offended the goddess by promising her a sacrificial animal and then failing to fulfil his promise. Greek gods certainly never mind taking their revenge on a later generation. One ancient scholar, writing about the now-lost epic poem the *Cypria*, says that Agamemnon is responsible for a hubristic slur.[10] After shooting a deer, the Greek king boasts that not even Artemis could have done a better job, and this kind of statement rarely goes down well on Olympus. Pseudo-Apollodorus suggests both causes are in play: Agamemnon claimed to be as skilled a hunter as the goddess of hunting, and his father had failed to keep a promise to sacrifice a golden sheep.[11] My opinion of Agamemnon is notoriously low, so I am always tempted to assume that he is in the wrong, but do draw your own conclusions.

Either way, the Greek priest Calchas interprets the wrath of Artemis as requiring a sacrifice from Agamemnon. And this sacrifice is not metaphorical, but horrifyingly literal. As the Euripides play begins, under the advice of his priests, Agamemnon summons his own daughter, Iphigenia, to Aulis. He instructs Clytemnestra, mother of Iphigenia, to bring their daughter under the pretext that the girl is to be married to Achilles. But having sent the letter ordering them to come immediately, he has a change of mind. He writes a second letter in which he reverses his previous instructions and gives it to the old man to take to Clytemnestra. Iphigenia can get married another year, he says. Don't bring her here.

The old man sets off to deliver the letter, but he bumps into Menelaus, Agamemnon's brother and Iphigenia's uncle. Menelaus must have been suspecting that his brother would try something like this, because he immediately grabs the letter, breaks its seal, and reads its contents. The old man berates him for taking a letter which isn't addressed to him. Menelaus responds that the old man shouldn't have been carrying something which was bad for the whole of Greece.[12] At the very least it is bad for Menelaus's attempt to get his wife back from Troy, which we can conclude seems to him to be the same thing. The sons of Atreus rarely downplay their importance in any situation, so this conflation of what Menelaus personally doesn't want with what is terrible for all Greeks is entirely in character.

Menelaus pockets the letter and storms off to argue about its contents with his brother. Agamemnon had been, he says, *asmenos* – pleased or happy – to sacrifice his daughter to Artemis, as Calchas had suggested. He sent his letter to Clytemnestra *ou biai* – unforced.[13] But now he's decided he doesn't want to kill his daughter and he's sending secret letters. This often happens to powerful men, Menelaus observes. They work hard to get their position, and then ruin it all by being weak and incapable.

It is quite something to the modern ear to hear a man complain that his brother is pathetic because he won't carry out this perfectly simple task of killing his own daughter as he'd gladly agreed to do just a short time earlier. But throughout his long speech, Menelaus spends almost no time at all talking about the offence to Artemis. He literally mentions her once, when he reminds Agamemnon that Calchas had claimed Iphigenia must be sacrificed to the goddess. The rest of his speech is much more focused on politics than divinity. His rebuke doesn't concern itself with divine vengeance (*If you don't deliver the sacrifice as promised, Artemis will punish you further*) or even expiating the wrongs already done which incurred divine wrath in the first place (*We're already on her bad side, which is why we can't sail*). He is much more worried about the loss of status his brother will experience in the eyes of the men he is supposed to command. Whether this is Menelaus's own most pressing concern or whether he simply believes this is his brother's greatest fear and is playing on that in order to get what he wants is open to debate.

Either way, he doesn't provoke the response he was presumably expecting. Agamemnon isn't at all worried about losing face in front of his men or anyone else. He claims not to be able to understand why his brother is so annoyed when he's finally had the good luck to lose a wife he couldn't trust anyway. He asks the question we are probably all thinking: Why should I, the one who didn't screw up, pay the price for your problems?[14] He correctly identifies that Menelaus just wants his good-looking wife back. I made a bad decision before, he says. And now I've changed my mind to a good one. And then, using a formula echoed by siblings through the ages, he continues: Am I mad? You're the mad one.[15] You mind your own affairs; I won't kill my child. Again, he seems to have no concern at all for Artemis, to whom his daughter is apparently owed as a sacrifice. He doesn't mention the goddess, or any wrong that he (or his father) might have done her. He sees one cause for the demand for his daughter's life, and that is his brother's inexplicable desire to be reunited with his straying wife. He doesn't seem to see any reason to discuss why the army is unable to sail, or why he might be the one to sacrifice his child to change it. Like Menelaus, his discourse is conducted at an entirely human level.

The chorus acknowledge that Agamemnon has reversed his decision, but they agree with him that he shouldn't kill his child. Menelaus – in a display that would make even a hardened Helen-hater think she should have left him years ago – says that Agamemnon should really care more about his brother's feelings, since they both have the same father. The question we're yearning for Agamemnon to ask here is surely: *Would you do something so horrific to your own daughter, to Hermione? Would you do it to get your wife back? Would you do it so that I could get my wife back, assuming she had abandoned me the way yours has left you?* Would Menelaus really be able to answer yes?

But the questions go unasked and unanswered, because a messenger arrives onstage to say that they have brought Iphigenia and Clytemnestra to the camp, as well as Agamemnon's infant son Orestes. Agamemnon is horrified: having summoned his daughter to a phony marriage, he had somehow not realized that her mother might accompany her so swiftly and bring the baby along for the ride. It is immediately clear to Agamemnon that he will now have no choice but to kill his daughter. He has summoned her here for a sham marriage that only he, Calchas the priest, Odysseus – the brains of the operation – and Menelaus know about. Not even the pretend bridegroom Achilles has been told that he is the lure to draw Iphigenia to her death.

But surely he could simply confess that he had told a stupid lie? For a modern audience, this moment in the play can be frustrating. Just because you said there was a marriage and there isn't doesn't mean your only alternative course of action is murder. Even Menelaus doesn't seem to feel that way, and it would be helping his cause to pretend he does. Unexpectedly, he draws back from his earlier position and tells

Agamemnon that he now realizes he has asked too much. Iphigenia is his niece, after all, so his compassion may be belated, but it is understandable. But Agamemnon is resigned to the killing; he is forced to, he says, by *anankē* – necessity.[16] Who can force you to kill your own daughter? asks Menelaus, apparently forgetting that he argued for this only moments earlier. The whole camp full of Greeks, replies his brother. So it seems Menelaus's argument had its desired effect after all. Agamemnon cannot lose face in front of all the men he commands. Menelaus suggests he simply send Iphigenia straight back home. But Agamemnon knows he won't get away with it: Calchas would tell the men his reading of the situation, and his proposed murderous solution. What if we killed him before he could do that? wonders Menelaus. That won't work either, says Agamemnon, because Odysseus knows about it too. And he'll tell everyone. He'll say what Calchas said I had to do. And – and this is the kicker – he'll tell them I promised to make the sacrifice to Artemis, and that I lied.[17]

It is only now that we can truly understand the impossibility of his situation. It isn't that he promised his brother he would kill Iphigenia, it is that he promised Artemis. Agamemnon is not a great keeper of promises (as we have seen in this play, the first third of which he spends trying his utmost to break a terrible promise he never should have made). But he cannot deceive a goddess the way he was quite happy to deceive his wife and daughter, by promising them a marriage that was never going to happen. Or rather – since we know he was willing to take his chances until Menelaus intercepted his second letter, countermanding the first – he cannot be seen by the mass of Greeks to break a vow to Artemis. We've seen that he and his brother don't seem to care much about her, but they both know the rest of the Greeks do.

And they both know how dangerous Odysseus is to Agamemnon, because of his persuasive way with crowds. The Greeks consider persuasion to be such an important skill that they have a goddess who represents it. Peitho is the goddess you appeal to when you want to be rhetorically convincing, either in front of a large group – a jury, an army – or in private. She is often shown as a companion of Aphrodite, part of a deep tradition in Greek and Roman art and poetry that you have to persuade someone to love you. We might find this a rather troubling concept, since one woman's persuasion is another woman's coercion. But it is not an idea which is questioned in the ancient world – better to appeal to Peitho and hope to learn her skills.

And this is something Odysseus has achieved. If he cannot persuade Achilles back onto the battlefield in Book Nine of the *Iliad*, he can at least manage to stay on relatively good terms with both parties in the quarrel. Here, Euripides is showing us a glimpse of how he might do that. Agamemnon and Menelaus are afraid of his persuasive way with a crowd, and they both believe he would turn it against them. As Agamemnon has it: He would stir the men and order them to kill you and me, and to slaughter Iphigenia.

We see this argument made by other child killers in Euripides, most notably Medea. *Whatever I do, someone is going to kill my child, so it's better if I do it.* It's a stretch to see this argument as altruistic when Medea makes it, but it's impossible to do so when Agamemnon does – not least because he is more concerned with his own life. They'll kill you and me. And even if I flee to Argos, he adds, they'll come after me, tear down my walls, destroy my land. This is my nightmare.[18] There is no action Agamemnon believes he can take to save his daughter. The only element of choice is whether he dies too.

The play unfolds as we might expect. There are somewhat farcical elements: Clytemnestra and Iphigenia talking at cross-purposes with Agamemnon; Clytemnestra introducing herself to her daughter's bridegroom Achilles when the latter has no idea who she is, or that anyone has been promising him in marriage to her daughter; the old man whom Agamemnon earlier entrusted with his second letter finally giving up the truth about the sham wedding. But the play never descends into farce, because at its core is something deadly serious. And yet, the tragedy does not have an unhappy ending, which may come as a surprise. Iphigenia goes willingly to her death, accepting that Artemis demands her life. She does not rage about the unfairness of it, though she knows she doesn't deserve it.[19] Instead, she asks the women of the chorus to raise a hymn of praise to Artemis. In her sacrifice she expects to incur victory-bringing salvation for the Hellenes.[20]

Considering that Artemis ends up backing the Trojans in the war, for example in Book Twenty-one of the *Iliad*, this is an optimistic prayer that Iphigenia delivers. Although even if Artemis had backed the Greeks, it doesn't appear that she is an especially useful ally in a war: according to Homer, she loses her bow and arrows after an attack by Hera. Her mother, Leto, collects them from the battlefield and returns them to her daughter on Olympus. Artemis, it seems, is a much more deadly friend than foe.

Perhaps she does answer Iphigenia's prayer in her own way, however. She couldn't bring victory to the Greeks in the Trojan War even if she chose to support them, because – as we discover in the *Iliad* – the war's course will be dictated by more powerful gods than she. But she can do something about Iphigenia's death. Moments after the young woman has gone to be sacrificed, a messenger rushes onstage. He describes an astonishing scene. He has watched Iphigenia give herself willingly as a sacrifice both to her father and to the goddess. The men have gathered around to watch her die, though the messenger tells us that when the moment came, they all looked down at the ground rather than witness her killing. No one says it, but the war-bedraggled audience who watched this play in 405 BCE had direct experience of conflict across twenty-five years of the Peloponnesian War between Athens and Sparta. Surely this audience could understand exactly why men who would soon be fighting to the death on the battlefield would prefer to look away from the murder of a young woman. Why see more slaughter than you must?

The messenger did the same as the rest of them: looked down and shuddered as he heard the blade fall. But then he heard the priest shout out, and he – like the rest of the gathered men – looked up to see that Iphigenia had disappeared, spirited away by Artemis. In her stead lay a dead deer, its blood spattered all over the altar. Calchas proclaimed that the goddess had chosen the deer to replace Iphigenia so that her altar wasn't stained with her noble blood. An ungenerous person might now ask the priest how come he had been so sure about killing Iphigenia to appease Artemis in the first place, if the goddess herself was so against the idea that she resorted to switching victims. But perhaps Artemis – much like the men in the play – sees the sacrifice as one made by Agamemnon rather than by Iphigenia.

Artemis never appears in this play (though we can see her onstage in Euripides's *Hippolytus*, for example). But her presence hovers over the characters as much as if she were a *dea ex machina*, flying above the stage in a deer-drawn chariot. Every character is pulled into the plot of the play by their response to her perceived demands. And Agamemnon can congratulate himself on a good day in charge: he has decisively offered to kill his daughter, briefly wavered in his resolve but only in private, carried out the sacrifice as instructed, and finally discovered that his daughter isn't even dead. We can be considered blessed with regard to our daughter, he tells Clytemnestra right at the end of the play. She's now keeping company with the gods. But a moment earlier – before he arrived onstage – Clytemnestra couldn't believe what the messenger was telling her. Her assumption is that it is a lie to try and stop her from mourning. Because what use is it to Clytemnestra, the easy belief that their daughter now dwells among the gods? What parent of a disappeared child would be comforted by this? We already know the answer: Agamemnon.

The audience watching this play might have remembered another of Euripides's tragedies, first performed a few years earlier. *Iphigenia Among the Taurians* shows where the daughter of Clytemnestra and

Agamemnon found herself after the deer switch had saved her life. Contrary to what Agamemnon chooses to believe, Iphigenia does not wake up to find herself swanning about on Mount Olympus, pouring nectar and serving ambrosia to her divine roommates. Instead she finds herself a priestess of Artemis in the land of the Taurians – we know it better as Crimea, in modern Ukraine. She is deeply resentful at being cut off from her Greek roots: she doesn't only miss her family, but also the life she led as an Argive woman; singing hymns to Hera is only one example of what she resents missing out on. As for her life in this new place, she describes it with a list of negatives. She is *agamos, ateknos, apolis, aphilos* – unmarried, childless, without a city, without a friend.[21] Her emotions are muddled and contradictory with regard to her birth family; they could hardly be anything else. She remembers quite clearly that Agamemnon had promised to sacrifice the most beautiful child born in a particular year and that Calchas had proclaimed that child to be her. In this version, Odysseus was in on the whole story; indeed, the sham marriage to Achilles was his idea.

Even if her personal circumstances were less wretched, Iphigenia would still be wildly unimpressed at her new home, living in a land ruled by Thoas, a barbarian among barbarians. And she herself has been drawn into barbaric behaviour: as priestess to Artemis, she conducts human sacrifices. We are surely meant to make the connection that Iphigenia does not. The barbarians worship an Artemis who demands horrifying payment in human lives, but this was also true of the Greek soldiers massed at Aulis all those years before, including Iphigenia's own father. The apparently civilized Greeks have identical values to the barbarians whose customs so appal Iphigenia.

Moments after Iphigenia has delivered her monologue, two Greeks arrive on the shore. By wild coincidence, it is Iphigenia's younger brother, Orestes – now a grown man – and his friend Pylades. They have been sent to this part of the world by Apollo, so perhaps not so much of a coincidence after all. Apollo has charged Orestes with retrieving the statue of Artemis from the temple where Iphigenia serves (though Orestes doesn't know the priestess is his long-lost sister). Orestes must do this if he wants to be rid of the Furies, who still pursue him for the murder of his mother, Clytemnestra.

This part of his backstory would have been familiar to Euripides's audience, because the fall of the house of Atreus had been dramatized many times before, most famously by Aeschylus in *The Oresteia*. Agamemnon kills Iphigenia (or, in Euripides's version, is willing to do so, and is only saved from this dreadful crime by the miraculous substitution of a deer). In return, Clytemnestra waits ten years for her husband to come back from Troy and then murders him. Orestes and Electra, her younger children, then murder her in revenge for their father's killing. The Furies pursue Orestes for the unforgivable crime of killing his own mother.

In this Euripidean version too, the Furies are persecuting Orestes, and in desperation, he has asked Apollo for help. Apollo's answer is that Orestes must travel to the land of the Taurians and take their statue of Artemis back to Athens. Orestes and Pylades are confident in their mission; Apollo could hardly send them on a quest and then allow them to be killed before they've completed it.

The Taurians keep a lookout for foreigners landing on their shores, and two Greek men fulfil the criteria for perfect sacrificial victims. A herdsman rushes to report their arrival and capture to the priestess, who receives the information with a bloodthirsty interest. The altar of the goddess hasn't yet been reddened by streams of Hellene blood, she says.[22]

It takes a little time for the siblings to be reunited, which luckily happens before Iphigenia murders her brother or his friend (although I have often wondered what the Furies would have done if the man they pursued for blood guilt was then murdered by his own sister, in service of a goddess and ignorant of the man's identity. Perhaps they would have felt honour was satisfied and retired to the country). After a simple ruse to lay their hands on the statue, the three Greeks escape from the angry Taurians by boat, only to find a vicious wind blowing them back towards the shore.

Iphigenia prays to Artemis to save them. Save me, daughter of Leto, your priestess, bring me to Hellas from this barbarian land, and forgive me my theft. And as you love your brother, goddess, trust that I love mine.[23] But moments later, the Taurian king is pleading with the same goddess for the opposite result, praying that the ship will be driven back to his land. The clash of cultures could hardly be more explicit: his Artemis would want her statue returned to her temple; the Greek Artemis would want her statue taken to Athens.

This impasse of cultural relativism is brought to an abrupt halt by the goddess Athene, who appears high above the stage, a position of divine authority. She reassures the (Athenian) audience that the statue has been removed (the Taurians might well think looted) on Apollo's orders. His sister's statue must indeed be taken to Greece, where Orestes can build a temple to contain it. And when they hold festivals to celebrate Artemis Tauropolos (Taurian Artemis), the priest must cut a man's throat just slightly, to pierce the skin. Even in her respectable new Greek home, this statue of Artemis will still enjoy the taste of a little blood.

And what will become of Iphigenia, the surviving sacrificial victim and sacrificing priestess? She will serve at the shrine of Artemis at Brauron (modern-day Vravrona, about thirty miles east of Athens). This place of worship gave Artemis another of her cult titles: Artemis Brauronia. But the connection between the Brauronian Artemis and the Taurian one – through Iphigenia as priestess at both places – is made explicit by Pausanias. He observes that a shrine to Artemis on the Acropolis is named after Brauron, because they still have an ancient wooden statue of her. It's definitely the one that Iphigenia and Orestes stole from

Tauris and brought to Athens, because Pausanias adds that the statue is called Taurian Artemis.[24]

At Brauron, Artemis was served by acolytes who blurred the line between human and animal, just as Iphigenia had done before them, although the animal has changed. The female chorus in *Lysistrata*, Aristophanes's comedy of the sexes, reminisce about their time in service to the divine. When they were seven years old, they carried sacred baskets; at ten, they started grinding sacred corn. And then, they say, they served as bears at Brauron.[25] These young devotees seem to have worn yellow dresses to recall yellow-brown ursine fur. Exactly what being a bear at Brauron entailed is open to some debate, but dancing appears to have been a major feature. Many statues of little girls performing this religious role have been found at Brauron and are displayed in its Archaeological Museum: if anything, they look even younger than the age given by Aristophanes's women, perhaps only seven or eight years old.[26]

The rites of passage in young female lives are routinely connected to Artemis, and she is often linked with other deities, including Selene, the moon goddess. Plenty of scholars have observed that the moon is seen as Artemis's domain for no better reason than that the sun (which also has its own god, Helios) is connected to Apollo. As his sister, therefore, Artemis must be linked to the moon. There is, of course, another reason why young girls might be interested in a moon goddess, but it seems to have been a step too far for male academics of previous centuries to note that menstruation is often linked to lunar cycles (so much so that you can buy a menstrual cup called Selena, although I suppose you can call it whatever you like).

In her poem 'The Moon Writes a Love Letter to Artemis', Nikita Gill has the moon feeling as though she doesn't belong with the goddess Selene. Instead she adores Artemis, an untamable girl child, for her wildness, her animalistic nature. How could I ever resist falling in love with you, she asks. Like all lovers (and particularly those in Greek and

Latin literature – Gill is a ferociously well-read poet), the moon has one question on her mind: Tell me, Artemis, do you love me too? Love is all very well, but reciprocated love is what we all really want. Gill also offers a neat explanation for this love affair. When Artemis was still a child, her father, Zeus, asked her what she wanted. The goddess had only one request: Give me the moon.[27] So the moon is desired while experiencing a mirror desire of her own. And the unapologetic ambition of Artemis – even as a child, the woods and mountains aren't enough for her; she wants the moon itself – is part of her nature too.

Gill's lovelorn moon has been watching over Artemis since the very beginning of her existence. It is from seeing the newborn goddess serve as midwife to her mother for the birth of her twin, Apollo, that the moon first falls for her. And this part of her story explains why Artemis is also connected with Eileithyia. At first glance it seems contradictory that Artemis – a goddess most often linked to young, unmarried girls, wild animals and landscapes, and the moon that shines down on them all – should also be linked to the process of childbirth, although women in ancient Greece would certainly have been mothers at a very young age. But the apparent contradiction is explained away by one story of Artemis and Apollo's birth.

According to Callimachus, in his *Hymn to Artemis* from the third century BCE, Artemis is given the task of coming to the aid of women suffering labour pains by the Fates themselves. They order it, she explains, because her own mother (Leto) suffered no pain when giving birth to Artemis.[28] Pseudo-Apollodorus also has the newborn Artemis helping her mother to deliver Apollo.[29] So although Eileithyia is often a separate goddess, there is also this mingling of her role with the daughter of Leto.

But by far the most common image of Artemis that we see in ancient sources – in literature, vase paintings, and sculptures – is that of the archer, as we saw at the start of the chapter. Our earliest literary sources define her in this way: the *Homeric Hymn to Artemis* is barely ten lines long, and it twice calls her 'the arrow-lover'. First she is 'the arrow-loving maiden', and then four lines later she is 'the far-shooting arrow-lover'.[30]

It is this aspect of her nature that has proved most influential in modern culture. The female archer is a perennially popular character, as recently illustrated by *Hawkeye*, the 2021 miniseries from Marvel Studios. Hawkeye, the world-weary sharp-shooter (of arrows), was played by Jeremy Renner in the recent *Avengers* movies. He is human rather than superpowered, but he takes his place alongside gods and monsters to save the world, and specifically New York, from alien invasion. His astonishing ability to aim, fire, and hit makes him the equal of almost any foe. And yet, as we have seen throughout the film franchise, he is not just Hawkeye, hero and saviour of the world. He is also Clint Barton: a family man, a man who wants to be in his isolated home with his wife and kids, far away from the glamour of global hero worship.

The miniseries introduces us to the child who will eventually take on the responsibility of being Hawkeye. Kate Bishop has a couple of things in common with Artemis. She likes wild animals, at least if her large toy giraffe is anything to go by, and she longs for a bow and arrows. If Artemis can ask her father for weapons (they are usually then provided by Hephaestus), Kate wants arrows precisely because she can't ask her father for them: he was killed during the aforementioned alien invasion. Kate has fixated on the loss of her father and at the same time developed a fascination for the man she watched on the news, shooting his arrows with precision and no fear. She wants to be able to protect herself and her mother in the same way.

We next meet Kate as a young woman, played by Hailee Steinfeld. We soon see that – after years of practice – her aim is every bit as impressive as that of her idol, Hawkeye. She can shoot an arrow with such precision that she can ring a bell, although she does bring the bell tower down as well. But no one ever said that resisting alien invasion was going to be a tidy business.

The series follows a classic buddy-movie formula, in which Kate wants to team up with Barton and he wants this irritating young super-fan to leave him alone so he can get on with his life and be back with his kids for Christmas. As the episodes progress, the two archers manage to thwart a crime and solve a murder. In the final battle sequence, they both let arrows fly in unison, hitting their targets with precision. The music swells and we realize we are witnessing Kate's epiphany. Her first major battle will be the first of many. Her archery skill is now matched by the discipline and experience she has gained from working with her idol and mentor. The series concludes with the passing of the baton: Clint retires from the role of Hawkeye, and Kate takes it on in his stead. The reluctant hero is replaced by an eager new generation.

Delightful as this series is, Kate Bishop/Hawkeye is not the first person most people will think of when asked to name a woman who can fight to the death armed only with a bow and arrows. The cultural juggernaut that is *The Hunger Games* franchise has ensured that, for a generation at least, the name most readily associated with this particular skill is Katniss Everdeen. Suzanne Collins's novels are set in a dystopian future which has been heavily influenced by ancient Rome. The Capitol (a city, rather than one of seven hills in a city) rules over twelve districts, each of which has its own speciality. District 12 – where Katniss lives – is the coal-mining district. Although her neighbours are involved in this dirtiest aspect of the industrial revolution, the life of Katniss and her family is closer to that of mediaeval serfs. She hunts in the nearby forest for meat, because she and her mother and little sister, Prim, would otherwise starve. The technology powered by their coal is all in the hands of the Capitol.

The country is a futuristic alternative America, with a toxic power imbalance. It is called Panem, in case anyone was in any doubt of the nod to imperial Rome. The Roman people, as the satirist Juvenal once complained, sold their votes for *panem et circenses* – bread and the circuses.[31] The bread Juvenal is referring to is a grain dole, handed out to voters, who were adult male citizens of Rome. Women couldn't vote, so they had nothing to sell for grain; they needed a man in the family to qualify. This is essentially the condition in which Katniss finds herself growing up. Her father is dead, her mother paralysed with shock and grief. In order to keep her remaining family alive, Katniss must become the hunter-gatherer they need. There are times when she is so close to failure that only charity from the boy who works at the nearby bakery prevents their starvation.

Juvenal's epigram is twofold, and so is the misery endured by the citizens of the twelve districts of Panem. If a lack of bread keeps the masses hungry, desperate, and docile, the games remind them that they really do have no control over their lives whatsoever. Every year, two children are selected by lot from each district: twelve boys and twelve girls. They are taken to the Capitol as tribute. This part of the story may well remind us more of Greek myth than Roman history. It is certainly reminiscent of the young boys and girls sent to Crete for the Minotaur to kill, as described by several authors, including Pseudo-Apollodorus[32] and Pausanias, who also gives numbers: seven boys and seven girls.[33]

Katniss is not chosen by lot; she volunteers when her little sister is named as the luckless girl. The selected children are all taken to the Capitol, which is ruled by a president rather than an emperor. Once there, they are trained to fight in the gigantic bio-dome of an arena, much like the gladiators of ancient Rome. Some are ruthless warriors; others are tiny children without hope of survival. There can be only one winner, and the entire battle is televised for the gratification of the gamblers of the Capitol and the subjugation of the districts.

Katniss isn't a highly trained warrior, but she is a hugely experienced hunter with expert aim and impressive survival skills. She has multiple echoes of Artemis: the familiarity with the natural world, the extraordinary talent for archery. She even matches the impassive expression that Artemis wears as she slaughters the children of Niobe. Katniss knows she is being watched most of the time, by agents of the Capitol regime as well as by the cameras that are trained on each of the tributes throughout their terrible ordeal. For Katniss, showing emotion – even to her family as she bids them farewell – is a risk she prefers not to take. She has learned to 'turn my features into an indifferent mask so that no one could ever read my thoughts.'[34] And although Katniss has a younger sister rather than a twin brother, she also has friend and fellow hunter Gale, who 'could be my brother.'

We watch Katniss – inventive, fearless, and kind – struggle to survive the Games. She wins the hearts of the audience with her bravery and her choices to protect a smaller child and to help heal Peeta, the boy from the bakery in District 12, who had kept her and her family alive with his stolen bread long before the two of them entered the arena. When she does attack other tributes, she does so using her Artemisian skills: setting mutant hornets on her most aggressive competitors, she is surely as much the *potnia thērōn* – queen of wild creatures – as the goddess she resembles. Katniss is slower to turn her arrows on the other players, though she shoots and kills the boy from District 1 the moment she sees he has killed Rue, the little girl with whom she had forged a sisterly bond.

Throughout the Games, Katniss never forgets the inhumanity of all the adults who are collaborating to kill innocent children. In this, we might note that she resembles not Artemis but Euripides's Iphigenia, who becomes her priestess. Katniss and Iphigenia both despise their current circumstances while fondly remembering a more innocent and kindly homeland. Yet as we saw above, Iphigenia's beloved Greeks were just as capable of human sacrifice as the Taurians. And though Katniss is undergoing this horrific ordeal because of the ruling president and his cronies in the Capitol, she was only saved from desperate hunger in her own district by the kindness of another child, one she didn't even know. We might well wonder where the adults were who could have shared some of their own meagre rations with two small children. Even the good people of District 12 would apparently have watched Katniss and Prim starve to death. So the parallels continue: no matter where you are in futuristic Panem, or in Iphigenia's Bronze Age home, you are not protected by those who surely should protect you.

But this Euripidean echo aside, Katniss is a natural descendant of Artemis. She is most comfortable alone or with her quasi brother Gale, out in the forest where the normal rules of society are suspended and the rules of the natural world replace them. She is a hunter of wild animals and, when necessary for her own survival, a reluctant killer of other children. She takes no pleasure in killing, however. When Peeta is boasting of her skill to their mentor as they prepare to fight, he reveals more than he perhaps intends. Katniss is a great shot, he explains to Haymitch. She has been selling rabbits and squirrels to his father for years, and the baker has commented before on how skilled she is. She never pierces the animal's skin, because she always shoots them straight through the eye. She is ruthless, in other words, but she doesn't ever want a creature to suffer, even if she takes its life.

Nothing has perplexed me more, in exploring Artemis worship across the ancient Greek world, than the apparent contradiction between her connection to animals and girls and her remorseless taking of their lives. It took a conversation with a travel writer to remind me that I was looking at things from a modern, European perspective, and a vegetarian one at that. Of course I think of animals as being in need of protection: I have only lived in a time and place where human damage to the animal kingdom – the vast extinctions that have occurred because of us – have been undeniable. Even when I was a child (and one young enough to serve Artemis), I felt this jeopardy: being asked to Save the

Whales, being aware that pandas might run out at any moment. I have never lived outside a city, nor in countries with wildlife that can kill you. When people talk about hunting, I think of posh people on horses chasing a tiny fox, or suburban men with assault rifles looking proud of themselves next to the carcass of an obliterated lion. My travel-writing friend has no problem with the notion of someone loving an animal they will hunt and kill. I have had to rethink my position and accept that it is not a universal response to seeing a lion or a bear, believing that it is in need of protection from you. For most people throughout history, the opposite would have been true. Especially with regard to the bear, since they can climb trees.

There is a beautiful *krater* in the National Archaeological Museum in Florence. It is known as the François Vase and is dated to around 570 BCE. It was made by Ergotimos and painted by Kleitias; both names are signed on the vase. It is decorated with multiple friezes showing different stories from Greek myth, including both the wedding of Peleus and Thetis and the funeral games of Patroclus. Tiny name tags are painted beside many of the characters: Diomedes, Achilles, Aias (Ajax). The designs go right up and over the sturdy handles, each of which has a Gorgon on the inward curve above the rim of the pot. On the outward-facing side of one handle is the figure of a winged goddess flanked by two wild creatures, a panther on her right, a deer on her left. This is Artemis *potnia thērōn* – Artemis, queen of wild animals.[35] She holds both animals by the neck, and while the deer looks quite perky, springing up on its hind legs and pawing at her with its front legs like an excited puppy, the panther looks rather less delighted. It too has its front paws raised, but Artemis has lifted it off the ground, so its back legs dangle and it seems to be scrambling to get a grip with its rear claws. It's a long time since I owned a cat (or it owned me, whichever seems more accurate), but I foresee a snagged dress in Artemis's imminent future. The panther's body faces the goddess, but its head is turned towards us, giving it a look of twisted discomfort. Perhaps this is how Artemis rules the wild animals: a choke hold on the predators to keep the deer alive to pull her chariot.

The body of the vase shows another scene from Artemis's myth, although we are lucky we're able to see it. Any object surviving from the ancient world will likely have a chequered history; we can read of countless finds wrecked by their discovery or damaged in harmful attempts to conserve them. But the François Vase has had an unusually difficult life. It was broken into many pieces in antiquity. In 1844, some of its many sherds were discovered by Alessandro François at Chiusi, not far from Perugia in northern Italy. The legend goes that François had to excavate an area the size of the Colosseum to find as many pieces as he did.[36] The pot was rebuilt and displayed for the next fifty years, until disaster struck it again – literally – in 1900, when the pot found itself in the way of an angry museum guard. He threw a wooden stool at it, and even though it was covered by protective glass, the vase was smashed into 638 pieces. It was restored by a man named Pietro Zei in 1904, whom we can safely say must have been an absolute demon at jigsaws. It was rebuilt again in 1973 to incorporate a missing piece that had been returned.[37] This must be a rare instance of a vase having more lives than the cat painted on its handle.

The Artemis myth on the rim of the vase is that of the Calydonian boar, a cautionary tale for why you should never do as a man named Oeneus did and fail to mention Artemis – and Artemis alone – in your prayers. Either he forgot her, or it didn't occur to him, Homer says.[38] It causes him great harm, either way. Artemis Arrow-shooter (even this epithet reminds us that she could easily have killed Oeneus where he stood) is furious. She sets a wild boar loose in his orchard. The huge creature uproots trees and causes carnage of a slightly different kind from that we have seen before. It is the trees, their fruit, their blossoms that the boar destroys, an agricultural plague rather than the kind which picks off men and animals (Artemis's brother Apollo sends just such a plague to devastate the Greeks in Book One of the *Iliad*). Meleager – a Greek hero – manages to kill the boar eventually, but he needs help from many other hunters (he couldn't have done it with just a few, adds Homer).[39] Even then the damage is not over: the men all fight over who gets the head and skin of the boar.

But there is another story which tells of an even more ruinous instance of Artemis's rage against an erring mortal. This one has been the inspiration for centuries of writers and artists. Actaeon was born into the royal house of Thebes, which should sound a warning sign if you're expecting him to live a happy life and die of old age. His grandfather Cadmus, founder of the legendary city, is cited by Ovid as an example of the dictum (borrowed from the Greeks) that you can call no man happy until he's dead.[40] The reason for this late-life reversal of fortunes is the loss of two grandsons: Pentheus (whose demise at the hands of his mother and other women maddened by Dionysus is dramatized in Euripides's *The Bacchae*) and Actaeon. It is to Actaeon's story that we now turn.

He is the son of Autonoë, one of Cadmus's four daughters. He did nothing wrong, Ovid assures us. Why punish a man for a mistake?[41] The exact nature of Actaeon's mistake depends on the source. Euripides offers up a variation on the hubris theme: he says Actaeon boasted about being a better hunter than Artemis.[42] As we have seen time and time again, the gods have no interest in whether you were making a humourous exaggeration, or speaking figuratively, or any nuance whatsoever. But Ovid has another explanation, and one which fits well with his slightly grubby persona as a love poet.

He takes us straight to the scene of the mistake. It's a mountain, in the middle of the day, and a bunch of huntsmen have covered their weapons with blood. Their leader Actaeon reckons they've done enough and they'll hunt again at dawn tomorrow. The men all do as he asks and call a halt to the day's exertions.

Nearby is a valley with a spring where Diana (Artemis's Roman name) likes to come and bathe after she has been hunting.[43] On this particular day, she arrives and hands her spear, bow, and quiver to a nymph. Another nymph takes her dress as she strips; two more take her shoes. One named Crocale, who is the expert on hair, ties her hair back. Five more nymphs are ready with their large jugs of water to help give their goddess the bath she desires.

The juxtaposition of these two scenes is absolutely perfect. We know that a character who is completely at home in one environment is about to crash straight into a neighbouring environment where they won't belong at all, at which point all bets will be off. It reminds me of the opening scenes in a TV murder mystery or hospital drama, where we see an innocent boy flying a kite near a disused and flooded quarry, and then the camera flicks to a pylon sparking with ominous electricity, and we try to guess whether the hapless child will suffer near-death from electrocution, drowning, or strangulation by kite string before the tension is resolved and our heroic doctors can step in and save the day.

Ovid knows he has built up a theatrical amount of tension, because he continues, Look! There goes Cadmus's grandson, wandering through this unknown bit of the woods.[44] That's where the Fates have carried him. Ovid is clearly having huge fun telling this story, but he's also redrawing its boundaries. We have those other sources where the plot is subtly different: that Actaeon was comparing himself favourably with Artemis as a hunter, or that he had ambitions to marry her,[45] or even that he was trying to seduce his aunt Semele, on whom Zeus was making his moves.[46]

These varying depictions of hubris make Actaeon responsible for his own downfall. But Ovid is offering us a version (derived from the earlier Greek poet Callimachus) where no one is at fault except the Fates, where it is just bad luck for Actaeon that he's wandering about in the wrong place at the wrong time. Even as he's building up to the terrifying climax of the encounter, Ovid can't resist adding a little humour.

Actaeon could just lumber into the scene and see Diana naked, but Ovid can't miss out on the fun of the nymphs seeing a man and screaming in shock, their cries echoing and filling the entire wood. The nymphs flock around Diana to protect her from this stranger's wandering eyes, but she's a goddess and they're only nymphs. So she stands head and shoulders above them, meaning that Actaeon can still get what we might term as an eyeful. Diana blushes the colour of the sunset or sunrise, Ovid adds. That's Diana *sine veste* – without her clothes on – by the way, in case you'd forgotten the crucial information for your daydream.[47]

In this whole story, there's not much I like more than the unspoken assumption that goddesses are taller than nymphs. This isn't particularly surprising: gods and goddesses are often much bigger than mortals, and nymphs tend to be human-sized. But Diana isn't gigantically bigger than her attendants; just enough taller for this scene to be mortifying for her. It's funny and sexy and seedy all at once, which is not the only reason to enjoy Ovid's poetry, but it's a good one.

The nymphs close in around her, trying to shield her from view, and Diana herself turns sideways to try and reduce the amount Actaeon can eyeball. She wishes she had her arrows close to hand, but of course she gave them to a nymph before she had her bath. Instead – in a moment which seems lifted from a *Carry On* film – she throws water in Actaeon's face, spattering his hair with *ultricibus undis* – vengeful waves.[48] Ovid is clearly exaggerating the quantities involved, again for comic effect. But then she speaks, and her words promise catastrophe to come. Now, if you want to tell people you saw me naked, you can give it a try, she says.

And he will try to speak, at least. But he won't succeed. Because where the water has splashed on his head, he grows antlers. His ears grow pointy, his hands become hooves, his arms turn into forelegs. *Additus et pavor est* – then she added terror.[49] Actaeon flees until he sees his reflection in a pool, his changed face, his horns. He tries to speak, but *vox nulla secuta est* – no voice came. He groans, and tears flow down his face. His mind has remained the same, even as his whole body has changed. He has no idea what to do, however: Try to go home, to the royal palace? Hide in the woods? There's shame one way and fear the other. Actaeon's mind might have remained intact, but there is more than a hint here, as his mind darts from one possibility to the next, of the way a deer panics.

The comical nature of the previous scene is now a world away and Ovid ramps up the horror of Acteon's condition in the next line. *Dum dubitat, videre canes* – while he was trying to decide, his dogs caught sight of him.[50] And then Ovid pulls out another rhetorical trick: he lists the entire pack of dogs by name. Some are harder than others to translate, as they are made-up Latin names with Greek origins. So the first one is called Melampus – using two Greek words to create Blackfoot. But then the next is a made-up word – Ichnobates. It is obviously meant to recall the Greek word *ikhnē* – tracks – so, Hunter. My favourite by far is Pamphagus – eats everything. Others are compared to winds, mountains, and monsters: Harpy is a great name for a dog. The fast ones are given wings, the noisy ones named for their barks and howls. The list goes on for twenty lines: it is a huge pack of dogs, well over thirty.

Actaeon flees the hounds, and they chase him through the woods, just as he had chased his quarry before. He wants to cry out, 'I am Actaeon – recognize your master!' But the words go missing from his mind, and the air fills with barking. Ovid's ability to turn these scenes of transformation into horrifying nightmares is extraordinary, and often centres on a loss of voice. As we saw when poor Io was turned into a cow, there is no quicker way to be robbed of power than to lose your capacity to speak. And nowhere is this more true than of Actaeon, desperately trying to communicate with his own dogs but unable to say a word.

The first dog to sink its teeth into Actaeon's flesh is called Blackhair. The next is called Therodamas, an impressively opaque reference, even for Ovid. But perfectly chosen: Therodamas was a Scythian king who fed human flesh to his lions. As the rest of the dogs sink their teeth into him, Actaeon makes a sound, a terrible groan, which no human could have made.[51] But nor could a stag ever make such a noise. Actaeon is truly caught between his old self and his transformed one. But his body is tearing apart as the dogs attack, encouraged by Actaeon's friends, who have now caught up. They call his name, asking where he is and wondering why he doesn't appear to see their prize. Actaeon dies in this form: *falsi . . . cervi*, a false stag.[52]

Again, Artemis has acted to defend her honour, and she does so with the same swift inhumanity that we saw in the case of Niobe and her children at the start of this chapter. We can see an earlier version of the Actaeon myth on a bell *krater* held by Boston's Museum of Fine Arts.[53] The vase has been decorated by the Pan Painter, and it dates to around 470 BCE. This Actaeon has not been transformed into a stag, but his hunting dogs – who answer to a higher authority than their erstwhile master – have turned on him just the same. Three of them scamper over his body; a fourth is biting at his left arm, which is supporting his weight. He has collapsed to his knees, and he raises his right arm to the heavens as if in supplication. His head is thrown back. One of the dogs has already sunk its teeth into his throat. In front of him Artemis fits an arrow to her bow. She is wearing a deerskin cloak and a long tunic which hangs in drapes down to her ankles. She has a quiver slung over her shoulder and a spare arrow in her left hand. Her left foot is extended, toes pointed. The foot actually strays into the border of the vase painting. The meander pattern (also called the Greek key: a repeating geometric pattern of right-angled loops) is used to represent the ground on which Actaeon has fallen. But the goddess's elegant toes block a little corner of it from view: the abstract decoration has become part of the overspilling scene. Even the conventions of artistic expression have to obey Artemis, it seems. It's a glorious way to convey her absolute lawlessness, her insistence that everyone subscribes to her view of the world or pays the price.

And once again this Artemis – ready to kill a man whose dogs are already attacking him – has a completely serene expression. There is no suggestion that her emotions are engaged at all by the killing she is about to commit. It is a scene that has been painted countless times, by everyone from the Pan Painter to Titian,[54] and her unemotional pursuit of this man's death is always a remarkable feature. No matter how many different aspects of Artemis we examine, it all comes back to this. She is a true predator. And – like the great white shark in Steven Spielberg's *Jaws* – she has a doll's eyes: empty of expression, fixed on death.

DEMETER

WHEN FACED with a female figure of undeniable power and strength who is nonetheless beset by a grief she can't describe, Iambe makes an interesting choice. The figure is the goddess Demeter – disguised and living among mortals – and the grief is because her daughter Persephone is missing, kidnapped by Hades, lost in the Underworld, his dark realm. The story is told in the second of the *Homeric Hymns*, and it is not a pretty one.

It begins with a brief precis: Demeter of the lovely hair has her slender-ankled daughter snatched by Aidoneus (a poetic variation of Hades), and Zeus gave her to him.[1] That these three deities are siblings, so that it is Demeter's brothers who are conspiring to kidnap her child, goes unmentioned. So does Persephone's name, although her youth is referenced obliquely because she is *paidzousan* – playing like a child – with the daughters of Oceanus. The scene is all bucolic innocence: girls picking flowers in a field together. But even the earth is in on Zeus's deception. Gaia – the earth goddess – causes a huge blossoming of narcissus flowers to act as bait for Persephone. She is still unnamed, but here called *kalukopidi* – the girl with a face as beautiful as a flower.

This introduction sets a deeply sinister scene. Not only is Zeus in cahoots with his brother Hades, but Gaia is in on it too. There are a couple of points to note here. First that Demeter is not Mother Earth, a role we can more accurately ascribe to Gaia. Rather, Demeter is the goddess of grain, of agriculture. In other words, she specializes in the plants which feed hungry mortals. Gaia – from an earlier generation of gods – is mother to giants and Titans, but shows little interest in the fate of human beings. In fact, she is pretty keen to get rid of some of them, according to the lost epic poem *Cypria*.[2] In a fragment quoted by a scholiast on the *Iliad*, Gaia and Zeus decide that there are too many mortals and set events in motion to cause the Trojan War. There's nothing like ten years of fighting to reduce human numbers. The second point is how horrible it is that it's the narcissus flower – representational of a young man who was cursed with self-infatuation, from which he wasted away and died – that is used to trap Persephone. There is no indication that she is even slightly self-aware about her beauty: her behaviour is that of a guileless child. But the gods conspire against her all the same.

Persephone is drawn to this miraculous bouquet: a hundred flowers bloom from a single root. But as she draws closer, the earth splits open and the many-named son of Kronos (that's Hades again, at the risk of contradicting his epithet) drives his immortal horses at her.[3] He snatches Persephone against her will – *aekousan* – and she screams as he carries her away. She shrieks, calls out for her father, the best and loftiest son of Kronos. But no mortal or immortal heard her voice.

The scene has become increasingly disturbing. There is no suggestion that Persephone is anything but terrified and appalled by her uncle suddenly appearing from beneath the ground to take her away. The hopelessness of Persephone's position is only emphasized by the use of 'son of Kronos' to describe first her uncle, Hades, and then her father, Zeus. Why would one of them help her when the other is kidnapping her? From Persephone's perspective, these two deities are – as the Greek text makes plain – essentially the same. One god rapes her, the other agrees to it.

It's a scene captured in a dramatic fresco discovered in northern Greece, in a tomb within a burial mound at Vergina, the site of the ancient city of Aigai, which was once the capital of Macedonia.[4] White horses pull the chariot of Hades, and they're working hard. The fresco is damaged in part, so we cannot see the detail of the horses' expressions. But we can tell they're moving at speed: one chariot wheel has bounced clear off the ground. Hades holds a whip in his right hand, his dead eyes gazing straight ahead. He has scooped Persephone up in his left arm and holds her pressed against his chest. Her robe has fallen away in the chaos, so he is joylessly groping her left breast. Her body curves away from him, and her arms are thrown above her head. She is reaching out in silent supplication; the bangles on her wrists look like manacles. Her hair streams above her head, so quickly is the chariot moving. The edge of the fresco is degraded, so that her reaching hands seem to fade into nothingness. And this poignant absence reflects her new, unwanted existence: Persephone is now little more than a ghost, haunting the realm of the dead.[5]

The kidnapping of Persephone – or Proserpina, to give her her Roman name – was not a subject tackled just by ancient artists, but was a wildly popular theme in Renaissance art too. Between 1621 and 1622, Bernini carved an extraordinarily lifelike statue called *The Rape of Proserpina*. It now stands in the Galleria Borghese in Rome.[6] This version of Hades (or Pluto) has dispensed with his chariot and is grabbing Proserpina as he stands. He looks like a ballet dancer: strong muscles bulge in his thighs as he takes all his weight (and Proserpina's) on his left leg. His right leg extends behind him. Every tendon in his feet is visible, as is the vein that runs down his inner thigh. The robe which is sliding off Proserpina as she squirms in his arms is covering his groin, which presumably saved the blushes of the statue's commissioner, Cardinal Scipione Borghese. Proserpina's breasts are exposed as a consequence, but no one ever seems to blush at that. Pluto's arms are carved with the same remarkable attention to detail: biceps, triceps, veins, tendons. This is the body of an incredibly strong man, an athlete at the peak of his form. But the woman he is clutching isn't another dancer, relishing her moment in the limelight. It is a young woman in visible distress, desperate to escape.

Unlike her uncle's muscled form, Proserpina's body is soft. This may seem like a perverse thing to say about a marble statue, but it is the main reason why this sculpture is so compelling. Pluto's left hand grips Proserpina at the waist. He has long, elegant fingers, which always makes me wonder whether Bernini's model was another artist. Proserpina's legs are scrambling in midair as she tries to free herself. Just behind Pluto sits his three-headed dog, Cerberus. One of his mouths is open as he snaps at Proserpina's heels. Even if she could wriggle free, she wouldn't be safe.

Proserpina's left arm extends as she tries to push back against her attacker. Pluto's bearded face is turned away from his niece as she forces the heel of her left hand into his head, just above the cheekbone. Her right arm is stretched out behind her, hand upraised, as though she might ward off another attack from the air. Her expression is one of terrible distress: her mouth is slightly open; a small marble tear runs down her cheek. But it is her left thigh that grabs the viewer's attention. Her uncle's hand is sinking into the soft flesh of her leg: it dimples beneath his fingers. Look further up at Proserpina's torso and we see the same thing happening there. His index finger pushes into her ribs, his middle finger caught in the roll of flesh at her waist as she struggles to break free.

It is a breathtaking work of art, in more ways than one. Looked at from a modern perspective, it depicts a profoundly harrowing and all-too-familiar scene: a very young woman trying to escape the clutches of an older, much stronger man. And yet you cannot look away from it. The skill on display is astonishing, the illusion of living flesh is complete. I can well understand why someone might wish to avoid looking at something so brutal, but – for me at least – the beauty is undeniable. For almost every art form, I find I can imagine where the artist began. The first words of a story that demands to be told, the distant musical refrain in an ear, the dash of colour in a mind's eye. But I can't even begin to think how a sculpture like this is created – where Bernini must have started, how he proceeded to capture these bodies in motion. I almost find it easier to believe he used real people and somehow turned them to stone.

Let's return to the *Homeric Hymn*, where Persephone was screaming for help as Hades snatched her, but going unheard among both gods and mortals. Not even the olive trees, bearing beautiful fruit, heard her cry, says the hymn.[7] But two gods do hear her. Hecate (a goddess associated with witches and night) in her cave hears Persephone cry out. And Helios, the sun god, also hears her calling out to Zeus. But Zeus is busy in a distant temple receiving offerings (far be it from me to use the word *alibi* at this point) and so Hades is able to abduct Persephone. The Greek is unequivocal – *aekazomenēn* – against her will.[8] The focus stays on Persephone for a moment longer. While she can see the sky and the sun, she still has hope of seeing her beloved mother and the other immortal gods again. And this hope comforts her brave mind. She continues to cry out, and the sound echoes off the peaks of the mountains and in the depths of the ocean.

And it is this cry that Demeter hears. A sharp pain seizes her heart. She begins an extensive search for her missing daughter, over land and sea. But no one – not mortals, not gods – wants to tell her the truth. Deo (an alternative name for Demeter) travels all over the earth for nine days, carrying flaming torches in each hand. Although we can assume this is to aid her in her search when it's dark, it also reminds us of the way the Furies pursue those who have committed a terrible blood crime, always armed with torches. Demeter doesn't eat ambrosia, drink nectar, or wash.[9] It's interesting that her behaviour here is very much like ritual mourning practices we still see today, when the bereaved pause the simple habits of daily life in order to mark a terrible loss.

This part of Demeter's ordeal always seems to me the most desperate. Not knowing the fate of a loved one is a catastrophic double loss, where imagination forces those left behind to grieve again and again. The couple at the centre of Ian McEwan's *The Child in Time* suffer exactly this nightmare when their daughter, Kate, is snatched from a supermarket. Her father, Stephen, cannot move on with his life or even sustain his marriage, because he is so riddled with guilt and the agony of not-knowing. But the kidnapping alone is terrible enough. The most famous of Agatha Christie's novels, *Murder on the Orient Express*, has as its victim the perpetrator of a child kidnapping and eventual murder. Christie was very astute when it came to knowing what kind of crime a person would have to commit before she could make them the focus of such a remarkable murder. We all know that killing a child is just such a horror. And no one sheds a tear for the dead man, especially once his vicious past is revealed.

On the tenth day, Hecate arrives to console Demeter. She explains that she also heard Persephone cry out, but could not see who took her. The two goddesses go straight to Helios and ask him what has happened to Persephone. The sun, of course, sees everything. Helios finally offers Demeter the information she needs. No one else is responsible, he says, but Zeus the cloud-gatherer. He's the one who gave her to his brother Hades, to be his wife.[10] And Hades has taken her to his dark kingdom, even though she was crying so loudly. But you must stop being angry – it doesn't do you any good. Hades isn't a shameful son-in-law, even if he is your own brother.

Helios might see everything from his lofty perch in the sky, but he doesn't understand Demeter at all. Her grief is now more terrible, more savage. She leaves Olympus, abandoning the divine existence she has previously known. She disguises herself, conceals her divine beauty, and walks unrecognized among mortals. Eventually, she arrives at the house of Celeus, king of Eleusis (which is about thirteen miles northwest of Athens). She is now disguised as an old woman, resembling the nurse someone like Celeus would have to look after his child. She settles herself by a well, and four of Celeus's daughters soon appear to collect water. They kindly suggest that this old lady would find company and shelter in their city. Demeter responds by telling them a tall tale – very similar to those spun by Odysseus in the *Odyssey* – that she was once a privileged young woman, until she was kidnapped by Cretan pirates, from whom she had to make her escape. Could they tell her which house she should go to, to find work? She could nurse a new baby, for example, or make beds. The girls advise her to try their own father's house. No family would turn her away, they add, because she is *theoeikelos* – like a goddess.[11] They don't realize how right they are, but they're excited anyway, and they run home to tell their mother about the wonderful old woman they have met. Their mother Metaneira is as thrilled as they are – she has a baby this lady could nurse. So she sends her older daughters to collect the stranger and bring her to their home.

When Demeter arrives at their house, she is not as well-disguised as she might be: her head almost hits the ceiling, and she fills the whole doorway with her brightness.[12] Metaneira is filled with reverence and offers this imposing figure a seat. But Demeter – the bringer of seasons, giver of shining gifts – won't sit on the ornate couch she is offered. The Eleusinians can't know it, of course, but this goddess is in mourning, and a beautiful, comfortable seat isn't appropriate for her. Demeter says nothing, but keeps her gaze averted.

And then trusty Iambe gives her a plain stool with a bright white fleece on it. Demeter accepts, veils her face, and sits in silence, at one with her grief. She doesn't smile, or eat, or drink, all of which a guest would be expected to do. She just sits there missing her daughter. But the family don't chivvy her or complain about her silence. Nor does Iambe leave her to grieve alone. As I mentioned at the beginning of the chapter, she instead makes an interesting choice. Faced with a grieving stranger, she decides to make jokes. She continues to do so until this devastated woman begins to smile, and then laugh, and ease her gracious heart.[13]

It is hard for me to overstate how much I love this part of the poem. Firstly, it reflects what I have always believed to be true (and important) about jokes: we don't need them when our lives are going well. I mean, we don't shun them in the good times either. We have those times with friends when we're laughing so hard about something so nonsensical that we begin to wonder if we'll ever be able to stop. But we don't need them then; we just enjoy them. The jokes which reach us when we're in the bottom of a dark pit, the ones that make us give a reluctant half smile at the absurdity of it all, even as we're struggling to climb back up to normality? Those are the ones we need. It is these jokes – delivered by friends or strangers who may have no idea of the torment we're enduring – these ones that put solid ground beneath our feet and carry us back to who we are, and were, before we landed in the pit. Iambe is one of those extraordinary people who doesn't shy away from the crippling weight of grief in another person, and a stranger at that. She isn't horrified by Demeter's sorrow; she doesn't treat it as a contagion that might spread to her. She reaches right down into the chasm of grief where Demeter has found herself, and she lights the way so that the goddess can climb out again.

It is an incidental source of delight to me that Iambe is a woman, of course. If I had the energy, I would print out this part of the *Homeric Hymn* and I would send it to every witless fool who has ever claimed with sincerity or irony, which is – as I have doubtless said before – sincerity but with raised eyebrows, that women aren't funny or can't tell jokes. Here is Iambe to prove them all wrong: a woman living in a deeply patriarchal society who responds to what comedians might well describe as a tough crowd with a series of gags. It's not a one-off performance either, as the next line explains that in later times too she would ease Demeter's spirits.

Once Demeter has softened with smiles and laughter, she is willing to accept wine from Metaneira. She rejects the wine as it is offered, however: it must be mixed with water, grain, and herbs before it is acceptable to her. When Metaneira has followed the goddess's recipe, Demeter drinks this new concoction, which the hymn describes as holy.[14] The reference here is to the Eleusinian Mysteries, a religious or cult practice that honoured the goddess Demeter, and was obviously centred on this part of her story, which takes place in Eleusis. Frustratingly for us, the rituals of this cult are largely unknown. Most aspects of mystery religions were kept secret by their worshippers; to reveal any details – in speech or in writing – would have been deeply blasphemous. So we will have to imagine what Demeter-worshippers got up to in their secret gatherings. Suffice it to say, their wine sounds vile.

Metaneira has concluded that her guest is nobly born, even if she is now an itinerant nurse. She invites Demeter to raise her son, who is late-born and much longed-for. In other words, Metaneira has spent years wishing for a son after her girls were born, and her prayers have recently been granted. If he reaches manhood, thanks to Demeter caring for him, Metaneira will richly reward her.

Demeter gladly accepts the job. The baby's parents are delighted by how quickly their son grows, and how handsome he is. They have no idea that Demeter isn't feeding him food and milk, but ambrosia. She is raising him not as a mortal man, but as a god. Perhaps Metaneira and Celeus wouldn't have minded if they had known this. It is working, after all. But there is another element to Demeter's childcare routine that they do mind, when Metaneira discovers it. Demeter hides the boy at night, placing him in the fire like a log. We have other examples of goddesses burning the mortal weakness from a demigod or, like this boy, a heavily favoured mortal. In some versions of the childhood of Achilles, for example, his mother Thetis holds him in a fire, rather than dipping him in water. The fragile heel is the only part of him which isn't then made strong.

Metaneira sees Demeter put her son into the fire one night, and she cries out in horror. Demeter is so angered by this lack of faith that she pulls the boy from the flames and drops him on the ground. (I hope it doesn't need saying that you should try literally none of Demeter's childcare tips at home.) She tells Metaneira that her son will now not be immortal, but will remain mortal and eventually die, like his parents and siblings. Only now does she introduce herself and explain that they have been lucky enough to have Demeter herself as their son's nurse. She demands that the Eleusinians build her a temple and promises to teach them her mysteries. She finally sheds her disguise and allows herself to be young, beautiful, fragrant, and gleaming once more. And then she leaves.

The Eleusinians build the altar to Demeter, as requested. But no amount of worship can comfort the goddess in what is still her time of grieving. Did she find that nursing Demophoön, the baby of the house, distracted her from her terrible loss? The hymn doesn't say so, but certainly now that she no longer has a child to care for, her grief seems to rebound. For a year, she makes the all-nourishing land barren. No seeds sprout, no crops grow. Her desperate famine would have destroyed the entire human race and – crucially – deprived the Olympian gods of all the sacrifices and offerings mortals give them. Not one to be concerned by trivial things like conspiring to kidnap his own daughter for a forced marriage, Zeus discovers he cannot tolerate something as dreadful as the loss of prestige and gifts he will experience if all humankind is exterminated by famine.

First of all, he sends Iris – the goddess of the rainbow – to plead with Demeter and ask her to return home. Iris tries her multicoloured best, but Demeter is unmoved. So then he sends the other immortals, one after another, to offer her presents, but she remains angry in her heart and she holds firm against their entreaties.[15] The message she sends back is always the same: she won't return to Olympus and she won't allow the crops to grow until she looks into her daughter's eyes again. This is one of very few occasions when anyone holds their ground against Zeus – and certainly against all the Olympian gods – and wins. And Demeter does win. Zeus sends Hermes down to the Underworld to explain to Hades that he must release Persephone from the murky depths and allow her to come back to the light, back to the gods, and back to the sight of her mother, and thus end Demeter's anger.[16]

Hermes does as instructed and scoots down to Hades. His role as psychopomp – a figure who escorts the living to the world of the dead – means that this journey is a great deal easier for him than it is for most. He finds Hades in his dingy palace and notices Persephone, now described as Hades's *parakoitos* – bedmate. There is no mistaking her demeanour, it seems: she is described as very much unwilling, longing for her mother. And – the poet knows how to build suspense – her faraway mother is devising plans.

This hymn is to Demeter, so we have pulled our attention away from Persephone for the last three hundred lines in order to focus on Demeter and her response to the loss of her daughter. The last time we saw Persephone, the ground had split open and Hades had appeared in his chariot. She was crying out in fear and begging for help, but no one came. And because our attention moved away from her to follow her mother's quest to find her, we haven't thought to ask what it was like for her when she arrived in her new, unwanted home. But luckily, the poet A. E. Stallings has brilliantly imagined the scene for us in her poem 'Hades Welcomes His Bride'.[17] The avuncular (and deeply sinister) Hades begins his address to Persephone with the words 'Come now, child.' He guides her around this clammy, claustrophobic vision of the Underworld, where 'The pale things twisting / Overhead are mostly roots.' He tells her she will be his queen and – by extension – queen of all men. 'No smile?' he asks her, and you can practically hear the threat beneath the apparently kind enquiry. He details the elaborate thrones he has commissioned for them both, then takes her downstairs to her quarters, where, he casually notes, it's easier to breathe. Persephone is a goddess, of course, so he can't mean it literally; she doesn't need breath to live. But he has apparently noticed that she needs to breathe in a less literal sense and that she struggles to do so when he is present.

So he has had this room prepared for her with a loom – weaving is always the most suitable womanly pursuit in Greek myth – and thread. The thread has been unravelled from shrouds, he explains, and all of it has been dyed black. 'Such pictures you shall weave!' he says. He has found three shadows to be her maids, because they won't be able to gossip about her – or talk to her, or hear her, as he doesn't need to mention. There's no time anyway, because he takes her straight into a palatial room where he has had the ceiling painted to resemble the night sky. The claustrophobia is crushing, and that's not even the worst of it. He points out the bed: 'Our bed. / Ah! Your hand is trembling! I fear / There is, as yet, too much pulse in it.'

The temptation when examining these parts of Greek myth is to focus on the female voice that has so often gone unheard. But Stallings finds a different, devastatingly potent way to draw attention to the treatment Persephone experiences. She has no voice at all in this poem, because it's Hades's monologue, and we can't help but notice. Her silence speaks more loudly than dialogue ever could, of a fear that is coming over her in waves: of the dark, of the damp, of the terrifying earthiness of the Underworld, of the labyrinthine nature of the palace, of the power of a king who can command diamond-encrusted thrones, of the isolation, of the tedium, of the imprisonment, of the rape. And we feel all this in the differing shades of silence to which Hades so carefully responds.

Back in the *Homeric Hymn*, we now see Persephone again – visibly unhappy – because we have travelled down to the Underworld with Hermes. The messenger god addresses Hades and explains that he has been ordered by Zeus to take Persephone out of Erebus (a dark region of the Underworld), because her mother will only let go of her rage against the gods when she lays eyes on her daughter once again.[18] Otherwise she'll exterminate the entire feeble human race by hiding the seeds in the earth and not allowing them to grow. She's so angry she shuns the other gods and stays in her temple in Eleusis.

Hades smiles, and tells Persephone to go back to her mother. Go, he says, but think and feel kindly towards me; don't be so angry with me. And then he reiterates the argument Demeter heard from Helios – I'm Zeus's brother, I'm a worthy husband for you, you're queen of every living thing, you can punish anyone who doesn't worship you. I despise Hades throughout this poem, and never more so than at this moment where he essentially says: *I mean, sure, I kidnapped you, but don't be all miserable about it – you like me, remember?* It's not even that he is a serial rapist that makes me hate him so much here, although that certainly contributes the largest part of my contempt. But the finishing touch is the way he is so needy for the approval of a young woman he's kidnapped and then assaulted. He has all the power in this relationship – he is literally king of the whole netherworld – and yet he is still wheedling and whining for approval. He's the real victim here, don't you see? Give me strength.

Well, that's what he said, continues the hymn. And wise Persephone rejoiced.[19] In the Greek, the verbs of him speaking and her rejoicing are right next to each other, so the connection between him offering her freedom and her delight is emphasized. But then, of course, it turns out that this poor, victimized, incredibly powerful deity is still conspiring against his niece. Having smiled at the orders of Zeus, having told Persephone she may go back to her mother, we now see that his apparent acquiescence was all a lie. He secretly feeds her a sweet pomegranate seed, because he's made a rule that if she eats, she won't be able to stay with Demeter permanently.

The word *lathrēi* – secretly – is extremely important in this telling of the Persephone story. We tend to know this myth rather differently, thanks to the way children's books often make Persephone responsible for her own imprisonment. She chooses to eat the pomegranate seeds, and often does so knowing that she must stay in Hades for a month for each seed consumed. This is a modern cleansing of the story. In most ancient versions of her myth, Hades force-feeds her the pomegranate seed. In this version, he does so in secret. The upshot is the same, either way: having robbed her of consent when he brought her to the Underworld, he continues to do so now. He will always do so.

The actor and writer Hannah Morrish played the role of Persephone (or Proserpina, since she was inspired by Ovid's account, which we looked at briefly in the Muses chapter above) in a short film called *Ceres* (Ceres being the Roman name for Demeter). Juliet Stevenson played the eponymous goddess, but in a modern, human world. This agriculture goddess is a gardener, a woman who belongs in the cold outdoors. When her daughter returns – expected and yet still a surprise – the women are jumpy and awkward with one another. Ceres tries to make plans with Proserpina, even for tomorrow or the next day. But her daughter won't commit, and soon we see why: car headlights flash through the kitchen window. Proserpina knows that her husband has chased her down once again and there is nothing either of them can do to change it. She cannot escape from his coercive control – it is as inevitable as the seasons.

The romantic ideal of so many love songs, films, and novels is still one which is deeply questionable: the notion that persistence in the face of rejection is a signifier of profound love and not a disturbing refusal to hear the word no. And that is only compounded when the pursuer in the relationship is also the one with enormous power (or wealth, or vampiric tendencies, or all of the above. Vampires live forever, so they have terrific investment opportunities). Maybe if you just ask her enough times, or refuse to listen to her refusals, or kidnap her and take her to the Underworld, she'll learn to love you the way you love her. Even when the man singing this tune has glittering eyes and razor cheekbones, I urge you to run rather than walk.

This romantic ideal has been retrofitted onto Persephone's story, because it fits a trope that is still appealing to many. He's old (well, ageless, but definitely old), and rich (*Pluto* literally means 'wealthy': he is rich in the souls of the dead), and she is young and naive. He can't ignore his feelings for her, and hey, at least she's a queen now. I'm sure you don't need me to tell you how unsatisfying your life would be if your status were decided entirely by your husband's choices. So let's instead turn to Book Eleven of the *Odyssey*, where Achilles tells Odysseus that he would rather be alive and working another man's land than king among the dead.[20] Death might be inevitable, in other words, but it's not worth swapping life for. Not even the hard life of an indentured land-worker.

And the undeniable truth is that Hades knows all this. Persephone has been with him for well over a year, because Demeter has been grieving and raging long enough to cause a famine. If he was hoping he could wear down her antipathy to him, and to the Underworld, he has had plenty of time to do it. Stockholm syndrome would have kicked in by now if it was ever going to happen. And he knows he has failed. And please, don't tell me he loves her. If he loved her, he would want her to be happy, even if it meant losing her. Wanting to own someone isn't love; it's just possession.

Continuing his deceit, Hades provides Persephone with the transport she needs to escape his clutches: the same immortal horses are ready to pull the same golden chariot as he used to bring her down here all those months before.[21] But this time it's Hermes who drives, and they are soon back above ground racing across oceans and mountains and valleys until they reach Demeter.

This scene is imagined by Carol Ann Duffy in a beautiful poem, 'Demeter'. Her goddess lives in 'winter and hard earth' unable to break the ice that surrounds her.[22] She even tries using her broken heart, 'but it skimmed, / flat, over the frozen lake.' It is not just Demeter's room that is cold stone, but her heart too. She sees her daughter coming 'across the fields, / in bare feet, bringing all spring's flowers / to her mother's house.' Persephone brings the thaw, and so Demeter answers her with a rush of new life. 'I swear / the air softened and warmed as she moved,' she says.

The anger, the boiling, murderous rage Demeter feels in the *Homeric Hymn* is a lesser emotion here. This Demeter is bereaved; she has grown numb from the cold of her grief. She doesn't choose to thaw when Persephone is returned, it's done to her: Persephone brings the warmth as she walks closer. The helpless love of mother for daughter is all the more moving when contrasted with the selfish desire to possess that we saw in that A. E. Stallings poem, and in the *Homeric Hymn*, to which we now return.

Persephone rushes into her mother's arms, although the manuscript is somewhat corrupted here, so some of this section is conjecture by textual experts. Demeter must ask Persephone if she ate anything while she was in Hades, however: we can deduce her question from Persephone's reply (by which point the manuscript is legible again). If she has eaten something – however small – she will be condemned to spend part of the year in the Underworld forever.

If you're wondering why the hymn is harder to read at this point, incidentally, it is because every translation, every emendation, every variation of this poem all stem from the discovery of a single manuscript, which was found in Russia in 1777, by a man named Christian Frederick Matthaei. Often we have multiple manuscripts of an ancient poem to compare and contrast, so if there's a damaged section in one version, that part might be clearer in a different manuscript. But the *Homeric Hymn to Demeter* was considered lost until the 1770s, though it had apparently spent many years in the Imperial Archive in Moscow. Matthaei, however, claimed to have found the manuscript in a farmhouse, covered in straw and surrounded by chickens and pigs. I'm afraid I cannot tell you what route it might have taken from one location to the other. So while we're entitled to feel aggrieved at the damage this manuscript has sustained, let us all issue a brief hymn to Demeter in gratitude that her poem was obviously not tastier than whatever else the pigs had to eat.[23]

Persephone says she will tell her mother everything. When Hermes arrived in the Underworld to say that she – Persephone – could leave so that Demeter would lay eyes on her again and let go of her anger and her terrible wrath, Persephone leapt up with joy. But Hades secretly placed a sweet pomegranate seed in her mouth. He compelled me, she says, unwilling, with force, to eat it. Then she goes back to the moment of her kidnap: she was playing in the meadow with a long list of girls and goddesses, including Calypso, Athene, and Artemis. There were lots of beautiful flowers, Persephone picked the lovely narcissus, and then the ground opened up and Hades snatched her and took her under the earth. She was very much unwilling and cried out in protest. Everything I'm telling you is true, she concludes, though it pains me to say it.[24]

Since this is the first time we've heard Persephone's account of these events, it's worth examining this speech in some detail. The encounter with Hermes is exactly as it was described to us: she jumped for joy when she was told she could leave the Underworld. She is under no illusions that Zeus has ordered his brother to allow her to leave because he is concerned for her well-being. She knows that her freedom is contingent on her mother's rage. The word she uses to describe Demeter's fury is *mēnis*.[25] This is the same word used to describe the wildly destructive rage of Achilles in the first line of the *Iliad*. Demeter's anger has the same murderous quality as that of the notoriously raging Greek hero.

Interestingly, both these examples of wrath are provoked by the removal of a young woman. Achilles is prompted to his great rage when Agamemnon removes Briseis – the woman awarded to Achilles by the Greek army in recognition of his mighty victories. Achilles loses honour when he loses his prize (I wish I could tell you the *Iliad* considers Briseis's feelings, but we don't even hear her speak until Book Nineteen, so we are obliged to think of her as a possession conferring status to an owner, as well as a human being, because otherwise the poem would make no sense at all). And Demeter loses her daughter, which obviously causes her enormous pain. Unlike Achilles, she doesn't seem to be particularly bothered about the disrespect that is certainly implicit in Persephone's kidnap: if Zeus or Hades had been afraid of her response, they would surely not have conspired in this plan. It's only when Demeter has given free rein to her wrath that Zeus begins to regret his earlier behaviour. This is precisely the same dynamic we see in the *Iliad*, when Agamemnon offers to return Briseis alongside quantities of other treasure only once he sees the damage done to the Greek army by Achilles's withdrawal from battle. We so often think of Demeter as being a maternal figure – kindly, nourishing, protective – that we sometimes lose sight of the fact that her rage is terrifying, even to gods. She is described in the *Homeric Hymn* and elsewhere as *chrusaoros* – which could mean 'Demeter of the golden sword'.[26] In the past, I have tended to translate it as 'of the golden sickle', because of her most obvious connection to the harvest. But now I think a more ambiguous translation – golden-bladed Demeter – might be a better option. She wields the best weapon she has – famine – with the same murderous intent as Achilles wields his spear.

But then comes the most painful part of Persephone's description, where she recalls the pomegranate scene. Again we have the word *lathrēi* – secretly – so we remember that Hades is being deliberately deceptive. We might have concluded from the first use of the word that the person Hades was trying to deceive was Persephone. But the rest of her sentence makes it clear that was not the case. Hades has to force her to eat against her will. There are three words – all conveying this abuse – in one line: unwilling, by force, compelled. Hades has not tricked Persephone into eating; he has physically pushed the seed into her mouth. The person from whom he was concealing this can only be Hermes. There are plenty of horrible scenes in Greek literature, but not many more chilling than this: an all-powerful god – the king of the dead in the heart of his domain – pretending to the messenger of Zeus that he is doing what has been asked of him while force-feeding a girl he has already kidnapped and raped so that he can reclaim her every year for ever.

Persephone's story then jumps back in time to the day of the kidnapping, when she presents an innocent bucolic scene of her and her girlfriends playing in a meadow together. There is a lovely moment when she has named all the other girls – Leukippe, Phaino, Ianthe, and many more – and then last on the list come everyone's first choice for a playful afternoon in the country: fight-rousing Athene and arrow-shooting Artemis. The moment where the earth splits open as Persephone reaches to pick the narcissus flowers is still dramatic and shocking, even though we know it's coming. Then she concludes her account with a reminder that she was taken against her will, crying out. Again, we know this part of the narrative from the earlier third-person perspective, so we have no reason to doubt Persephone's word about any of this. The saddest part is perhaps the terrible reversal in mood as she speaks, beginning with the most recent moment when Hermes arrived and she was leaping up, elated. And then becoming more and more wretched as she continues, taking us back in time to the day when she was first snatched by Hades, though she was unwilling and weeping. There is nothing but unhappiness for Persephone in the Underworld, and the violence and deceit of Hades have ensured that she will always have to endure it. The relationship between Hades and Persephone is one that has inspired countless artists and composers, but I find it very difficult to see the romance. For me, it will always be closer to the A. E. Stallings poem: constant threat beneath a veneer of civility.

And the contrast is never more stark than in this reunion scene between mother and daughter. Their relationship is the opposite of the one Persephone has with Hades. The two goddesses are *homophrōn* – same-minded, they think alike. This is the quality that Odysseus and Penelope share in the *Odyssey*: they look at the world from a common perspective.

The language is positive and repeated: they're of one mind, they take joy from one another, they embrace each other and soothe each other's sore hearts, misery left their souls, they delight in one another.[27] Then the goddess Hecate arrives (who had heard Persephone being kidnapped) and she too is overjoyed to see the girl again. After all the vocabulary of pain and unwillingness when Hades entered the picture, there is only delight in his absence. Zeus now sends another messenger – this time the goddess Rhea – asking Demeter to rejoin the other immortals. Rhea is the mother of Zeus, Demeter, and Hades, so it really does seem that Zeus has sent his mum to apologize for his crummy behaviour because he was too scared to own up to it in person.

He offers a compromise, that Persephone should spend one third of each year in the Underworld and two-thirds aboveground with her mother. It's a compromise that Demeter is likely to accept, which is lucky given that the poet tells us that the once-fertile Field of Rharus no longer provides food but is bereft of its leaves. Rhea and Demeter have another joyous reunion when they see one another, taking great pleasure in each other.[28]

There are marked differences in this poem between the way men greet one another (Hermes and Hades – unemotional salutation), the way men greet women (Hades kidnaps Persephone; Hermes doesn't speak to her directly at all, only to Hades), and the way women greet one another (joy, embraces, delight): this is the third such happy reunion in quick succession. The author of this hymn – written in overtly and unquestioningly patriarchal times – nonetheless understands the value of women's relationships with one another. They bring comfort, consolation, joy, and warmth, in the face of every injustice.

In 1994, the Irish poet Eavan Boland published a collection called *In a Time of Violence*, which featured her exquisite Demeter (here called Ceres) and Persephone poem, called 'The Pomegranate'.[29] For Boland, this story is the only myth 'I have ever loved . . . And the

best thing about the legend is / I can enter it anywhere. And have.'
It's a beautiful observation and one which feels incredibly true, not
least because Carol Ann Duffy and A. E. Stallings seem to feel the
same way. You really can enter this story anywhere, depending on who
you are when you encounter it. All three of these contemporary poets are mothers of daughters, as well as being daughters. No wonder
they were all drawn to this particular myth, in which a woman wins
a partial reprieve for her trafficked daughter by simply refusing to do
what so many women are expected to do and tolerate the abuse of
powerful men. Zeus and Hades obviously never consider what Persephone might want, but they also disregard Demeter in their plot, even
though she is their sister. They simply decide between themselves that
Hades should have whatever he wants and assume that Persephone
will get used to it, since she can't escape it. And yet Demeter – mother
of this young woman and therefore firmly occupying the space where
women become invisible to the eyes of predatory men – doesn't accept anything. She weaponizes her rage, flexes her tremendous power,
and forces them to do what they should have done all along: consider
Persephone's feelings and consider her own.

Boland recalls the time when she first read the story, saying 'and at
first I was / an exiled child in the crackling dusk of / the underworld'.
But then many years later she goes searching for her own daughter one
evening, and she summarizes every parent's anxiety in a single sentence:
'When she came running I was ready / to make any bargain to keep her.'
The poem concludes with Boland accepting that this story or legend will
be the same for her daughter as it has been for her, that one day she too
will be Demeter.

My experience with this myth is similar to Boland's: I also read it
when I was young, and I identified with Persephone, of course. Not only
is she young, but also tragic and an outsider, someone who can never
fully belong in either world because she must divide her time between

both. She is every quirky teenager millennia before they exist. But now I am far more focused on the power of Demeter, the incredible price she extracts from her two brothers by withdrawing from the divine sphere. I would slightly prefer her to blast them with thunderbolts, but age confers wisdom, I suppose, and I have learned to accept that you can't always get what you want.

She would, I might add, be well within her rights to attack Zeus even before he and Hades conspire against her and Persephone. Hesiod tells us in the *Theogony* that Demeter had a passionate fling with a mortal man named Iasion.[30] But in Book Five of the *Odyssey*, the goddess Calypso tells us how that worked out for everyone. She is fuming because Hermes has arrived with a message from Zeus, telling Calypso she needs to send her mortal lover Odysseus on his way home to Ithaca. She is shaking with rage by the time he's finished speaking, and her words rush forth.[31] You gods are vicious, she says, you exceed everyone in your jealousy. She mentions how they took against rosy-fingered Dawn when she chose (the mortal) Orion to be her lover, and sent Artemis to shoot him with her arrows. And then there's beautiful-haired Demeter, who fell for Iasion and made love to him in the thrice-ploughed field. As soon as Zeus found out, he killed him by throwing a bright thunderbolt. Given the number of times Zeus helps himself to a mortal lover, Calypso would seem to have a point about Dawn and Demeter. It's interesting that Hera is the one who gets the reputation for destructive jealousy, because she is so quick to punish Zeus's lovers and victims alike. But Zeus doesn't even pause before obliterating Demeter's lover, doesn't even subcontract by sending another god, like Artemis or Apollo, to carry out the death sentence for him. He reaches straight for the thunderbolt. His jealousy is just as vicious as Hera's, but the trope of the jealous husband is less pervasive in Greek myth than that of the jealous wife. Not that Zeus is Demeter's husband, but he is the father of Persephone. Iasion, incidentally, is the father of the minor god Ploutos – Wealth – according to Hesiod. So perhaps fathering a god is another factor in Zeus's extreme response. But either way, Demeter had a legitimate grievance against him long before he gave Hades the nod to kidnap her daughter.

There are some beautiful vase paintings and sculptures that illustrate moments in the intertwined existence of Demeter and Persephone, although they can be frustratingly difficult to identify with certainty. The east pediment of the Parthenon frieze – still held in the British Museum at the time of writing – has two goddesses seated together, one leaning to her right, the other half embracing her.[32] Or at least, the goddess on the viewer's left rests her forearm on her companion's leaning shoulder. And the two goddesses sit casually, their tunics draping between their spread knees. There is something careless and relaxed about these two figures (the heads are missing, as are the hands and some of the forearms). Although we can't be sure of their identities, Demeter and Persephone are the likeliest fit: the pediment depicts the gods witnessing the birth of Athene. And they are seated on what look like wooden boxes, which might be *cistae* – chests or boxes used in Eleusinian cult worship – which adds a further identifying clue. You can see a more ornate example of a cista on the head of a caryatid – a priestess who holds the weight of the temple quite literally on her head – from the sanctuary of Demeter at Eleusis. The statue and her box are now held in the Fitzwilliam Museum in Cambridge. This may all seem like a bit of a reach, but when you have so little evidence to identify these figures on the Parthenon, you tend to take what you can get.

The very last section of the *Homeric Hymn* focuses on the story's happy ending. And that is not only the limited victory that Demeter has wrested from her brothers, but also the improvement this brings to the lives of humans. Rhea has asked Demeter to give up her anger towards Zeus, reminding us all that there is nothing more dignified than sending your mother to fight your battles for you. And her final plea is for us – give a fruitful harvest to mortals.[33] And fine-garlanded Demeter did not ignore her. She hastened the crops; the whole land was full of leaves and flowers.

But bringing the world back to life isn't the only way Demeter decides to improve our lot. She goes to four kings: Triptolemus, Diocles, Eumolpus, and Celeus (in whose house she stayed during her bleakest time). She teaches these men the sacred rites of her cult religion. And Triptolemus in particular is associated with Demeter-worship: the two appear alongside one another on various artworks. He is named by Pseudo-Apollodorus as the elder son of Metaneira and Celeus; his youngest brother is Demophoön, the baby Demeter burnished in the fire like an animate log.

We see Triptolemus as a young man on a skyphos – drinking cup – from the early fifth century BCE. The cup, made by Hieron and painted by Makron, is now held in the British Museum.[34] It's a small red-figure vase, just over 21 centimetres tall, showing Triptolemus in the centre of the scene, seated on a winged chariot with snakes at its wheels. He holds five stalks of wheat in his left hand and a wide, shallow bowl in his right. In front of him is Persephone, offering him wine from a jug. She holds a torch in her left hand, and her dress is ornate: a mass of folds and ruffles. Behind Persephone stands Eleusis – the goddess personification of the place – who is watching the scene intently, as though she too wants to learn the sacred rites. At the back of the chariot is Demeter, holding a torch in her right hand like Persephone and stalks of wheat in her left hand like Triptolemus. The torch reminds us of the ones she carried when searching the earth for days and nights looking for her beloved Persephone. Demeter wears a simple crown, and she is draped in the most spectacular mantle – it's covered in delicate horizontal patterns of tiny flying people, figures rushing along in chariots pulled by horses, and dolphins leaping in the air, as well as ornamental spirals and palmettes. The artist must have had a model for this, because he has replicated exactly the way a pattern distorts as the fabric creases. Poseidon is sitting behind Demeter, his head fully turned to eyeball her incredible outfit. He's literally holding a dolphin in his left hand, and he still looks underdressed in comparison. Even the dolphin looks a bit put out.

No one can blaspheme these sacred rites of Demeter, the *Homeric Hymn* goes on to explain. Nor question them, nor even speak of them. Don't ask me how you know if you're blaspheming these rites if no one ever speaks of them; I suppose that would be an ecumenical matter. But the hymn is quite clear on the advantages of knowing and practising the rites. A mortal who has seen them is blessed, and those who haven't seen them will get no share in the good things that he (the true believer) will have after death.

This is a surprising moment, no less so because it appears so near the end of the poem. We might well have assumed that worship of Demeter is a very earthly affair – her interest is in the growing of grain, as we see both in the poem and in that beautiful skyphos, where she is holding wheat stems and Triptolemus is holding them in imitation of her. The Eleusinian Mysteries may be shrouded in secrecy (the torches held by Persephone and Demeter suggest they might take place under cover of darkness) but they are closely connected to something communal and tangible: the harvest. And yet here also is a glimpse into the afterlife, and the promise of a better life after death for those who practise a particular religion. This will obviously become a commonplace in seven or eight centuries' time, when one of the draws of Christianity is that its adherents will have a better afterlife than everyone else. But it's unusual to find such a promise in the context of a polytheistic and individualistic worldview (as we usually see in Homer and in the *Homeric Hymns*). We're accustomed to seeing – in the *Odyssey* for example – an afterlife which focuses on individuals and the particular circumstances of their lives, deeds, and deaths. So a person's mighty deeds might place them in the Elysian Fields after they die in battle, and terrible wrongdoers might find themselves punished for all eternity in Tartarus. But here, the hymn seems to suggest that something much less epic – participating in the Eleusinian Mysteries – will enhance your existence both before and after death.

The poem is almost at its end, and Demeter and Persephone now retreat from the mortal sphere, returning to Olympus. They live there together (for two-thirds of the year, anyway), alongside Zeus. Any person who experiences their love will be glad of it, because they'll send Ploutos – the god Wealth, son of Demeter and her lover Iasion – to their home. The poem concludes with a plea from the poet for Demeter and Persephone to look on him kindly.

The Demeter of Knidos was carved several centuries after the *Homeric Hymns* were composed. She is from the mid-fourth century BCE. She's about 150 centimetres tall, carved from white marble and seated on a throne, now in the British Museum.[35] Her chair looks a lot less regal than it once did: both the back and the arm rails have broken off. And the goddess herself has suffered a similar fate. Her arms have also been broken above the elbow joint. Her nose and chin have been damaged too, but that hasn't changed her serene expression as she gazes, sightless, at the viewer. There is a veil over her hair, which is worn in a simple style: pulled back from the face, over the ears. Locks of her long hair rest on the front of her tunic, which is worn high with a *himation* – mantle – pinned just below the collarbone. She is the calm, patient mother figure we expect from a goddess associated with harvests and agriculture.

You have to look hard to see the other side of her, given the damage sustained to the lower part of the statue, where you can see the folds of her dress draping over her knees, but much of the detail is missing. And yet, if you look at her from the side, you can see that she isn't sitting quite as serenely as her face suggests. Her right foot extends beyond the footstool where it should be resting. She might be still in this moment, but she is readying herself to rise and move. This is the mother of Persephone, after all. If her daughter is threatened, she's ready.

One last point about this mother who never gives up. In the version of the story of Persephone and the pomegranate told by Pseudo-Apollodorus, Hades doesn't force-feed his unwilling bride.[36] Instead, he simply gives her the pomegranate seed, but doesn't tell her the consequence of eating it. So she eats. And then – when the question arises of whether she ate anything during her captivity, and the enormous impact this will have on her future existence – it turns out that there is a witness to testify against her. This is Askalaphos, son of Acheron and Gorgyra. His evidence condemns Persephone to her fate. So Demeter drops a large rock on top of him, squashing him where he stood in Hades.

Men and gods try their best to interfere in the existence of Persephone, also called Kore, the archetypal innocent young woman. But Demeter never gives in, even if she has to cause a famine to make them reconsider their behaviour. No life matters as much as her daughter's life. And if you rashly decide to go against her, she will crush you like a bug.

HESTIA

THERE COMES a time in every author's life when she has to accept she may not have made the absolute best possible decision. And the day when I blithely promised ten thousand words on a goddess who is barely mentioned in any ancient source, who makes no dent on the Renaissance, who has inspired virtually no classical composers, no modern artists, nor even any philhellenic sci-fi writers to create work inspired by her? That may turn out to have been just such a time. There is a children's book named after this goddess (one of a series by Joan Holub and Suzanne Williams), and when someone told me about it, I briefly raised my hopes. Then I read the title – *Hestia the Invisible* – and wondered if they were mocking me.[1] Now I'm beginning to think the question of how an omnipresent goddess can just disappear is fascinating in itself. So all I have to do is persuade you of the same thing.

Hestia was once one-twelfth of the Olympian pantheon, the biggest names among Greek gods. As we've already seen, the family tree of these gods is more of a dense thicket, given the complications that ensue when – for example – Zeus gets married multiple times, including to his sister, and that is before we try to decide on a birth order for gods who are born, immediately swallowed by their father, and then regurgitated in reverse order. And, as discussed in the chapter on Hera, this is what happens to the offspring of the two Titans, Rhea and Kronos. According to Hesiod's *Theogony*, Rhea gives birth to the following children in this order: Hestia, Demeter, Hera, Hades, Poseidon, and Zeus.[2] Kronos swallows each of the first five deities, and Rhea is understandably consumed with grief. She consults her parents – Gaia and Ouranos, Earth and Heaven. They tell her to go to Crete to give birth to Zeus, the youngest of her children.[3] Rhea gives birth and then plays a trick on Kronos: instead of giving him their youngest child to consume, she gives him a rock, disguised as a baby. The inability to even register the difference between a god and a rock suggests Kronos was not just a terrible father, but also an inattentive eater. He vomits up the stone and then his older children. If Zeus is the youngest of these gods – as Hesiod clearly states – then Hestia must be the eldest.

We might reasonably expect her to be as central to the peaks of Mount Olympus as most of her siblings: Hades occupies the Underworld, which is usually considered too far from Olympus for him to be counted among their number. There isn't a canonical list of Olympian gods (some major gods like Hades aren't there, and plenty of minor or earlier gods take up residence there too). But in most of our sources, Zeus and Hera become king and queen of Olympus. Their siblings Demeter and Poseidon are up there alongside them. Aphrodite's birth is contested, as we saw in her chapter, but she is always an Olympian too. Zeus's offspring form the next group: Apollo and Artemis (his children by Leto), Athene (his daughter from Metis), Ares (his son by Hera), and Hermes (his son from the nymph Maia). Hephaestus is the son of Hera (sometimes with Zeus as the father, sometimes just hers). That's eleven Olympian gods, which leaves one more spot for Hestia. But it's a spot she has to share with another of Zeus's sons, the youngest Olympian, Dionysus. Perhaps unsurprisingly, when Hestia has to battle the god of wine and theatre to get our attention, he usually comes out on top. It's easy to forget about a quiet goddess when a raucous god presses a drink into your hand and offers you days of free entertainment.

The Greeks themselves considered Dionysus to be a late addition to their pantheon: Euripides's *The Bacchae* is set in Thebes, a city-state in Boeotia, as this new religion (worshipping Bacchus or Dionysus) takes hold. It is regarded with suspicion by the king of Thebes, a young man named Pentheus. Dionysus incites his followers to tear the king to pieces, as punishment for his blasphemous doubts. These two opposing characters – order and chaos, mortal and divine – are technically cousins through their respective mothers: Pentheus is the son of Agaue, and Dionysus the son of her sister, Semele. Pentheus sees Dionysus as a threat to his status as king, but as the play unfolds we soon discover he is far more dangerous than that.

So – at the risk of offending a god who has a proven track record for obliterating his detractors – let's examine the role Hestia plays in Greek religion before she's displaced by this flashy latecomer. Hestia shares her name with both the Greek word for *hearth* and the fire that burns within it. The Greek notion of a hearth had the same metonymic quality that the English word has: *hearth* is often used to mean 'house' or 'home'. It is also a place of sanctuary, the part of a house where a supplicant would make their case. It can be a metonym for the building we call home, but also for the people who make it our home: so *hestia* can be the household, as well as the house. It is the hearth of a god when found in a temple (and so is sometimes used as a metonym for altar), and it is also a civic location, the hearth of a town hall that provides the focal point for a city's administrative life.[4] The word *focus*, incidentally, is the Latin word for *hearth*.

If you have ever come home and found warmth – literal or metaphorical – you have had an encounter with the goddess Hestia. In other words, every ancient Greek home contained a shrine to Hestia: if you lit a fire, cooked food, burned a sacrificial offering to any god or goddess, you were using her name, recognizing her divinity. In this polytheistic society, it's hard to imagine any deity could be more central to daily life – domestic, civic, and religious – than Hestia. She was the goddess who received the first part of a sacrifice to any god, and heroes swore by her name just as they did by that of her brother Zeus.

So in Book Thirteen of the *Odyssey*, Odysseus arrives back on Ithaca, the island he calls home. We are only halfway through the poem, and our hero has many more trials to endure before he can truly be said to be home: that time will only come when he is in his palace, reunited with his wife and son, reestablished in the eyes of his people as their king, and reintroduced to his ailing, elderly father. Coming home is not just a geographical act; it's a question of being recognized for who you really are. Odysseus is home in the former regard, but still has a long way to travel in the latter.

The goddess Athene disguises him as an old beggar and sends him to the hut of Eumaeus, the kindly swineherd who has done his best to remain loyal to Odysseus and his family, even as the years have slipped by and most Ithacans – Eumaeus included – believe Odysseus must be dead. Odysseus does as instructed by Athene, and receives the first of many double-edged welcomes. Before Eumaeus can even greet this stranger, his guard dogs rush to attack the disguised hero. Eumaeus calls them off before they can hurt him, but we have already seen one terrible consequence of Odysseus's long absence: not even the dogs can remember him (there will be one tragic exception to this rule later in the poem). Eumaeus makes the stranger welcome, sharing his food and his warm blanket without hesitation. Odysseus casually enquires after the queen of Ithaca as he shares the swineherd's meat and wine, and Eumaeus tells him that he thinks the queen should accept her husband's death and remarry.

Odysseus then finds himself in a characteristic logical fallacy. I loathe like the gates of Hades the man who because of poverty starts lying, he declares.[5] Since Odysseus never sees a truth he wouldn't bend – in richness and poverty alike – this cannot be true. *I honestly hate liars*, says world-class liar barely capable of honesty. But then – even as his disguise is a lie, a fiction, even as he is pretending to be an interested stranger rather than the king, he tells the truth. Odysseus is coming home, he says. And to make sure Eumaeus believes him, he swears it by Zeus, by the table of *xenia* (the guest-host friendship that characterizes so many Greek social encounters), and by the hearth of noble Odysseus: he is coming home.

Swearing by Zeus is a long-held tradition: Zeus is both king of the gods and the god who punishes those who perjure themselves, casting thunderbolts their way. Swearing on the relationship of guest-friendship is another reflection of societal values: the Greek word *xenos* is used to mean both a stranger and a friend. This is one of those times when you really notice that different languages can capture concepts that barely exist in your own mother tongue. In English, stranger and friend are practically opposites; in Greek they are the same. You have an obligation to make someone welcome in your home with food, wine, and a bed for the night, and they have the obligation to return the favour. You might begin your encounter as strangers, in other words, but you will treat each other as friends just the same. This deeply sacred bond is often marked with an exchange of gifts. Breaking the rules of hospitality might be a minor faux pas in our society, but for Bronze Age Greeks it was a much deeper breach of the social contract. These two solemn oaths are insufficient for Odysseus, however, which is why he also mentions the hearth. This part of the royal house of Ithaca – of the palace which belongs to the very man swearing by it as he pretends otherwise – this is the third sacred pillar on which he can rest his oath. By Zeus, by *xenia*, by *hestia*.

The hearth of Odysseus's palace performs both a literal and a metaphorical role in the second half of the poem. Odysseus is soon reunited with his son, Telemachus, and the two hatch a plan to allow the Ithacan king to return to his palace. Mindful of the fate of Agamemnon – who returned home to his wife only to find she was armed with a new boyfriend and a sharp blade – Odysseus decides to be cautious. Still disguised as an old beggar, he and Telemachus return home separately. The suitors who have invaded his palace (all hoping to woo Penelope on the understanding that Odysseus is dead) are showering her with presents, each believing that the value of his gift will improve his chances with the hesitant queen. The suitors set up *lamptēras treis* – three portable stoves to fill the hall with light.[6] These braziers were tall and slender with three feet at the base and a small basin at the top to hold the flames. The fuel was made from splinters of pine wood.

While the suitors are prepared to set up these lamps, they don't concern themselves with the business of lighting them. That task is performed by *dmōiai* – slave women – belonging to Odysseus. And Odysseus himself is watching and – even though he is in disguise as an impoverished old man seeking food and charity – he cannot resist telling the women what to do. Go and look after the queen, he says, I can ensure there's *phaos* – light – for all these men. The slave women laugh at him and suggest he should be afraid to be in these grand halls among the suitors, one of whom will surely beat him up. Odysseus-the-beggar threatens to tell Telemachus what they have said, and they scurry away. He stands beside the lamps to keep them burning. One of the suitors mocks him because the *selas* – flame – is gleaming off his bald head.[7]

Archaeological evidence from Bronze Age Greece suggests that plenty of houses would have had these portable stoves or braziers as their primary source of light and heat. Not every building has revealed a permanent, immobile hearth. But the palace of Odysseus does have a proper hearth: Odysseus swore by it a few books ago. And the language has shifted each time these sources of light and heat are mentioned: lamps, light, flame. The king didn't hesitate to swear by the hearth, the centre of his home. But the pretenders to his throne are happy to use smaller, more mobile stoves to keep them warm. Odysseus likes his home to be unchanging and solid; even the bed he shares with Penelope is cut from a tree that grows through their bedroom. When Penelope tests his identity, this is how she tricks him, by asking her servants to move the bed. Odysseus is so distressed by the idea that his beloved immovable bed has in fact been moved that he reveals his true self straightaway.

Perhaps a more important part of this story for us, however, is the way that the shifting language of heat and light reflects shifting status. When Odysseus is in no danger and wants to swear an oath, he swears by the hearth – Hestia (or *Histiē*, to be completely accurate: Homeric Greek is a different dialect from Attic Greek, the literary language of Athens in the fifth century BCE). But the suitors – unwanted invaders in another man's home – don't claim the hearth or swear by it. They reflect their own impermanent role by using these temporary lamps that need constant resupplies of fuel to keep them burning. These men use lamps because – however much they may wish otherwise – they know the hearth isn't theirs and they don't really belong here.

There is another point to note about this sequence with the lamps: it is the slave women who are expected to fuel them and keep them alight. And when Odysseus offers to help, he is doing so while in character as a beggar. So the daily maintenance of heat and light in this Bronze Age palace is the territory of women in domestic servitude. They're only relieved of the chore by a man of even lower status. This reveals something extremely important about the role of the hearth, of fire and heat in the home. We all need it and want it, but the maintenance of it is dirty, menial work: gathering wood, chopping it, storing it, fetching it, lighting it, feeding it, cleaning up after it. The ineffable sacred flame cannot be separated from the ceaseless manual labour. It's a duality that we often see when someone describes something as 'women's work'. They never seem to mean 'work that can only be done by women because of the skills they possess'. They tend to mean something arduous and boring that they wouldn't choose to do, decorated with a patina of gender stereotypes.

It is a risk, of course, arguing anything from an absence of evidence. But I keep coming back to the same question: what if the reason Hestia is so often overlooked, even though she is a daughter of Kronos, a sister of Zeus and Hera and all the rest, is because she is associated with a part of the home that people of status benefit from, but never maintain? Everyone wants heat and light, cooked food and warm nights, but no one wants the boring, repetitive labour of collecting wood and cleaning ashes and soot. The hearth is both the sacred centre of Odysseus's home and the preserve of women and slaves. Odysseus swears grandly by the hearth when he's in Eumaeus's hut, but would he be tending braziers if he weren't a beggar? I doubt it.

Fire is always an amoral force: life-saving on a cold winter night, life-threatening on a hot summer day. And it has the same dual nature in the *Odyssey*. Telemachus asks for his father's weapons to be moved out of the hall before Odysseus reveals his true identity and cuts down the impudent suitors en masse. Obviously neither man wants the suitors to be able to reach out and grab the nearest sword. But the reason Telemachus gives for wanting the weapons moved is that the smoke is making them dirty.[8] It's an unarguable point. Yet at the end of Book Twenty-two, when the suitors are all dead and their blood has been cleaned from the palace floors by the same slave women who tend the fires (or who used to do these chores, before Telemachus killed them), Odysseus asks for fire so he can purge the evils from his home.[9] Fire from the hearth is both cleansing and polluting, noble and filthy, the property of kings and the province of slaves.

As mentioned above, the hearth has multiple roles in ancient Greek societies, and in addition to offering heat and light, it can also serve as an altar. Sacrifices – of animals and incense – were burned, and so the sight of smoke rising held some religious weight. And while it might be tempting to conclude – from the absence of temples dedicated solely to Hestia, and the absence of narratives concerning her – that Hestia was a forgotten goddess, it would be a mistake. She was probably the recipient of more offerings than any other deity, because she was the recipient of the first part of every sacrifice. And she was considered present in every home and every temple, not merely in a metaphorical sense but in a literal one. The *Homeric Hymn to Hestia* isn't a huge narrative affair like the one to Demeter, but it is very clear about her status. The homes of all the immortal gods (i.e., temples) and of all mortals allot you an everlasting seat, it begins, and *presbēida timēn* – the highest honour.[10] Without you, there are no feasts for mortals. The first and last offerings of honey-sweet wine are made to you.

So perhaps the reason Hestia doesn't have vast temples of her own is because she resides in all homes and temples and is present at all sacrifices to any and every other god. If you were planning to sacrifice to, say, Apollo to ask him to release you from the plague, you would first offer something to Hestia. When you had a cooked, social meal – from the grandest banquet to the most modest family gathering – you were doing so at Hestia's pleasure: no Hestia, no feast. Her apparent omnipresence and her status as the first and last (first born of Rhea, last freed from Kronos, and recipient of first and last sacrificial offerings) make her a goddess who must have been constantly referred to in daily life, even if not in grand mythological narratives. Hestia is, for example, traditionally omitted from lists of gods who fought the Titans or the giants in these two great battles where the gods come together to repel an existential threat. If you follow the scenes of the Gigantomachy on the extraordinary Pergamon Altar, now found in Berlin, you will see major and minor goddesses and gods fighting giants in every possible way. Artemis, Hera, Athene, and Demeter are there, but so are Leto, Selene, and Themis. Nyx – Night – is my favourite, for no better reason than that she is fighting a giant by lobbing a jar full of snakes at him.[11] But there is no sign of Hestia. She is a goddess of the house – everyone's house – so is rarely seen, or claimed, in other external settings.

But if we want to see her in her own home, we may be able to do so by examining the east pediment of the Parthenon, which we looked at in the previous chapter, showing the Olympian gods greeting the arrival of Athene. As with the figures identified as Demeter and Persephone, we cannot be certain who we can see. The statue is only tentatively named as Hestia by the British Museum.[12] She lacks a head and arms, but she is wearing a beautifully draped tunic and mantle. She is seated with her left leg in front of her, foot pointing outward. But her right leg is fully tucked underneath her, as though she is about to get up, or pivot on it to turn sharply to her left. I can't tell you with any certainty whether this is Hestia or not – she is notoriously difficult to identify, as she has no clear symbol, like Athene and her helmet or Artemis and her bow – but I like to think this figure is her. It's one thing to be missing from the Pergamon Altar, but the Parthenon scene is set on Mount Olympus, and depicts an archetypal family moment: the welcoming of a new member of the clan, a new daughter of Zeus. There is little reason to include Hestia in a battle, but she is the epitome of home and family, and (ridiculous as it no doubt sounds) I think she would be there to greet her niece.

By the standards of gods in Greek myth, not least her own family, Hestia seems to have been remarkably placid and good-natured. There are no stories where she annihilates some hapless mortal because he has delivered some minor slight, no fallings-out with other deities. This makes her virtually unique in Greek myth and certainly implies some superhuman capacity to neither give nor take offence. She manages not to offend the goddess of love, even though she is described as one of the three goddesses Aphrodite couldn't persuade or cheat, in the fifth *Homeric Hymn*.[13] In other words, Hestia – like her nieces Athene and Artemis – has no interest in a sexual relationship. Athene prefers the art of war to the art of love, the *Hymn* explains, and we have already seen that Artemis prefers hunting in the wild untamed forest to domestic life with another. But Hestia doesn't want to be a warrior or a hunter. Still, *aidoiē* – this word means 'revered' but also 'shy' or 'bashful' – Hestia avoids Aphrodite's affairs (if your euphemism klaxon is not sounding now, it should be).[14] Perhaps you're thinking Hestia might not have had any suitors, but you'd be mistaken. Because the *Hymn* goes on to say that Poseidon and Apollo both tried to woo her, but she wasn't interested and said so firmly.

This is an extremely unlikely scene – a goddess who shuns Aphrodite and her values of sex and desire, yet Aphrodite doesn't punish her by having her become besotted with a mortal or a pig or similar. Aphrodite is hypersensitive when it comes to those who aren't keen to worship her, as poor Hippolytus discovers in Euripides's play of the same name. Similarly prone to petulant rages are Poseidon and Apollo. But here they are, both making a play for the same goddess. She turns them down flat – by speaking sternly to them, something which generally goes quite badly for women in a patriarchal society – and yet there appears to be no animus between them. Hestia has somehow managed to reject three thin-skinned egomaniacs and fall out with none of them.

The *Hymn* continues: Hestia swears a mighty oath by the head of Zeus himself that she will remain a *parthenos* – an unmarried woman. And Zeus gave her a glorious gift instead of marriage (I can't tell you how disappointed I am that this tradition hasn't survived to modern times). He grants her a seat in the middle of the house and the fattest chunk of any sacrifice. On top of that, she will take honour in all the gods' shrines and in all the offerings made by all mortals to the gods.

The centrality of Hestia could not be made more clear than it is here. She isn't shoved to one side, as we might expect to happen to an unmarried woman in a conservative society. She doesn't become a threat to married women, or an irrelevance to men and gods alike. She is seated right in the middle of things, just like the hearth in a home. Greek gods usually occupy an allegorical space – in addition to their many other roles – and that is no less true of Hestia. She is not just the goddess of the hearth, she also is the hearth, seated at the centre of a house. Her connection with the home is so profound that Diodorus Siculus, writing in the first century BCE, says that she is the goddess who learned how to build houses and – by extension – taught mortals to do the same.[15] It is, he concludes, because of this *euergesia* – kindness, good deed – that virtually all men have set up shrines to her in their homes.

And on top of her architectural know-how, Hestia is capable of something even more miraculous: she is able to live alongside male deities without any difficulties. Because when we return to the *Hymn to Hestia*, we find an invocation to the killer of Argus, son of Zeus and Maia – we know him better as Hermes.[16] He is further described as blessed or happy, carrier of the golden staff, giver of good things, and the invocation continues: come and bring good luck, alongside your dear, shy friend. Live in her lovely house as friends to one another. For you both know the deeds of earthly men, come and help us in our minds and our strength. Rejoice, daughter of Kronos, and Hermes of the golden staff.

If your euphemism klaxon is still sounding, you need to switch it off. Because we know that Hestia isn't interested in a sexual relationship, at least according to the composer of the *Homeric Hymn to Aphrodite*. She doesn't want marriage or sex. And yet, she is here described – in her own hymn – as having Hermes as her friend and housemate. As Sarah Ruden notes in her excellent translation of the *Homeric Hymns*, Hermes is the perfect complement for Hestia.[17] He is always travelling. He crosses boundaries between life and death (as we have seen, he can easily make a trip down to Hades and back), and he crosses the boundaries between mortal and immortal. A god who is always in motion is the opposite of Hestia, who is forever still at the centre of the house. And yet – as with so much in Hestia's slight but beautiful story – this meeting of opposites doesn't cause friction, like it does when Aphrodite clashes with Artemis, for example, over the fate of poor Hippolytus. Instead, we have the delightful image of a house-share sitcom, where opposites attract, but not in a sexual way. You feel they are only moments away from solving cosy crimes together, or doing a crossword. I have been racking my brains to think of another instance of male-female friendship like this anywhere in Greek myth. It's a real struggle to think of even one.

I wonder if this is the image that Playmobil had in mind when they created a toy Hestia (complete with fire bowl, sacred fire, golden jug, and a plinth on which the latter stands).[18] She's wearing a white tunic with a lovely gold spiral decoration – known as the wave pattern – below a Greek key design around the neck. She has a bright blue cloak that is draped over her dress and pulled up over her hair. Just a little of her dark fringe is visible beneath it. In Greek statuary, this veiling usually conveys that someone is conducting a sacrifice. Playmobil Hestia has the most encouraging smile, and looks to be the ideal flatmate, particularly if you like barbecues.

And this is only echoing the image of Hestia we see on a kylix – a wide, shallow drinking cup – now in the National Archaeological Museum of Tarquinia.[19] This shows Hestia seated at a gathering of the gods, facing her brother Zeus, to whom Ganymede is offering wine from a jug. Hestia has a relaxed, benign expression: she holds a flower in her left hand and a small leafy branch in her right hand. The flowers or leaves of the branch are drooping in all directions. I'm not sure if any of the other gods present at this feast (which include Ares and Hermes) are thinking of making a pass at Hestia, but she certainly seems to be giving them an arboreal hint not to do so.

Not only does Hestia have an unusual ability to reject men without hurting their feelings and shun Aphrodite without causing offence, she also manages not to take offence where another deity might. So, for example, let's examine the case of Erysichthon, whose story is told by the poet Callimachus in his *Hymn to Demeter*.[20] Erysichthon antagonizes Demeter by running fully armed – with twenty axe-wielding attendants – into her sacred grove. The men chop down Demeter's favourite tree, which grieves her. The goddess sends a message to Erysichthon telling him specifically not to damage her sacred trees, as the last thing he wants is for her to be angry with him. He tells the goddess to do her worst: try anything and he'll attack her next. He's determined to have the wood from her trees, and he will use it to build a house for himself, where he will throw banquets for all his friends.

Provoked beyond her limits, Demeter tells him to go right ahead and enjoy the many banquets he'll be having. And then she gives him a terrible, gnawing, insatiable hunger. No amount of feasting could reduce his desperate need to eat more and more. Because Dionysus takes Demeter's side, Erysichthon also finds himself unable to slake his thirst for wine. He eats huge banquets prepared by twenty men, but still he hungers. His parents shut him away because they are so embarrassed by his desperate appetite. They refuse to allow him to eat in public; they lie about his whereabouts: he's away, he's been hit on the head, he fell from a chariot, he's been gored by a boar. Anything but admit the truth that Erysichthon has been cursed by a goddess and is eating everything in sight. And yet – Callimachus uses a haunting image – no matter how much he consumes, he grows thinner and thinner, like a wax doll melting in the sun.

The young man's father, Triopas, prays to Poseidon, asking him to either remove Demeter's curse or feed the starving young man himself, since Triopas has no more to give. His livestock have all been consumed. Poseidon ignores these pleas, and Erysichthon keeps on eating: the mules that are used to transport heavy loads, and then the cow that his mother is fattening up for Hestia.[21] Then he eats the racehorses, a warhorse, and an *ailouros* – the animal they keep for catching vermin. This word was usually translated as 'cat' when I was a student, but some archaeozoologists now think domestic cats were quite late arrivals in Greece, so an *ailouros* might actually be a weasel or a pine marten. Whatever it is, Erysichthon eats it.

There is no happy ending for this young man: he eats his way through the family store cupboards and then he sits at a place where three roads meet, begging for scraps and digging through refuse in the hope of finding more. And there, the hymn leaves him. Callimachus prays to Demeter, promising he'll never befriend anyone who has angered her. Not least, one presumes, because they might see him as a source of food. Ugly as this story is, it adds another dimension to the wrath of Demeter, which we previously saw in her decision to cause a famine to force Zeus to return Persephone. She will afflict a whole world with hunger, or just a single obnoxious man.

And in his hopeless attempts to stave off hunger, Erysichthon eats a cow that belongs to Hestia, or at least is being fattened up for her. And yet Hestia takes no revenge on him: she doesn't deprive him of fire to cook his endless food; she doesn't set him on fire. Perhaps you might think that's fair enough, since it's beyond his control. But that's not an argument that works very well for Oedipus, who ends up blinded and ruined even though he committed his crimes (patricide, incest) in complete ignorance. Perhaps we might think that Demeter has the whole divine wrath thing covered, but that didn't stop Dionysus from chipping in and adding wine to the list of things Erysichthon desperately craves. Hestia might even have been angry with Demeter for putting her delicious future feast of a burned cow into his ravening maw.

But she doesn't bear a grudge, as we can see if we look at the Sophilos Dinos – an extraordinary black-figure wine bowl held by the British Museum.[22] It was made around 580 or 570 BCE, in Attica, and the wine bowl is about 40 centimetres across, and 30 centimetres high. The painter has signed it: *Sophilos painted me.* The bowl has been decorated in registers. The lower friezes show animals, both real and imaginary, from lions to sphinxes. The upper frieze shows a procession of the gods arriving at the house of Peleus for his wedding to the sea nymph Thetis. They have their names inscribed beside them, so we know it's the messenger goddess Iris who leads the way in her winged boots. Behind her walk two pairs of goddesses who all seem to be wearing highly decorated tunics for the wedding. The dress of Hebe – who is a few paces behind them – is more visible because the vase is undamaged there, and she isn't wearing a cloak to cover any of it. Nor would I: it's a beautiful white peplos – a shift dress – covered in repeating patterns of animals, much like the lower portions of the vase. Deer, lions, and sphinxes all march around her body.

But move your attention back to those goddesses directly behind Iris: like all the gods on the vase, they are stylized, with pointed noses and strange, elongated fingers. The second pair are named as Leto and Chariklo. The two in front of them are also labelled. This is Hestia, and Demeter, leading the procession. You'll perhaps be expecting the inevitable: the vase is damaged, missing a piece right over their lower bodies, legs, and feet. There's a smaller gap where Hestia's neck and left arm would be. But her right arm is intact: she has strong shoulders and her arm is bent at the elbow, as though she's walking along at a comfortable pace. Both of Hestia's hands survive: her left hand is raised as though she's in the middle of an anecdote. Demeter has had the worst of the damage: we can just see the profile of her face and cloak as she advances towards the house of Peleus. But Hestia is right beside her, both of them apparently enjoying themselves, as the corners of their mouths turn up slightly. Their names are painted beside their heads: Demeter's is damaged, but both are still legible. So Hestia isn't angry here with her sister about the pilfered cow. They're side by side, having a great day out at a family wedding.

There is one story about Hestia which shows that days out with other gods aren't all fun and games, even if you are as patient as she is. It's told by Ovid in the *Fasti*, a poem in twelve books (though only six survive) about sacred days in the Roman calendar. Each book covers a month, and Ovid uses the changing days of the year as a peg for stories from Greek and Roman myth. As is always the way with Ovid, his capacity for irony is so subtle and comprehensive that it is difficult to know how sincere or cheeky he is being at any given moment. Certainly it is very like him to choose a mischievous story about a goddess who was held in very high esteem by the Roman emperor Augustus. We don't know if books seven to twelve were written and lost, or if they were never written because Ovid was only halfway through the project when he found himself exiled to Tomis on the Black Sea. The explanation he gives for this banishment in the *Tristia* (poetic epistles with a melancholy tone, hence their name – sorrows, sadnesses) is *carmen et error* – a poem and a mistake.[23] Classicists have been occupied with discussions of what either of these might have been for a very long time. The poem is probably Ovid's smutty guide to urban adultery, the *Ars Amatoria* – *Art of Love* – in which he tells his readers how to flirt with smart young city women, and how to take things quite a bit further than that. This jokey guide was at odds with the ostensible morality reforms which Augustus had ushered in after becoming emperor. Like so many reformers who concern themselves with other people's morals, Augustus's own personal life was a triumphant display of immorality, by the standards of any time. He had notoriously divorced his wife Scribonia in order to marry Livia, who was also – at the time they met – married, to a man named Tiberius Claudius Nero. In spite of the fact that both women were pregnant at the time, Augustus ditched Scribonia and forced Nero to divorce Livia.

And as for Ovid's error, we may never know. If it was political and he'd made any kind of threat against Augustus, he would surely have been executed rather than exiled. Augustus also banished his own daughter, Julia (and later, her daughter, also called Julia), so the temptation is to conclude that Ovid may have taken his interest in urban adultery all the way to the top. Just to add to your confusion, some scholars don't accept that Ovid was banished at all, but argue that the whole thing was merely a literary conceit. The problem with analysing writing full of irony and misdirection is that you can never really be sure if you've got the joke or missed the point.

We'll examine why Augustus might have been particularly delighted or irked by Ovid choosing to tell this story about Vesta – the Roman name for Hestia – in a moment. But first, I should probably tell you why Vesta is such a fan of donkeys. The gods are all invited to a banquet by the goddess Cybele, who hails from Anatolia – modern-day Turkey. Cybele was regarded by the Greeks as being roughly the same as Rhea, and then in turn by the Romans, who also called her Magna Mater: the Great Mother. Cybele invites all the gods, including the nymphs and the satyrs. Among other attendees is Priapus, a minor fertility god with an enormous erection. Ovid can't tell us much about the gods' banquet. It's not allowed, he says. They spent the whole night drinking.[24] This is another reason I love Ovid: bored by poets bleating on about divine banquets? Just tell the audience that you're not allowed to say much, but everyone drank a lot, and move on. Most of the gods can be found the next day lounging in verdant idylls. Among the deities sleeping off the night before is Vesta, who is lying on the grass, having a peaceful rest without a care in the world. Priapus catches sight of her. It's uncertain, Ovid says, whether he knew it was Vesta or thought she was a nymph; Priapus himself says he didn't know it was her. Look at any picture of Priapus from antiquity, and you will see why he might have had trouble focusing on anything beyond his own anatomy. One fresco in Pompeii shows him fully occupied with the task of weighing his gigantic erection on scales.[25]

He raises his filthy hopes, Ovid continues, and tries to sneak up on her, heart racing, on tiptoe (I find myself wondering how he doesn't tip up, which says a great deal about why I haven't pursued a career in academia). By chance, old Silenus (a satyr) has left a donkey close by which he found near a river. Just as Priapus is about to make his move, the donkey gives an unexpected bray. The goddess leaps up, terrified by the noise. A whole crowd comes together around her, and Priapus flees through hostile hands. Vesta is saved from violation by a guard-donkey.

Ovid likes this story so much, he tells it twice – once with Vesta being rescued by the appalled donkey, and once when the victim of Priapus's attentions is a nymph named Lotis.[26] But other sources – both literary and artistic – agree that Vesta is the goddess saved by Eeyore.

The love poet Propertius, a contemporary of Ovid, makes a passing reference to Vesta rejoicing in garlanded donkeys.[27] And Lactantius, an early Christian writer, composed his *Divine Institutes* at the beginning of the fourth century. In one chapter he bemoans the terrible practice of worshipping non-Christian gods and the bizarre means by which this worship was conducted (in fairness, some Roman writers, like Tacitus, described Christians as depraved criminals, so no one comes out of these exchanges tremendously well).[28] Lactantius has particular scorn for the way the Romans put garlands or crowns on a donkey at the Vestalia (a festival in honour of Vesta), precisely because it preserved her chastity with its timely braying. What could be worse, he asks, than if Vesta really did owe her chastity to a donkey? But he thinks poets invented these dreadful stories in order to conceal even worse ones.[29] It must be the only time Ovid has ever been accused of underselling deviant sexual behaviour.

However much Lactantius disapproved of this story, the connection between Vesta and donkeys does seem to have been a firmly affectionate one, and it's one that we can also see depicted on frescoes. If Hestia is often overlooked in the great narratives of Greek myth because she's almost taken for granted as sitting quietly at home, then Vesta is rather more visible. Not least in Pompeii, where numerous shrines to Vesta have been discovered in bakeries. Just when you thought you couldn't like her more, this versatile goddess turns out to be the patron saint of carbs.

There are a couple of wonderful frescoes of Vesta in Pompeii, which show her with her favourite animal. One niche lararium – a small shrine set into a wall to worship Lares, household gods – depicts Vesta beside a donkey or ass that has cartoonishly long ears (I find myself idly wondering if it could have been the same Pompeian artist who painted Priapus, as mentioned above. Perhaps he just had a weakness for gigantic appendages).[30] And there is a second example which shows Vesta seated on a grand throne and holding a cornucopia in her left hand. In her right hand is a patera, a bowl for libations. Wandering casually past in the background is another example of her beloved donkey, head down, apparently in pursuit of food.[31]

While Hestia might not have the most flamboyant mythus surrounding her, the Romans took her to their hearts and hearths: worship of Vesta dates back as far as the fourth or even sixth century BCE. Her altar was discovered at Lavinium, almost twenty miles south of Rome, and one of those places which occupies a double existence, in both myth and history. According to Roman myth, Lavinium was the city founded by Aeneas, one of the few men to escape Troy. The *Aeneid*, Virgil's epic poem, follows the storm-tossed journey of Aeneas (son of Anchises and Venus, as you doubtless remember from her chapter) as he searches for a new land where he and his fellow refugees can begin the next part of their lives. Eventually – and in accordance with Jupiter's plan – they arrive in Italy. Aeneas establishes the city of Lavinium, which is the mythical beginning of the Roman foundation story. The Romans didn't just syncretize their gods with the Greeks; they did the same with their myths, connecting their history back to the time of the *Iliad*. Some five hundred years after Aeneas founds Lavinium, a pair of brothers will find themselves suckled by a wolf not too far away, and Rome's other great foundation myth – of Romulus and Remus – will allow the great city to begin its story.

So Lavinium is both an early historic settlement near Rome and a mythical setting for the life and eventual death of Aeneas: a *heroön* – hero shrine – built over a tomb there was believed by some in antiquity to house the remains of Aeneas, though the first-century BCE historian Dionysius of Halicarnassus pointed out that if multiple tombs were said to be connected to the hero, they couldn't all contain him.[32] He gives a detailed account of Aeneas's arrival in Latium (modern Lazio), which includes a moment where Aeneas's ancestral gods appear to him in a dream and tell him to use persuasion rather than fighting to achieve his goal.[33]

Gods appearing to mortals in dreams is not an unusual phenomenon; characters in epic poems often receive advice from apparitions of one sort or another. Aeneas – who notoriously remembers to take his son, his father, and the shrines of his household gods with him as he flees the burning city of Troy, but somehow manages to lose track of his wife, Creusa – receives a divine visit from his mother Venus, encouraging words from the ghost of Hector, and permission to leave without going back to find the missing Creusa from her ghost, and that's just in Book Two of the twelve-book *Aeneid*.

The Romans were enormously keen on household gods – Lares and Penates – which were guardian spirits for individual homes. There were also public Lares to protect a civic area. Vesta is considered one of the Penates because she is present at the hearth of every home. And Vesta was also a public goddess, just as Hestia had been before her, so Rome had a hearth sacred to Vesta, just as individual houses did. But the public or civic hearth was on a much grander scale, and was tended by priestesses.

These priestesses were known as Vestal Virgins. The first of these, according to the first-century BCE Roman historian Livy, was a young woman named Rhea Silvia, whose regal father was murdered by her usurping uncle Amulius. We are back in mythic-historical time, before the foundation of Rome in 753 BCE, and Amulius was trying to ensure his niece wouldn't have any children who might overthrow him.[34] Rhea Silvia accepted her fate as a perpetual virgin, but then miraculously conceived twin boys. She sensibly claimed to have been raped by the god Mars rather than admit to a sexual liaison with a mortal man, as this would have provoked her uncle to kill her, as he had already killed her father. Maybe she really believed it, says Livy, sceptically. These twins will of course grow up to be Romulus and Remus.

So Vesta is intimately connected with Rome from its very inception. According to the Aeneas myth (which we would place around the twelfth century BCE, after the fall of Troy), his Penates accompany him to Italy to found the new city, and Vesta will be included among the Penates when Rome is founded. Fast-forward through Livy's version of history – a flurry of kings and backstabbings – and we find the second great Roman foundation myth rests on Romulus, the son of one of Vesta's priestesses. Mars may be the grandfather of Rome – and who could doubt that when Rome was such a proud martial power? – but Vesta, the quiet deity of the hearth, is its godmother.

Vestal Virgins – often known simply as Vestals, while the Greeks called them Hestiades – held huge symbolic value throughout Rome's history; assault on a Vestal was tantamount to an assault on Rome itself. These women were chosen when they were still children – perhaps between the ages of six and ten – to serve the goddess for at least thirty years. Their duties centred around the maintenance of the sacred flame of Vesta, which they were obliged to tend day and night. The punishment for letting this fire go out was physical and painful: a beating. And the punishment for losing their virginity – at least, if caught – was live burial. One of the many scandalous stories to attach itself to Julius Caesar was that a man named Publius Clodius Pulcher had infiltrated a women-only festival by disguising himself as a woman, in order to conduct a sexual liaison with either Caesar's wife, Pompeia, or one of the Vestals. When the story came out, Caesar divorced Pompeia, because, says Roman biographer Suetonius, Caesar declared that his family should be free even of the suspicion of guilt.[35] But at least Pomponia only ended up divorced, and not buried alive.

The life of a Vestal may seem restrictive and miserable to us, but they were treated with enormous respect, and it was in some ways preferable to the lives of other high-status Roman girls, who would be married off aged fifteen or so, often to a man who was a great deal older. Vestals had a role in public life when women were largely

excluded from this realm (unless they were highly ambitious and related to an emperor, anyway). Augustus granted rights to Vestals that
he otherwise extended only to mothers of three children, who were
given special honours for their commitment to the Roman populace.
Cicero even implies that the priestesses were allotted good seats at the
games.[36] And according to Pliny the Elder, Vestals also had miraculous
powers: he tells a story of Tuccia, from the third century BCE, who
managed to carry water in a sieve.[37] Other Vestals could, he claims, stop
runaway slaves in their tracks. Given the many bizarre and anachro-
nistic treatments Rome has received onscreen, it slightly surprises me
that the telekinetic Vestal Virgin bounty hunter TV series has yet to
be made.

These stories are fantastical to modern ears: tales of miracles and
virgin births often meet with scepticism, even in our ancient sources.
But if we want evidence of the Vestals' real influence rather than their
supernatural abilities, we need only look to the man who could always
spot power: the emperor Augustus. Carved on the great Ara Pacis –
Altar of Peace, which you can still visit in Rome today – are six Vestals taking part in a religious procession.[38] This sculptural monument
is just one way in which Augustus made a great public performance
of his power and generosity to the Roman people. Finally, peace had
come to Rome, ushered in by Augustus. Look at this magnificent altar
for long enough and you might even forget that Augustus had also
ushered in quite a lot of war to Rome before eliminating his rivals and
becoming emperor.

Augustus held multiple religious offices, along with political offices, that combined to enable him to become the most powerful man
of his time. Roman religion was fundamentally civic rather than personal, and being Pontifex Maximus – chief priest – was a political role
at least as much as a religious one. Once the Roman Republic had been
overturned in favour of an imperial system, the emperor held the role

of chief priest automatically. A pontifex is literally a bridge-maker, creating a link between mortal and immortal worlds. If you take on a position of supreme ruler, it makes a lot of sense to convey to people that the gods are on your side. And being Rome's chief priest was a shorthand for that. Augustus obviously couldn't serve as a priestess too (certainly not one claiming to be a virgin). But he did the next best thing when he introduced the civic cult of Vesta into his own home, on the Palatine Hill. What better way of showing you have Vesta on your side – and that you are therefore Rome's protecting ruler – than by turning your domestic hearth into the state hearth? For the Romans (and the Greeks before them), a temple is a literal home to a god, as well as a metaphorical one. And it would be a brave man who tried to assassinate or overthrow an emperor who lived alongside one of Rome's foundational goddesses. Even his eventual death didn't break him of the habit. Augustus was deified by his successor – having shared his home with a goddess during life, after death, he moved in with her whole family.

Worship of Vesta continued until 394 CE, when her sacred flame was finally extinguished. Christianity was now the official religion of the Roman empire, and a goddess who was practically invisible, virtually omnipresent, and whose acolytes had performed miracles including giving birth to the sons of a god must have seemed too pagan and old-fashioned for the new monotheism. The ruins of the temple of Vesta still stand in the Roman Forum today, although the building was destroyed and remade many times. Perhaps predictably, it burned down more than once.

Vesta retains a resonance of heat and light, even today (her name became a synonym for 'match' in the nineteenth century. If you're looking for an example, Sherlock Holmes uncovers a wax vesta from the mud in 'The Adventure of Silver Blaze'). But let's end where we began, back in Greece with the quiet figure of Hestia. In Plato's Laws, he describes the process of founding an ideal city. A lawgiver would start by finding a place near the centre of the country, somewhere which has the conveniences a city would need (like a water supply, fertile land etc.). Then he can start dividing up the land into shares for the citizens. But before he does that, he must set aside a sacred spot for Hestia, Zeus, and Athene.[39] Even for Plato, a citizen of the patriarchy of Athens, Hestia is mentioned before Zeus and before the patron goddess of his own city. And this is perhaps a nod to a proverb of Plato's time: *aph' Hestias arkhesthai* – to start from Hestia – means to start something from the beginning.[40] Because Hestia was always honoured first in sacrifices, everything starts with her.

And Plato doesn't just start with Hestia, he comes back to her more than once. In a dialogue called *Cratylus*, Plato's version of Socrates offers his companions a range of philosophical etymologies to explain why the gods have the names they do. Socrates – in every version of him that survives to us, from Aristophanes to Xenophon – is obsessed with definitions and subtextual meanings. It's no more evident than here, when he appropriately enough starts with Hestia. So why did men name her that? he asks. Well, the essence of something is called *ousia* or *essia* or *osia* (depending on dialect: these variations all mean 'being' or 'essence' in Greek). So it's completely reasonable, he says, that the essence of things should be called Hestia.[41]

At the beginning of this chapter, it seemed as though it would only be possible to define Hestia through a series of absences. The stories we don't have, the statues we don't see, the wrath she doesn't display, the battles she doesn't join. But – even if Socrates is a little tongue in cheek with these definitions – he does offer a different way to respond to Hestia, and it's one that rings true, for me at least. This is a goddess who doesn't often do, but always is. She is the heart of your home and mine, the heart of our cities and temples alike. She is our warm homecoming, our baked bread, our light in the dark.

ATHENE

A COLLECTOR would need deep pockets to own both the figurines that depict the two different facets of the character of Athene. The first is in her guise as goddess of wisdom. She wears a golden tunic and a diaphanous white cloak; a repeating pattern of gold palmettes decorates its border. A second garment of white gauze is wrapped around her body, pinned over the heart with an ornate brooch. Her head is crowned with a victorious laurel wreath; her earrings are palmettes again, picking up the pattern on her cloak. She wears a simple bangle on her left wrist and a glinting gauntlet on the right one. Perched on this is the compact body of a wide-eyed golden owl. Her hair hangs in very long plaits. Perhaps – in her wisdom – she has read about Rapunzel and this has influenced her own hairstyle.

The second figurine shows her in her role as a warrior goddess. This one wears an oxidized metal helmet, its horsehair plume resting atop her own chunky ponytail. Segmented armour plates her left arm and both of her legs. She holds a huge spear in her right hand and a round shield in her left. It bears her name in Greek letters – AΘHNA – and is decorated with the head of Medusa, all intense gaze and lion's-mane hair. Her aegis – or breastplate – has shrunk, but is attached to a large plate that covers the collarbone. In an audacious choice for a woman on the battlefield, her armoured boots have high heels. Looking at it, I can't help but think that if Cher were to play Athene, this is exactly the costume she would choose. If you wanted to buy both of these limited-edition Barbie dolls, you would get very little change from a thousand dollars. Honestly, though, I think you should save your money for Medusa Barbie, who presents as a goth mermaid snake-charmer, an all-too-rare overlap of these three usually discrete qualities.

Athene has always enjoyed an eye-catching sculpture. Her temple, the Parthenon, has rendered the skyline of the Greek capital instantly recognizable for two and a half millennia. It once contained a gigantic statue of the goddess, long lost now, but still visible when Pausanias was visiting Athens in the second century CE. Going into the temple they call the Parthenon, he reports, it's all about Athene.[1] Above the entrance (i.e., carved on the pediment of the temple) is the story of Athene's birth; at the back is her quarrel with Poseidon for this land (Attica, the area that includes Athens). The statue is decorated with ivory and gold. She has a sphinx in the middle of her helmet and griffins on either side. Pausanias goes on a brief tangent about griffins – their monstrous form and appetite for gold – before cutting himself short: I've said enough about griffins now.

He turns his attention back to the statue of the goddess. She's standing upright, and her chiton (tunic) comes down to her feet. On her breast is an ivory head of Medusa. In one hand she holds a Nike – Victory – about four forearms high (this is usually translated as 'cubits', but I find arms easier to visualize). In the other hand she has a spear. Lying beside her feet is a shield, and beside that is a snake. At the base of the statue is a relief of the birth of Pandora. According to Hesiod and others, Pausanias reminds his readers, she was the first woman.

Extrapolating from the height of Nike in this description, we can guess that the statue of Athene was well over eleven metres tall. And although the statue Pausanias is looking at is lost, we can see a small stone copy – about one metre tall – in the National Archaeological Museum in Athens.[2] This is a later, Roman statue made of marble, and it shows Athene much as Pausanias describes her: standing upright, her mighty helmet topped with a sphinx and two winged horses, rather than griffins (but enough about the griffins). The head of Medusa is placed in the centre of the aegis, which is decorated with small curling snakes. Her peplos drapes down to the floor, but it's caught at the waist with a double-snake-headed belt. She rests her left hand on her shield, beside which a large snake has coiled its sinuous body. The small Nike figure stands on her right hand, which – unlike the version Pausanias could see – is resting on a column. This is to support a figure made of a more inflexible material than the wood that would have formed the core of the Pheidias sculpture. She has a second support joining the shield to her left thigh. Traces of paint can still be seen on the marble so, – while it would have been undeniably less impressive than a statue eleven times its height and covered in gold leaf – it was once eye-catchingly bright.

Her giant counterpart was one of three Athenes created by Pheidias – the great fifth century BCE sculptor – that stood on the Acropolis. Pausanias tells us about the other two as well. The Lemnian Athene (dedicated to her by Athenians living on Lemnos) is considered by him to be the most worthy of Pheidias's works.[3] Annoyingly, we have no certain replica of this bronze statue, which was highly praised in antiquity.[4] But it would certainly have been dwarfed by the gigantic Athene Promachos – Athene at the front of the battle. This bronze statue was dedicated to celebrate Athenian victory over the Persians in the fifth century. Pausanias tells us the statue was so large that the tip of her spear and the top of her helmet were visible from the sea at Sounion, some forty miles to the south. Athens has always belonged to Athene.

Or almost always. Let's go back to the pediment sculptures that Pausanias mentioned as he walked us around the Parthenon. The first showed the birth of Athene, which is unusual even by the standards of Greek myth. Although there are some minor counter-traditions (according to Pausanias, the Libyans believe she is the daughter of Poseidon),[5] Athene is almost invariably the daughter of Zeus. And to hear Athene tell it, the daughter of Zeus alone: I don't have a mother, she says in Aeschylus's play *Eumenides* (which we'll discuss in more detail in the next chapter).[6] And the reason she can make this bald statement is because she was born from the head of Zeus. A goddess of wisdom could scarcely come from a more appropriate place than the head of the mighty king of the gods himself. But if you sense a misogynistic undertow there – in co-opting reproduction from the female sphere – you'd be right. Athene may be perfectly happy to have no mother, but no one thinks to ask what her mother, Metis, might feel about this dismissal of her role. Nor could they ask her even if they chose to. As Hesiod tells us in the *Theogony*, Zeus impregnates Metis, whose name means 'intelligence', 'wisdom', or 'skill'. So Athene's mother may also contribute something to her status as goddess of wisdom. In spite of her cleverness, Hesiod explains, Zeus manages to deceive Metis completely. He grabs her with his hands and swallows her, lest she give birth to one who proves stronger than his thunderbolt.

Well, well, well. The belief that you should consume your young on the off chance they're more powerful than you is obviously one that runs in the family – you'll recall that Zeus's father ate all his children from the same abiding fear. This is probably a question for a psychotherapist rather than a classicist, but there is something fascinating about the way the Greeks thought about intergenerational rivalry, at least among their deities. Now, I think, we would find the idea of our children surpassing us to be the opposite of threatening: the sign of successful parenthood is surely to raise offspring who are wiser, happier, healthier than the previous generation. On the rare occasions that we see a parent in direct competition with their child (usually over an informal sporting encounter in a public park, in my experience), we tend to feel an abiding sense of pity. Both for the parent, who apparently needs to boost their ego at the expense of a smaller and less coordinated child, and for their hapless offspring, who has an egomaniacal monster for a parent. But for the Greeks, the sight of, say, a grown man screaming at a toddler for not kicking a ball properly could have been strange for a completely different reason: you might want your child to be inferior to you, so demanding greater skill from them would seem wholly perverse.

Certainly Zeus is part of a peculiar family pattern, where son overpowers father and then lives in fear of the same thing happening to him.

From that perspective, Zeus's consumption of Athene – even while she is still inside the womb of Metis – makes perfect, if horrible, sense. It also allows us to look at Athene rather differently. If she had been born and raised by her mother, what might she have become? More powerful than the most powerful of the Olympian gods, perhaps? It's something Zeus fears so much that he swallows Metis whole to try to avert it, and he succeeds: the Athene born without a mother is indeed less powerful than he is. So although there is a certain quirkiness to the story of Athene's birth as it's usually told – springing fully formed from Zeus's head – it hides a deep-seated patriarchal anxiety that a child from the next generation might overthrow her mighty father.

Hesiod uses the language of giving birth to explain that having swallowed Metis, Zeus then produces Athene from his own body.[7] If we want to sustain the language of a more traditional birth scenario, then Hephaestus – who frees Athene from her father's head with a mighty blow from his axe – is the midwife. Athene is indeed cleverer and mightier than the other gods, but not so much so that her father has anything to fear from her. In fact, their relationship in, for example, the *Odyssey* is a close one, which we'll examine in more detail below. Zeus is usually able to rely on Athene to do his bidding, and she often goes to him to help her get what she wants, even at the expense of other gods.

Pausanias mentioned two sculpted pediments on the Parthenon: the first showed the birth of Athene, and the second her fight with Poseidon over the land of Attica. This second story is mentioned several times by Pausanias as he examines the Acropolis, and it's told by other sources too.[8] Poseidon and Athene both want to claim the land of Attica as their own. Neither is willing to yield in the face of the other's claim, and so they compete to win the votes of the other Olympian gods (appointed by Zeus to be their judges) or of Zeus himself. Poseidon's bid is represented by a sea wave in the sculpture Pausanias describes. The longer version of this story – as it appears in Pseudo-Apollodorus – has

Poseidon slamming his trident into the ground and creating a new sea. Athene's contribution is an olive tree. Less grand than an ocean, you may be thinking. But Athene is the first to plant an olive tree, and she has a witness to prove it. And just as olives are so intimately linked to Greece now, so they were in the ancient world. Equally, the Greeks were hardly short of seas, living (as Plato once puts it) like frogs around a pond.[9]

Whether the Olympians vote according to Zeus's wishes or whether he simply declares victory himself, Attica is awarded to Athene. Scholars have debated (and still debate) whether the city gave its name to the goddess or whether she gave her name to the city, but it is more likely to be the latter. Poseidon is so put out that he floods part of Attica in a fit of pique. So how appropriate it is that the Acropolis has so many depictions of Athene and of her protective role for the city – she must really cherish something she won against an older god. It also suggests another connection between goddess and city. Athene loves this city that worships her so fervently, and Pausanias is quick to remind us that the Athenians are much more enthusiastic in their attitude to the gods than other people.[10] And both city and goddess are intrinsically competitive: Athene loves to win and hates to lose. The Athenians meanwhile manage to spend decades at war with their neighbouring Sparta and are determined to see themselves (and ideally to be seen by other Greeks) as the preeminent military and cultural force of their time. A city doesn't need such spectacular architecture just to worship its presiding goddess; it builds a structure like the Parthenon to announce its supremacy to all who see it. Even if they're sailing past Sounion at the time.

There was a second temple to Athene on the Acropolis, incidentally, called the temple of Athene Polias – Athene of the city. This one has an olive tree which Pausanias has been told is the very one with which Athene won the contest.[11] Like all good divine gifts, it has proved itself miraculous in the past. When the Persians invaded Athens (in the early fifth century BCE), they set the city alight. The olive tree was burned down. And yet, it sprang immediately back to life, sprouting a huge new shoot on the very day it was incinerated. Invading armies cannot keep Athens from her olives, nor separate the city from their goddess's munificence.

The Parthenon is named after Athene in her role as a *parthenos* – a maiden, one who doesn't marry, a feature we've already noted she shares with Artemis and Hestia. It's fascinating that fully half of these six major goddesses have sworn off sex and marriage, given that they were worshipped during times when ordinary women had little choice about marriage, and almost no opportunity to reject it as a way of life. Perhaps the only thing we can read into this mismatch is that gods occupy a different plane from mortals and so would live unimaginable lives, and that being unmarried is as natural for a goddess (and unnatural for a mortal) as living atop Mount Olympus or being born from the foaming sea. But I can't help wondering if there is some sort of recognition for the idea that female gods – who held power and autonomy that female humans were not permitted to have – might well not want a male partner.

The three *parthenoi* are unattached to men in quite different ways too. Artemis lives an independent, almost feral existence away from cities and their societal norms, so her aversion to marriage is in keeping with the unbounded life she has chosen. Hestia – on the other hand – is right in the heart of city and society, yet she seems to prefer companionship to desire, a longer-term kind of domesticity. And Athene is different again. To return to the *Homeric Hymn to Aphrodite*, she is the daughter of Zeus who bears the aegis, *glaukōpis* Athene, who takes no pleasure in the works of Aphrodite. It's wars that delight her, the work of Ares: battles, fighting, and making gleaming works herself.[12]

Glaukōpis is the epithet applied over and over again to Athene in the *Odyssey*. Its literal meaning can be 'to have the eyes of an owl' – a *glaux* is the Little Owl, which is so closely associated with Athene that the ancient Greeks used the phrase 'bring owls to Athens' as English people once said 'take coals to Newcastle': to convey that there is such an abundance of this thing in this location that taking any more would be a futile act. Alternatively, it could come from the word *glaukos*, which is used to describe the sea, which can mean 'grey-blue' and, by extension (when applied to people), 'grey-eyed' or 'blue-eyed'. But 'bright-eyed' might be a better translation: the Greeks tended to categorize the visual world less by what shade it was than by how bright and sparkly it was. When Homer compares the sea to wine, we have struggled to translate it: 'wine-dark sea' is how it has often been rendered, but that entails us imposing our way of looking at colour onto the Greeks. For Homer, the sea isn't necessarily the same colour as wine; rather, it is like wine because of the way light plays on it as it moves, just as light glints off wine when we pour it into a cup. And gods' appearances often defy easy translation too. In the *Iliad*, Zeus accedes to a request by nodding.[13] We would probably say someone nodded their head, but Homer has Zeus nodding his eyebrows. Not only that, but his eyebrows are *kuaneos* – dark blue. We'd perhaps prefer 'blue-black' to avoid the slightly punk connotations of blue eyebrows, but *kuaneos* is the root of the lighter and brighter 'cyan'.

So to return to the *Hymn*, Athene has blue-grey-sealike eyes, or owl-like eyes, and the quality being described is bright and watchful, rather than a particular colour. And she takes no pleasure in the *erga* – works – of golden Aphrodite. Instead, she enjoys war, the *ergon* – work – of Ares. Let's consider Athene's battle prowess before we move on to the final quality the *Hymn* attributes to her: a love of making *aglaa erga* – shining or gleaming works – herself.

Athene is a much-beloved goddess, as we have seen from the sculptural and architectural evidence of her worship in Athens. This is not a quality that she shares with the god of war himself, Ares. The Greeks were fiercely aware of the cost of war: many of the men voting in the

Athenian Assembly in the fifth century BCE were those who had survived previous conflicts and were often voting to serve in future ones. War and its consequences permeated ancient societies: Aeschylus fought at the Battle of Salamis in 480 BCE (it would inform his play *The Persians*). Sophocles's family made their money from manufacturing shields and armour. Euripides was so admired by one of Athens's enemies, Syracuse, that some of the men who were enslaved in the aftermath of military defeat there won their freedom by knowing and quoting whole speeches from his plays. Plutarch tells us that when these grateful men returned to Athens, they rushed to thank the playwright for saving their lives.[14]

Every Athenian had experience of war, in other words: either because he had fought himself, or because he or she had lost a close relative in battle. So their devotion to Athene is not because she is – like Ares – associated with the madness and destruction of war. It is because she is associated with tactical cleverness and strategy in war. The Athenians were more than capable of making rash and ruinous decisions about conflicts, but they knew it wasn't Athene guiding them in those moments.

We can see her in action during a conflict if we examine her role in the *Iliad*. She is a constant supporter of the Greeks during the Trojan War, and she has an ally in the goddess Hera. We see them together in Book Four. A ceasefire was called in Book Three so that a duel could be fought between Paris – Helen's current Trojan squeeze – and Menelaus, her Greek husband. The plan was that whoever won would claim Helen once and for all and the war would be at an end. But the duel has proved inconclusive: Aphrodite intervened when it became clear that her beloved Paris would lose his life. She spirited him off the battlefield to keep him safe, but this has not decided the duel or the war.

At the beginning of Book Four, Zeus suggests that Menelaus has won and the war should be over. Do the gods really want hostilities to recommence? Perhaps they should call it a day and let Troy still stand. But Hera and Athene are sitting together, muttering and plotting terrible things for the Trojans.[15] Athene is so angry with Zeus that she doesn't even reply. She doesn't need to, however, because Hera is articulate enough for them both. She essentially evokes the sunk cost fallacy: I've put all this effort into a war and now you don't want it to finish? Fine, Hera says, but none of the other gods agree. What did Priam ever do to you, Zeus asks, that makes you so determined to destroy his city? Hera replies that Zeus can obliterate one of her favourite cities sometime, but he should listen to her now. They agree on a course of action: send Athene to trick the Trojans into breaking the truce and restarting hostilities. Athene has been dying to do this, and she races down from Mount Olympus.[16] By the time she arrives on the plain where battle has been paused, she is disguised as a Trojan man named Laodokos. She pulls up beside another warrior named Pandaros, and starts talking. Why don't you fire at Menelaus? she asks. The Trojans would all admire you if you killed him. Now's your chance.

Pandaros is no match for the wits of Athene, and he immediately does as she suggests. He prepares his arrow, takes aim, and fires. But Athene – who doesn't want Menelaus dead, of course – stands in front of the Spartan king and brushes the arrow away, like a mother swats a fly away from her sleeping child.[17] The arrow grazes him and blood flows, like when a woman stains ivory with red dye, according to Homer. Agamemnon is horrified when he sees his brother is injured. Menelaus assures him it's just a flesh wound, and the Greeks are soon stirred up to start fighting again. The Trojans are receiving divine encouragement from Ares, while *glaukōpis* Athene rouses the Greeks.[18] More goddesses – Terror, Fear, Strife – arrive in the midst of battle and add to the chaos. Men are soon killing one another with all the vigour Hera might have hoped for.

Not only is Athene the goddess you choose to go down and stir up battle when there is any risk of peace breaking out, she's also the one who can infuse a hero with strength and courage. Book Five begins with her doing just this to Diomedes, who now goes on a ferocious killing spree.[19] Once Athene sees the Greeks are thriving, she approaches Ares, takes his hand, and suggests they both leave the battlefield now, or Zeus will be furious with them for intervening too much. Ares – much less clever than Athene, it seems – withdraws alongside her, allowing the Greeks to continue their current success.

The hapless Pandaros now wounds Diomedes with an arrow, and the latter prays to Athene to help him with his revenge. She answers his prayer by filling him with superhuman strength and telling him to go berserk. The only thing he can't do is attack a god, unless it's Aphrodite. Her you can injure with your sharp bronze blade, Athene cheerily advises, before swooping off the battlefield once again. Homer doesn't mention the source of the animus she feels towards Aphrodite, but we might guess that losing the golden apple to the goddess of love must have hurt. Even by the standards of Greek gods, it is a remarkably ungenerous moment (albeit one that always makes me laugh). Diomedes kills Pandaros, injures Aeneas, the Trojan son of Aphrodite, then goes on to wound Aphrodite herself, and then Apollo. Finally, Athene joins him in his chariot as he tackles and injures Ares. The war god is so outraged by this that he heads straight to Olympus to complain to Zeus. Zeus has no sympathy, but Ares is soon repaired and bathed. The book ends with its focus on Hera and Athene, who return to Olympus, having stopped the man-killing Ares in his tracks.[20]

Athene now stands back from the battlefield for a while, as Zeus orders the gods to leave things alone. She does manage to offer a little encouragement to her favourites (Diomedes and Odysseus) but she doesn't intervene with the same vigour now that Zeus has ordered her to stand down. Her alliance with Hera was only temporary; the queen of the gods is soon getting help from Aphrodite and collaborating with Poseidon instead.

But when the Greeks really need Athene, she is there. So, Book Seventeen brings us the aftermath of Hector's killing of Patroclus. Menelaus is standing over his dead comrade to try to keep him from falling into Trojan hands. Hector has already stripped Patroclus's armour from his body, but they hope to seize him too so they can exchange him for the corpse of their own dead warrior, Sarpedon. This is a genuinely heroic moment for Menelaus, in a poem that doesn't have too many of those. But after a while – and with Apollo feeding energy to the Trojans surrounding him – he is starting to flag. Zeus once again sends his daughter to stir up the battle and encourage the Greeks.

Athene arrives this time disguised as Phoinix, one of the older, wiser Greeks. She tells Menelaus that he will be disgraced if the Trojans manage to seize Patroclus's body. Menelaus tells Phoinix – as he believes – that he would be fine if only Athene would give him extra strength. Thus he spoke, says Homer, and Athene rejoiced, because of all the gods he had prayed to her first of all. She fills him with strength and courage, just as she had done for Diomedes back in Book Five. Thanks to her help, and with permission from Zeus, the Greeks retain Patroclus and take him off the battlefield.

Book Twenty-one is astonishing in its violence, even within the *Iliad*. Achilles is slaughtering all who get in his way until he can kill Hector, the one who killed his beloved Patroclus. He chokes the river with corpses, and is nearly drowned when the river god punishes him. Achilles prays for help, and the gods are soon falling over one another to get involved. Hera sends her son Hephaestus to torch the plain. This forces the river god back within his banks. Apollo is soon refusing to fight Poseidon; Artemis mocks him for his inaction, and Hera punishes her. While all this is going on, Ares takes on Athene, calling her *kunamuia* – a dog-fly – and blaming her for the strife that has broken out among all these gods.[21] Still smarting about the way she encouraged Diomedes to attack him in Book Five, he decides to return the favour and stabs at her terrifying aegis (which not even Zeus could damage with his thunderbolt) with his spear. Athene is so angry that she picks up a gigantic stone and hurls it at Ares's neck. He collapses to the ground, and she laughs.[22] You child, she says, you still forget how much stronger I am than you. To add insult to injury, the word she uses here (which I have translated as 'stronger') is *areiōn*, derived from the name of the god himself. So a fully unpacked version of this sentence would be: *How much better at the things Ares does I am than you, Ares*. Aphrodite helps her injured lover off the battlefield, but this provokes Hera, who now sends Athene after her. Athene shoves Aphrodite hard in the chest and takes her off her feet too.

If we were looking to see why the Athenians or any other Greeks might want to pray to Athene and have her statue towering above their city, this poem shows us everything we need to know. Athene really is *promakhos* – she does stand in the front line of battle. She encourages the Greeks, she gives superpowers to her favourite heroes, she is passionately involved in every ebb and flow of the fighting. Apollo might be willing to stand aside and consider the whole human conflict to be beneath him, but Athene loves nothing more than a proper scrap. In addition to that, she fears no one, and nor should she. Who can take her on and injure her? Even the god of war himself comes off worse in an encounter with Athene: he can't hurt her, stop her, or even damage her breastplate. She has no problem humiliating him and his lover in quick succession.

By the time of the Trojan War, Athene has already honed her love of battle. The Olympian gods find themselves in two major wars in early Greek myth. The first is the battle with the Titans, who rebel against the rule of Zeus and hope to restore Kronos to the throne. But Zeus – with the support of Athene, Apollo, and Artemis – sends them straight to Tartarus. The rebel ringleader, Atlas, is punished by being made to hold the heavens on his shoulders for all eternity. Incidentally, it is from this story that we derive variations of the phrase 'carry the weight of the world on your shoulders'. But Atlas doesn't carry the weight of the world; he carries the weight of the heavens (which are still very heavy, if artistic representations of Atlas can be believed). I suppose this just goes to prove that alliteration is more compelling than accuracy.

The second great war is the Gigantomachy, the battle between the Olympian gods and the children of Gaia. Several locations are given for this conflict including Phlegra, according to Pseudo-Apollodorus, Strabo, and other writers.[23] Phlegra was both a real and mythic place in an area of what we would now call Greek Macedonia. But other writers believed it to be a location near Cumae, in southern Italy. Perhaps it doesn't matter too much where the actual fighting took place: the first-century BCE historian Diodorus Siculus considers it a war with multiple battlefields (Pallene in Macedonia, the Phlegraean plain near Cumae, and the island of Crete).[24]

The children of Gaia are usually called *giants* in English, although their defining feature is not always their size. In early sources, the giants are human in form and godlike in scale: there is a red-figure kylix from the late fifth century BCE, now in the Antikensammlung in Berlin. It shows Athene wearing her aegis – which here extends far beyond her torso, covering her left arm. As so often, it has the face of Medusa at its centre and is also decorated with twisting snakes along its edges. Athene's plumed helmet covers her hair, and her peplos is belted at the waist and drapes down to her feet. Her right arm is drawn back and she is aiming her spear directly into the flesh of the giant Encelados. He has already lost his footing: his right leg extends too far in front of him, and his left knee is about to slam into the ground. He's trying to draw his sword but he is too late. His shield hangs useless behind him. Whoever he was protecting himself from, he has missed the threat which is about to cost him his life. If Athene stabs him to death with a spear, it will be a comparatively undramatic death. Pseudo-Apollodorus has her crushing Encelados by throwing Sicily at him. The Greeks often placed angry giants under active volcanoes such as Etna to explain the pulsing fury beneath their eruptions.

This kylix is wonderful, as are many other vase paintings that show scenes of gods and giants at war. But by far the greatest depiction of the Gigantomachy is the magnificent Altar of Zeus from Pergamon, in what we would now call Turkey. It is absolutely vast, frieze after frieze depicting scenes from the battle, in which the giants are losing, and losing badly. The altar has sustained some damage, of course, but not so much that you can't see how between that fifth-century kylix and this second-century BCE sculpture, the giants have changed form, growing snakes for legs. They have ordinary human torsos, and the younger ones still have human legs, but the muscular thighs of the older, bearded giants twist into curling, scaled reptilian bodies.

Athene appears alongside Nike, whom you may remember she was holding in her hand in those great Pheidias sculptures. Here, however, the two goddesses are more equal in size, and more than a match for the giants sprawling on the floor at their feet and the goddess Gaia – mother of the giants – who rises up from the earth between them in a futile attempt to save her children's lives. Athene has lost her face on this frieze, but she is identifiable nonetheless, thanks in part to the confident way she handles her shield. This is a goddess who understands how to fight. She is also wearing the aegis across her breast. Confusingly, it has the face of Medusa at its centre. Yet if you follow the frieze round from the east side to the north, you can see three figures who have been identified as the Gorgons – all very much alive – fighting more giants. They are ably assisted by a lion taking a large chunk out of the enemy's arm.[25] It is one of the quirks of Greek mythology that one artwork or text routinely contradicts another. But one wall of an altar showing the severed head of a character who appears alive on an adjoining wall of that same altar is relatively unusual. The timing of the Gigantomachy is hard to place when so many of its participants are immortal. So perhaps we should simply accept that both its time and place are destined to be mysterious to us.

The winged figure of Nike, to the left of this scene, hovers above the ground. The giant beneath her has collapsed: only his folded arm is visible. In front of her is Gaia, pleading for her son's life. Gaia's elbow is almost touching Athene's knee as the warrior goddess powers forward. Athene's shield is on her left arm: any minute it might come crashing down on Gaia's unprotected head. Athene's right arm reaches behind her, wrenching at the hair of another giant. His left arm reaches out to try to grab at her weight-bearing left leg, and his right hand is wrapped around her right forearm. He is obviously trying to make her let go of his hair, but his face – the only one that has survived in this section of the frieze – is a mask of pain and misery. His brow creases with the effort it is costing him to resist. And yet his body is already collapsing to the ground. This fight was over before it even began – no wonder Nike is there to crown Athene in her victory. In some versions of her myth, Athene skins a giant and uses his hide as a shield.[26]

So much for the warrior goddess. Athene is also the Olympian most likely to be helping a hero in whatever tricky circumstances he finds himself, whether on the battlefield or far from it. That is especially true of her relationship with Odysseus, for whom her support is so determined that it must feel like persecution to those around him who are less favoured. He has her backing during the Trojan War, as do all the Greeks. But when the threat from the Trojans diminishes, Athene continues to pick Odysseus even in more minor conflicts against his fellow Greeks. We see an extreme example of this in the Sophocles play *Ajax*.

Before we go any further, I should tell you that there are actually two different Greek warriors called Ajax, and they both fight on the same side in the Trojan War. To add to the confusion, neither is actually called Ajax, which is the Romanization of a Greek name – Aias. Odysseus competes against both men for two different prizes, and Athene helps him both times. Neither Ajax survives his encounter with an angry god. So, a quick diversion around the fate of Locrian Ajax, also known as Ajax the Lesser. I know, everyone's a critic. This is the smaller of the two Ajaxes (or Aiantes, if you prefer the Greek plural. I'll stick with the Roman one for now), and he comes from a place called Locris. In Book Twenty-three of the *Iliad*, Achilles holds funeral games for his beloved Patroclus. This tradition may seem peculiar now, but when Greek warriors lost a great hero, they celebrated the life with athletic contests offering prizes – gold, silver, horses, and more.

Odysseus has already been joint prizewinner in a wrestling bout (with the other Ajax. I really am sorry about this). Now comes the foot-race. This time, Odysseus lines up alongside Locrian Ajax, who has an excellent start.[27] Odysseus pelts after him, so close behind that his breath is touching the other's head. As they enter the home straight, Odysseus offers up a quick prayer to Athene, begging her to help his feet.[28] Every runner has this moment in a race, I think. But we don't all receive instant divine assistance. Athene springs into action – no request too trivial – and makes Odysseus's feet and hands feel light. Is this a way of describing the sudden rush of energy that can hit an exhausted runner in sight of the finish line? Well, perhaps. But then Ajax slips over because Athene trips him. Not only that, but she does so at the exact point that will ensure he lands face-first in ox manure. Athene may be ageless, but she isn't very mature.

Odysseus wins first prize, but Ajax isn't one to take defeat lying down. He cries foul, correctly identifying the culprit: The goddess tripped my feet, he shouts. She's standing beside Odysseus like his mother, just like she has before, always helping him.[29] This is obviously a risky position for Ajax to take, however accurately he is describing events. But Locrian Ajax will not die at Athene's hands for this insult, nor for the far greater blasphemies he commits during the looting of Troy at the end of the war. As the Greeks swarm through her city, Cassandra – priestess of Apollo –

takes refuge in the temple of Athene. She is holding the statue of the goddess in a position of supplication when Ajax drags her away from it. In some versions of this scene, he rapes her.[30] Athene loathes Ajax so much that on his return from Troy to Locris, she takes the rare step of hurling a thunderbolt at his ship (this is usually her father's prerogative). The ship is splintered and sinks and yet Ajax survives, clinging to a rock. You might think at this point it would be wise to do some pleading and praying, but Ajax decides his better course of action is to boast that he has survived in spite of her wishes.[31] Poseidon is so irritated by this mortal upstart that, according to Homer, he slams his trident into the rock to which Ajax clings. In a sequence which is pure cinema, the rock splits. Part of it remains intact, but the chunk on which Ajax is sitting collapses into the sea. He dies, the passage concludes, drinking salt water. Athene and Poseidon have their differences, but despising Locrian Ajax is one thing they can agree on.

So now let's turn our attention to Athene's treatment of Telamonian Ajax, also known as Ajax the Great. Sophocles's *Ajax* is set in the days immediately following the death of Achilles at Troy. His weapons and armour – much-prized – were desired by two equally high-status men: Odysseus and Ajax. The weapons have been awarded to Odysseus by Agamemnon.

The play begins like a good murder mystery (I've argued elsewhere that Sophocles is the originator of the whodunit). Odysseus is exploring the scene of a crime, following the footsteps he has uncovered to try and discover the perpetrator. Athene compares him to a Spartan dog (a theatrical ancestor of Toby, the dog used by Sherlock Holmes to track the scent of a one-legged murderer and his accomplice[32]). Tell me what you're looking for, she urges. I know things – you can learn from me.

Oh, this is the voice of Athene! Odysseus speaks to her so often, he recognizes her immediately. The most beloved to me of all the gods, he adds.[33] He has no doubts. I can't see you, he says, but

I hear your voice and I get completely carried away. The relationship between Athene and Odysseus is always fascinating: sometimes she protects him like the mother of a small child, as in that footrace in the *Iliad*. At other times they seem like a young couple in love. We know that Athene rejects a life of marriage and domesticity, while Odysseus longs to be home with his wife, Penelope. But the connection between goddess and mortal is one which seems to exceed all others: she's always listening out for his prayers; he knows her by her voice alone.

She has guessed correctly. I'm tracking a man who hates me, Odysseus explains, shield-bearing Ajax. And the reason is that the Greeks have discovered that someone has slaughtered their valuable livestock while they slept. Not only the flocks, but their shepherds have been killed too. And everyone thinks Ajax did it.[34] But we don't know for certain. Some of these footprints are definitely his, but some I'm not sure about. Did I mention that everyone thinks it was him? And that one of our night watchmen saw him with his sword dripping and told me about it? So it's lucky you came when you did.

Athene says, Yes, I've been here for a while, watching you. And yes, it was Ajax. He did it because he was raging about Achilles's weapons.

So why did he attack the flocks? asks Odysseus.

He thought it was your blood on his hands, comes the chilling reply.

His plan was to kill the Greeks? Odysseus can scarcely believe it.

And he would have succeeded, if I'd not been paying attention, she says.

Did he get close?

Yes, Athene replies. He was right outside the tent of Agamemnon and Menelaus.

How did he stop himself, asks Odysseus, if he was so desperate to kill?

I stopped him.

In spite of the many atrocious ways Athene behaves in this and other myths, she is often my favourite goddess. Never more so than when she begins her whole speech with the word *egō* – I.[35] She claims full credit with all the confidence of someone who is the recipient of desperate men's prayers. I covered his eyes, she explains, so that when he saw the flocks, he thought he was killing the sons of Atreus (Agamemnon and Menelaus) and more of the Greeks. I encouraged him. He's tying up cattle at the moment, thinking they're men. I'll let you see him, but he won't be able to see you.

More literally, she says she'll avert the beams of his eyes from Odysseus's face. Fifth-century views on scientific matters could permeate into the world of Bronze Age myth on the dramatic stage. Sophocles, Euripides, and Aristophanes all reveal an interest – sincere or mocking – in these new ways of thinking. And at this point in the philosophy of perception, one popular theory of seeing claimed that beams of light emanated from the eyes in the same way they do from the sun. That's what made things visible.

But nothing is visible to Ajax, who is still in the grip of madness. Athene calls for him to come out and join her.

What are you doing, Athene? Odysseus is alarmed into brusqueness. Don't call him outside!

You have to have a tremendous amount of confidence in your relationship with a goddess to speak to her in this way. I can't think of many people in Greek myth who could speak to their tutelary deity like this and live to tell the tale, let alone to keep her favour. As noted above, Athene has an incredibly indulgent attitude towards Odysseus, but her reply is pure mean girl.

Be quiet! I hope you're not about to show yourself to be a coward.

But Odysseus is genuinely afraid. And after he's seen all those butchered bodies, we probably don't blame him.

What's the problem? Athene asks. He's still the man you know.

He was my enemy then and now, Odysseus replies.

And here we get to see a little more of Athene's character. Is there any laughter sweeter than laughing at your enemies? she asks.[36]

She might not know the word *schadenfreude*, but it doesn't stop her enjoying it. This is evidently a pleasure that can be experienced by a goddess in a way that even a warrior like Odysseus can't share. He despises Ajax, but he's still afraid of the man's power and murder-lust. For Athene there is nothing about Ajax – or any mortal – that can scare her. So she can simply take her ungenerous pleasure as she finds it. A man experiencing hallucinations is funny to her. The slaughter of the flocks, of their shepherds, the tying up of cattle in the belief he has hostages: all of this would be disquieting to us, as it is to Odysseus.

I'd rather he stayed indoors, he replies.

Do you shrink from seeing a raving madman? It's up to an actor how she plays this line, of course, but I think she is completely sincere at this point. Her question is a genuine one: *Why wouldn't you want to see your enemy in this state?* Odysseus replies rather defensively.

I wouldn't shrink from seeing him if his mind wasn't deranged.

Athene understandably assumes this response comes from a place of fear. He won't be able to see you, she says.

How can that be true if he's still got eyes? Odysseus asks.

I'll lay darkness over them, she replies.

He concedes the point: gods can do everything.

Don't make a noise, and stay still, she says.

I'll stay still, he agrees; I wish I was somewhere else.

Perhaps Athene's reading of the situation is correct and Odysseus is simply afraid of this man in his murderous insanity. But I find myself thinking that it's the madness Odysseus is afraid to witness, more than the risk to his life. He really doesn't want to see this man, this enemy, in a delusional state. Perhaps he's afraid he'll get hurt or killed, but I think there is something more. Odysseus has fought on the same side as this man for a decade. They have been allies, even if they've never been friends. They have shared a common enemy. Yet now – after a public humiliation over their dead friend's belongings – Ajax has been driven from his mind. It's a sudden and terrible fall from grace. And while Athene can take pleasure in that, Odysseus seems to see a reflection of his own human frailty. It's no wonder this play has resonated in modern times as a depiction of the horrifying consequences of war for those who have to fight in it. [37]

Where Athene sees hilarity, we might see post-traumatic stress disorder, a man for whom the horrors of what he has seen can no longer be tolerated. The reality Ajax has experienced can't change, so his mind rejects it and replaces it in order to try and keep him alive and functioning. The Greeks had a very limited language of psychology, so their gods often stand in for psychological states; we saw this with Aphrodite afflicting someone with overwhelming desire. And here – though Athene is assuredly a character in her own right – it is also possible to read her as a malevolent abstract force, the overwhelming effect on a warrior of seeing so much killing, so much blood, of escaping death so many times. We are accustomed to thinking of war as something won and lost, but there is no winner in hand-to-hand combat, just a survivor.

Athene calls Ajax again, asking why he's ignoring his *summakhos* – ally, literally one who fights alongside you. Ajax now appears onstage.

Greetings, Athene, he says, child of Zeus, always there for me. I'll make you offerings of pure gold to thank you for this quarry.

She thanks him, and continues the pretence. Have you dipped your sword in Argive blood? she asks.

He doesn't deny it.

She is not going to let this go lightly: the sons of Atreus, did you get them?

They'll never dishonour my name again, he replies.

You've killed them, she asks.

They're dead, he confirms. Now let's see them try to take my armour from me.

I see, she says. And the son of Laertes? Did he escape you?

That cursed fox, he replies.

Yes, she says, I'm asking about Odysseus.

He's with my other prisoners inside, Ajax answers. I'm going to tie him to a pillar and beat him to death.

Why are you so set on doing harm to the wretched man? she asks.

I'm usually happy to let you guide me, he says, but Odysseus will receive this justice and no other.

Well, you'd better put your back into it then, she says (though in Greek it's your hand that determines effort).[38]

I'll get to it, Ajax replies. And don't ever stop being my ally, he adds, as he leaves the stage.

This scene makes my heart hurt. A heavily armed, highly trained killer is nonetheless a pathetic figure when his grasp on reality is so fractured. Watching Athene toy with him is like watching a cat batting its paw at a vole moments before she unsheathes her claws. And once Ajax has gone, she turns straight back to Odysseus to gloat a bit more. Did you see, Odysseus? Did you see how powerful the gods are? Did you ever know a more cautious or practical man than Ajax was?

She could not be enjoying more this comprehensive collapse in a man's sanity and standing. Again, Odysseus can't share her mirth.

No, he says, I never knew a more capable man. I feel compassion for the poor wretch – even though he hates me – because he's bound to misery now. I'm not thinking of his fate more than my own. I can see we live as nothing more than ghosts or flimsy shadows.

Odysseus has not become a new man. His sympathy for Ajax is bound up in thoughts of himself: he is as tightly yoked to self-absorption as Ajax is to delusion. But that makes him more sympathetic in this moment, not less. We know that Odysseus is always looking out for himself; we've seen plenty of examples of his treachery and slipperiness in the Trojan War, not least in the *Iliad*. If he suddenly became a paragon of caring for others, we wouldn't believe it. It would just be another trick, another disguise. This response – at the devastation done to the mind of his enemy – rings completely true. But for the grace of this goddess, he might be in the same condition himself. And the final words of Ajax to Athene, where he confidently thanks her for her help and asks her to continue to be his ally, these are the words that really twist the knife for Odysseus. From the inside, Ajax feels exactly the same as he does: blessed to have the support of Athene. Who's to say who is right, when she can bestow madness on a man who nevertheless feels sane? Odysseus has suddenly seen that his life is no more solid than the flitting shades in the Underworld.

But Athene is not remotely quashed by Odysseus's failure to share her delight. Well, since you've seen what's happened to him, she says, make sure you never say anything arrogant to the gods, or become swollen with pride. A single day can raise you or crush you. The gods love sensible men and they hate the bad ones.

And with these reassuring words, she leaves the stage. So does Odysseus, because what could he possibly say now?

He will not return until the end of the play, after Ajax has taken his own life with his sword: a great warrior finally turning his weapon upon himself. It is worth pointing out that since 2001, roughly four times as many members of the US armed forces have died by suicide than in military operations.[39] The causes are complex, but a report for Brown University's Costs of War project suggests that the trauma of conflict and crisis of conscience are two important elements.[40] No wonder the Theater of War organization – which has staged dramatic readings of Sophocles's *Ajax* and *Philoctetes* for civilian and military audiences to great acclaim – has found such connections within these plays.[41] I am often asked why Greek tragedy retains such a hold on us today, and I always give the same answer: because the unit of currency in tragedy is a human being. No matter what else has changed across thousands of years, I think that remains true.

But to explore Athene and Odysseus's relationship in greater detail – and across years rather than moments – let us turn back to Homer, and the *Odyssey*. At the beginning of the poem, we find Athene with her father, who is agonizing over the fate of Aegisthus, who had killed his cousin Agamemnon (with Clytemnestra's assistance) and has now been killed in turn by the couple's son, Orestes. Yes, yes, says Athene, he deserved it and so does everyone else who behaves that way. But what about poor Odysseus? He's breaking my heart in two. He's trapped on an island, surrounded by sea, held by the daughter of Atlas (the nymph Calypso). She's trying to get him to forget about Ithaca, but he just wants to see the smoke rise from his own land – he wants to die. And this doesn't touch your heart even now, does it, Olympian? Wasn't he always making sacrifices to you at Troy? So why are you angry with him now, Zeus?[42]

I mentioned above the shifting relationship between goddess and mortal, and here she reminds me of nothing more than the besotted teen who turns every conversation round to the object of her affection (rest assured this is definitely behaviour I have grown out of myself) and for whom any slight failure to share her obsession is treated as proof of an indefensible animus. *Oh, are you thinking about Aegisthus? You know who that reminds me of? Odysseus – why do you hate him, why?* She chooses emotive language to describe Odysseus's plight: to her, he is held in a watery prison, about to die of misery. And not only that, but no one even cares! Except her, his one true friend.

It is no accident that just before this exchange, Homer tells us that Poseidon is busy at a gigantic feast held in his honour by the Ethiopians. In other words, the god most likely to dissent from Athene's viewpoint – because Poseidon loathes Odysseus – is absent. She uses and repeats vocabulary of islands and the sea, so we cannot miss her subtextual meaning. It may be the daughter of Atlas who has taken Odysseus into her home, but it is the watery surroundings of that home which mean Odysseus can't escape without help. And Zeus doesn't miss that either.

My child, he responds, how could I forget Odysseus? He's got more sense than other mortals, and he makes more sacrifices to the gods than anyone else too. The problem is Poseidon, who hates him for maiming and blinding his son, Polyphemus. So come on, we need to think about his *nostos* – journey home – and how he can get there. Poseidon will have to let go of his anger; he can't fight against all the gods.[43]

Athene is delighted with this response, and her only additional request is that they hurry. Let's get Hermes flitting off to Ogygia (Calypso's island), she says. So he can tell that nymph with the good hair – *euplokamōi* – to let Odysseus go. Meanwhile, I'll head to Ithaca so that I can offer encouragement to his son Telemachus. I'll make him speak out against those greedy suitors, and then I'll send him to Sparta and Pylos so he can find news about his father and acquire a bit of fame for himself.[44]

She ties on her golden sandals – which allow her to travel over land and sea alike – and picks up her bronze spear. She goes straight from Olympus to Ithaca. By the time she arrives there, she resembles Mentes. He is a man who is guest-friend to Odysseus's family. In this, he is subtly contrasted with the suitors who are lording it over Odysseus's household, eating his livestock and drinking his wine. The themes of the *Odyssey* – of homecoming and of what it means to (mis)behave in your own and another's home – are laid out from the start of the poem. Telemachus soon notices the disguised goddess and hurries to welcome this visitor. The two of them sit apart from the suitors, to avoid being deafened by the noise. A bard starts singing, and Telemachus leans close to Athene so the suitors can't hear him speak. He asks who this *xeinos* – stranger, guest, friend – might be. Athene responds with the first of many tall tales told by her and Odysseus about who they are and where they've come from. I'm Mentes, she says, lord of the Taphians, and our fathers are friends from long ago – ask your grandfather. I heard your dad was back but now I see he is kept from here, undoubtedly *aekonta* – against his will. You mark my words, he'll be home soon, even if he's held by iron chains. He'll think of something. You really look like him, by the way.⁴⁵

Well, stranger, Telemachus replies, my mother says Odysseus is my father, but I've never known for certain. No one can know his father. I'd like to be the son of someone really lucky, growing old in his own home. But I have the unluckiest of men as my father, since you mention him.⁴⁶

It is a pleasing irony that of all the people he could be talking to, even though he doesn't know it, Telemachus is speaking to the one who can be completely sure who her father is, having appeared from his own head. But Athene doesn't mention this, she simply changes the subject to ask who the men are who are making such a racket and behaving in such an overfamiliar way. It is surely the case, though, that this sharp-eyed, sharp-minded goddess has noticed the doubts besieging Telemachus, who has never really known his father since he was a baby when Odysseus left. She remembers – as do we, since she and Zeus were discussing it only a few moments before – the horrors that can befall a man who arrives home without being sure of his welcome. Odysseus needs a son who accepts his parentage; otherwise there might be a second bleak homecoming among the Greeks who commanded men at Troy.

But if Telemachus has expressed doubts about his father, they are halfhearted ones. As soon as the subject of the suitors is raised, he is quick to convey to Athene that there is no candidate in his mind for a replacement father. He bemoans his particular fate: it would be easier to cope with his father being dead than missing. If he'd died at Troy, it would have been a hero's death and it would have brought renown to Telemachus, who would have grieved for him accordingly. But as things are, the family is stuck in limbo: no one knows where Odysseus is. The winds have snatched him away, says Telemachus, unseen and unheard. The only thing he has left me is sorrow.

The Greek concept of *kleos* is hard to fully realize in another language. It's usually translated as 'fame', but that makes Telemachus sound unfairly petulant and shallow, even to my ears (and I am not always a fan). He doesn't want his father to have died so that – as his child – Telemachus would have benefitted from the fame or glory that his father had accrued in life. *Kleos* is something more than mere celebrity. A man will fight and die in pursuit of *kleos*, as Achilles does. It is an explicit choice for him: short life with *kleos*, or long life in obscurity? For a hero, this is no choice at all (although Achilles speaking after death in the *Odyssey* rejected the decision he made during his life).

Kleos is not just fame and celebrity and a good reputation. It is immortality in a time before alphabetic writing, when no one can make a record of their deeds to pass down to future generations. It is what there is in a time before written history can preserve your name. Instead of that, perhaps you could live a life of tremendous daring in battles and adventures, and thus win *kleos* for yourself and your descendants. Bards – like the one who is playing while Athene and Telemachus have this conversation – will compose songs about your exploits and men everywhere will hear of you for as long as those songs are performed. And while men are introduced with patronymics (as 'Son of Laertes', for example), a man's name casts a long shadow.

But any sympathy I feel for Telemachus goes straight up in smoke as he goes on to blame his mother for the invasion of suitors in their home. She doesn't refuse a hateful marriage, he complains, but nor can she make them leave.[47] He shows not even the slightest concern for his mother's position: if she believes Odysseus is alive, then of course she will not remarry. But with no evidence that Odysseus is returning home, she presumably feels just like Telemachus does – stuck in limbo. And how is she supposed to make more than a hundred men leave her home if they don't want to?

Athene cuts right to the heart of the problem. You really need Odysseus to come home, she says. She wishes for the return of the king, and his swift dispatch of the indolent suitors (something she will do a great deal to encourage as the poem progresses). She outlines her plan. Firstly, Telemachus must call a meeting tomorrow and tell the suitors to leave. Secondly, if Penelope wants to remarry, fine. (This is the second time Athene has been irritable about women connected to Odysseus who aren't her, and we're not even three hundred lines into a twenty-four-book poem yet.) Thirdly, Telemachus should prepare a ship and sail to Pylos, and then to Sparta. You can't keep behaving like a child, she says. You're a bit old for that now.[48] You've heard about the *kleos* Orestes won for himself? By killing Aegisthus, who killed his father. You need to win praise for yourself like that.

This is certainly one response to Orestes's actions. Others vary, and we'll look at a powerfully different one in the next chapter. But Telemachus takes the words to heart as she tells him she must leave. Having been disguised as a mortal man for their whole encounter, she chooses to exit the hall by flying up in the air like a bird. She places courage and daring in his heart (just as she did to Diomedes in the *Iliad*). Wondering at what has just happened, Telemachus realizes that he has been in the company of a deity. No wonder his confidence is increasing. He has a goddess on his side. She will reappear in the next book (disguised as a man once more) to give him a further pep talk. When he still seems to be dallying, she raises the stakes higher again: disguising herself as Telemachus, she organizes the ship and the crew on his behalf, switches disguises once more, and goes to collect him. Athene is capable of drastic and total changes of heart, but not when it comes to Odysseus, or his son.

She continues to guide and support him on his voyages and adventures, but we'll rejoin her in Book Five when she has a second meeting with her father. Having already told him that they need to compel Calypso to free Odysseus as soon as possible, she repeats and reinforces her point: Odysseus is on an island, he doesn't have a ship, he can't leave without help, the suitors are planning to kill his son. Zeus knows his daughter: What a thing to say! he says. Wasn't this the plan you were devising in your mind? So that when Odysseus returns he can take revenge on them? As for Telemachus, you can guide him home skilfully and make sure he's safe. Those suitors won't succeed.[49] Athene might get her wiliness from her mother, but Zeus is no slouch either. And he is quite right about his daughter: she is indeed spoiling for a massacre of the suitors.

And she will get her own way, as so often. Her early appearances in the poem set the tone for a series of interventions in various guises to Telemachus and, of course, to Odysseus. In this story of twisting paths and narratives, of truths and lies, of adventures and homecomings, she will be a constant source of help and comfort to these two men. And Poseidon will have to let go of his rage against Odysseus, because Athene and Zeus have arranged things that way. Even the bereaved families of the suitors slaughtered by Odysseus and Telemachus will be compelled to accept their fate when Athene tells them it is time for peace. The last four lines of the poem are focused on her: she orders the suitors' families and Odysseus's family to swear oaths of peace. And in case you thought she or Odysseus were now committed to a straightforward life, she is still in disguise, this time as a man named Mentor, when the poem ends. No wonder so many Greeks in myths never seem quite sure if they've encountered a god or not.

But Athene's passion for weaving elaborate stories is not just a narrative skill. It's a physical one too. She is as accomplished at creating intricate textiles as she is aliases and disguises. And this brings us to the story of Arachne, whose fate you may be able to guess from her name alone. This is told by Ovid in the sixth book of the *Metamorphoses*. Athene has just heard the Muses sing of their revenge on the Pierids, which we looked at in the first chapter. And now, she concludes, it's time I received some praise. No one should be able to scorn my divine power without punishment.[50]

This isn't a particularly controversial position for a god to hold. As we've already seen, showing contempt or even insufficient honour to any deity is a dangerous choice. But as far as Athene is concerned, scorning her power is something someone can do almost by accident. And this is what happens to Arachne, a young woman from Maeonia, in Lydia, in what we now call Turkey. Athene turns her attention to Arachne because she has heard that Arachne doesn't yield to Athene in praise for her skill at weaving. It's an odd construction in English, but it just means that when someone praises Arachne for her weaving talents, she says *Thanks very much* instead of the more appropriate (in Athene's eyes), *Oh, this old thing, it's just a rag, really, you should save your praise for the goddess Athene, she's the one who can weave.*

Arachne's fame didn't come from the place she grew up or from her family (she is the daughter of a wool-dyer), but from her art. One incidental delight: Ovid says her father dyes *bibulas lanas* – thirsty wool.[51] If there's a better way of describing a substance that absorbs an unexpected amount of liquid, I don't know it. Arachne lives in a small house in a small village, but her weaving is so remarkable that even nymphs abandon their vineyards and streams just so they can come and admire her work. They don't just come to look at the finished fabrics either, but to watch her in the act of making them, so impressive is her skill. The whole process is mesmerizing: shaping the raw wool, turning balls of fluff into soft yarn, embroidering with a needle. You would know, says Ovid, that Arachne learned all this from Athene.[52]

But – and this is where her trouble really starts – Arachne denies it. Not only that, but she puts herself in what we know to be dangerous territory. Let's have a competition, she says. I'll give up everything if I'm beaten. Athene promptly disguises herself as an old woman, giving herself fake grey hair and wobbly limbs so she has to use a stick. She approaches Arachne and tells her that there are some advantages to being old: you gain experience. Now, don't reject my advice. You should seek fame for being the best mortal weaver. But yield to the goddess and beg forgiveness for your rash words before. She'll forgive you if you ask.

If we have learned nothing else from myths, folklore, and fairy tales, we should at least know this. If an old woman approaches you and asks for anything, or suggests anything, you always, always say yes, and thank you very much for asking. There is an almost zero chance that she is an actual old lady and not a goddess, a witch, or an enchantress in disguise. You either change your offending behaviour immediately or – and this is the best-case scenario – you find yourself stuck in a castle full of singing furniture, with one erratic houseplant your only hope of salvation.

Arachne has not learned this lesson, so she stares at the old woman angrily and is scarcely able to restrain her hand from hitting her. You stupid old woman, she says. Living too long is bad for you. Your daughter or daughter-in-law might want this advice, but I can advise myself. Don't think you've achieved anything by warning me – my opinion is unchanged. Why doesn't the goddess come here herself? Why is she avoiding this contest?

Oh, she's come here, says Athene, and her old woman disguise disappears. The nymphs and women around her start venerating her. Arachne alone is unafraid.[53] She blushes, but only briefly, and she stands her ground. So does Athene. The weaving contest is on. There now follows a tense action sequence where the two women both set up their looms and start weaving their patterns in a thousand colours, shot through with gold thread.

Athene – as you might expect – weaves a story that is all about her. Specifically, she weaves the story of how she beat Poseidon to claim Athens as her city. She weaves a version of herself wearing helmet and spear; she shows the moment she causes the olive tree to sprout. And then – because it wouldn't be Athene without an ever-present threat – she weaves into each of the four corners a different set of mortals who tried to rival gods and came off worse. One couple was transformed into twin mountains, two women were turned into birds, and one particularly unlucky one was converted into a flight of stairs. Finally Athene adds a border of olive branches, as a symbol of peace.[54] No matter how good the weaving, it's hard to imagine it could outclass the passive-aggression.

But Arachne isn't intimidated by either. She weaves a series of scenes illustrating exactly why she might not be willing to worship the Olympian gods, and particularly the daughter of Jove (Zeus). First she shows Europa, carried off to sea by Jove in the form of a bull. Then she weaves Asterie, trying to escape Jove in the form of an eagle. Leda is lying beneath the wings of Jove when he is a swan. The next part is Jove as a satyr, impregnating Antiope with twins. Then he appears to Alcemene (the mother of Hercules), disguised as her husband, Amphitryon. He impregnates Danaë (mother of Perseus) as golden rain; Aegina he tricks by hiding in fire. He appears as a shepherd to Mnemosyne (mother of the Muses); to his own daughter Proserpina, he is a snake.

But why stop there? It's not like Zeus is the only god who rapes and impregnates women and goddesses at will. So Arachne continues. Here's Neptune (Poseidon), disguised as a bull to assault Canace, daughter of Aeolus. He turns into the river Enipeus to father the giant Aloidae. He's a ram for Bisaltis, a horse to Ceres, a bird to impregnate Medusa with Pegasus, and a dolphin for Melantho.[55]

And she still isn't done. Here's Apollo disguised as a hawk, lion, shepherd accosting Isse. Bacchus pretends to be a bunch of grapes to deceive Erigone (please don't ask for more details, I honestly can't imagine. You can, however, see an engraving of this sinister fruit bowl by the seventeenth-century Flemish artist Cornelis Vermeulen in the National Galleries of Scotland).[56] Here's Saturn (Kronos in Greek) fathering Chiron the centaur, while pretending to be a horse. And around the outside, Arachne too produces a delicate border, but hers is of flowers and ivy.[57]

This entire sequence is extraordinary. The *Metamorphoses* is filled with examples of gods assaulting nymphs and mortals; you can become numb to it after a while. And it becomes easy to assume that ancient authors didn't see this, didn't think at all about consent or sexual agency or anything so modern. Certainly not Ovid, who cheerily composed poems about how to seduce women and how he has seduced women, where the very concept of consent is entirely absent. And yet, here he is listing god after god who has deceived and tricked, cajoled and forced himself on woman after woman. There was once (in some quarters, there still is) a tendency in academia, as elsewhere, to diminish rape and sexual assault when it happened far away, or in the past or both. The underpinning belief is that since these societies didn't share our values, they didn't see such behaviour as problematic. There are ways of framing these nonconsensual liaisons as a sort of meta-assault: it's not quite the same as assault because one party is a god, the assaulted woman usually gets a demigod baby out of it, if you were alive in the Bronze Age you would probably be raped by someone, so a god is better than most attackers because women often accrue status in the aftermath, and so on, and so on. I wish I were inventing these spurious arguments rather than paraphrasing ones I have heard and read too many times.

It shouldn't need saying that it simply doesn't matter what values a society has if you are the one who gets assaulted and hurt. Societies have a tremendously high tolerance for war, but it doesn't mean you'd think it was fair enough if your home was invaded and your family killed. Would you be half expecting such a thing to happen because the threat of war was ever present? Perhaps. Would it dull the pain? I suspect not.

Ancient societies have some constants which horrify us, like the total acceptance of slavery. Very few ancient writers or thinkers questioned it; most assumed it was the natural order of things. And yet – though in the abstract slavery was considered natural for some people – no one wanted to be a slave, and even slaves might cling to a status that marks them out as essentially unslavish. So in the *Odyssey*, we see a distinction being made between those who were born into slavery and those who were just unlucky – on the losing side in a war, say – who were enslaved after an early life of freedom. Eumaeus the swineherd wants Odysseus to know that he was the son of a king until he was kidnapped by his nanny (herself a woman of high status enslaved by pirates) when she ran away with sailors.[58] In other words, he is not a slave by disposition, just by ill fortune. So where are the slaves who were just born for that life and no other? It seems that while ancient writers and thinkers could believe in an abstract sense that such people existed, there aren't many of the enslaved – historical or imagined – jumping up to claim that status.

And the same thing is true of sexual assault. Just because it happens all the time doesn't mean someone doesn't mind it happening specifically to them: quite the reverse, in fact. I wouldn't claim for a moment that Ovid's description of this scene means that he understands that sexual assault is morally reprehensible. He is far too distant as a literary persona for me to claim anything very definitively about his beliefs as either poet or human being. Perhaps he is giving Arachne this tapestry to further illustrate her terrible arrogance: what kind of awful mortal woman thinks a divine visitation from Zeus himself is something to complain about?

But even if his sympathies are not with Arachne in this moment, he can still imagine that from her perspective these gods are nothing but rapists. She has been described to us as excessively arrogant about her own skills, even if her confidence is well-founded. And she has been shown to be short-tempered with an interfering old woman. But these aren't the characteristics of a fantasist or a fool. She isn't out of her mind, like poor Ajax. We can't simply dismiss her opinions as those coming from a disordered mind. Whether Ovid shares her views is unimportant. What matters is that he is perfectly aware of her feelings about the pain inflicted by these gods in their cruelty, and his version of Arachne is given the space to express it. *Look at the great gifts the gods have given you*, Athene's tapestry proclaims. Arachne's response is very detailed in its execution, but very simple in its message: the price is too high.

And Athene's reaction to her rival's tapestry is intriguing. Neither Pallas (Ovid prefers this name for Athene) nor Envy herself could find fault with the work, he writes. But surely if Athene disagreed with its central premise, she would find fault with that: a work of art isn't just judged by its execution, but by its theme (as anyone who has ever had to praise the costumes for want of anything generous to say about the script or the acting can confirm). Athene makes no such criticism. This cleverest Olympian is lost for words. And then, as Ovid says, the warrior goddess resented Arachne's achievement, and tore up the woven pictures, those *caelestia crimina* – divine crimes.[59] And surely here – though again I would hesitate to speak for Ovid himself – we can at least conclude that his Athene agrees with Arachne's view. Tearing up the evidence of something you don't want to accept is the behaviour of someone who can't refute it, not of a goddess in possession of the winning argument.

Her next action is no more mature. She raises the wooden shuttle she has used for her own weaving and hits Arachne on the head three or four times. The unfortunate girl can't bear it and fastens a ligature around her neck. Athene, pitying her, raises her up and says, 'Live then, even as you hang there, you impious girl!' She sentences Arachne's descendants to share her punishment and then she leaves, sprinkling drops of a potion made by Hecate as she goes. This magic solution causes Arachne to shrink and change, and she becomes a spider, hanging from a thread rather than a noose.[60]

The story concludes here, and Ovid moves on with a simple connecting device: someone who had met Arachne when she was still human was Niobe, who didn't learn from Arachne's terrible fate to avoid hubristic comparisons with a goddess. And yet, Arachne's hubris was rather different from that of Niobe, who did literally claim to be better than Leto because she had more children. Arachne is compared by other people to Athene, and denies having been taught to weave by Athene. Perhaps I'm being pedantic, but these don't seem to me to amount to Niobe's boast. Arachne is keen for a contest to prove herself the better weaver, which does stray into hubris, I suppose. But taking the chance to prove yourself against the best is behaviour we often see encouraged in men: no one punishes Diomedes when he attacks gods and goddesses on the battlefield at Troy, for example. Is it because he is caught up in the bloodlust of the moment? Or is it because wanting to prove yourself stronger than a god at war is a noble ambition for a mortal warrior, but wanting to prove yourself more skilled than the goddess of weaving is shocking and shameful for a woman?

I'm often asked who my favourite goddess is, and I usually (though not always – I am a fickle creature in these matters) say Athene. But I can't defend her against the charges of pettiness and gendered favouritism. She does tend to prefer men, even if she isn't keen to have sex with one; she doesn't tend to support women. Athene revels in being better than Ares at his specialism; she is competitive to her core. So I find myself wondering if Arachne's real sin in the goddess's eyes isn't that she challenges Athene to the weaving contest, but that the work she produces actually is superior. Athene doesn't hate competitiveness, she loves it. What she hates – above all else – is losing.

THE FURIES

DIDO HAS one of the greatest broken hearts in ancient poetry. As told by Virgil in Book Four of the *Aeneid*, she is abandoned by her lover Aeneas when he leaves Carthage for Italy to found a new colony there for the survivors of the Trojan War. Dido realizes he has been making secret plans to set sail without even telling her that he is going. She takes it about as well as anyone would, with a magnificent speech that begins, Did you really hope to deceive me, you traitor?[1] Aeneas tries to defend himself but Dido's sense of betrayal is undimmed. She wishes him dead in a shipwreck, calling out her name as he drowns. She anticipates her own death, and makes a chilling promise. I will follow you – though I won't be there – with black fire. When cold death separates my breath from my limbs, I'll still be near you in every place you go. You'll receive the punishment you should, you hateful man. And I will hear of it: the story will reach my shade deep in the Underworld.[2]

Aeneas does not drown at sea, though Dido does end her life when he leaves her. But one of the reasons this speech has stuck in my mind since I first read it thirty years ago is the imagery of pursuit that she uses. She doesn't threaten to chase after him like a hunting dog, a bird of prey, a storm sent by the gods. Virgil loves the natural world; he uses this kind of imagery throughout his poems. Instead, she says she will follow him even as she's absent, and she will carry black flames. She isn't comparing herself to any living creature, but to the three female deities who pursue those who have committed a variety of terrible crimes, often against family members: the Furies. It is Dido's ghost or shade that will persecute Aeneas in retribution for the great wrong he has done her, but it will have the tenacity of goddesses that personify revenge.

As it transpires, Dido doesn't get her wish. When they meet again in the Underworld in Book Six, Aeneas pleads with her to forgive him. She doesn't acknowledge him at all, and disappears into the shadows to be reunited instead with her first love, Sychaeus. Neither her ghost nor the Furies themselves are required to punish Aeneas for breaking his vows to her: her love for Sychaeus is greater than her anger with Aeneas.

But the wrath of the Erinyes – one of several names by which the Furies are known in Greek – is not so easily set aside as Dido's rage. The exact nature of these goddesses isn't fixed, and in earlier sources they are essentially personifications of vengeance or embodiments of curses issued by wronged parties. They soon develop identities and names of their own, however: Alekto, Megaira, and Tisiphone.

Their parentage is also unfixed. Sometimes – as in Hesiod[3] – they are the daughters of Gaia and Ouranos, formed by the drops of his blood that land on the ground after Kronos has castrated him. You'll recall that Aphrodite is the result of his semen spattering in the sea. I never feel enough is made of this blood-bond between two very different kinds of goddess, who nonetheless share a ruthless streak a mile wide. Later authors, like Aeschylus, have the Furies as the daughters of Nyx – Night.[4]

Our sources do converge on their appearance, though it can take those who see them some time to find the right words. Let's look at how they manifest themselves through *The Oresteia*, the trilogy of plays by Aeschylus in which they perform a starring role. In the first play, *Agamemnon*, they are spotted dancing at the house of Atreus by the Trojan priestess and visionary Cassandra.[5] She sees them engaged in a *kōmos* – an exuberant dance or revel. She's outside the palace when she spots them, so they are obviously visible from there, at least to one with Cassandra's powers. Wherever they choose to begin their revelry, they aren't easily expelled. The family of Atreus have committed so many horrific deeds at one another's expense that it's hard to know who exactly the Furies are here to punish. Cassandra believes their wrath has been stirred by historic crimes rather than more recent ones. She makes reference to Atreus himself, whose wife was seduced by his brother, Thyestes. His notorious response to this provocation was to slaughter

Thyestes's children and serve them to their father at a feast. Perhaps when they've slaked their thirst for retribution on this count, the Furies might get round to avenging Iphigenia, killed by her father Agamemnon – the son of Atreus – ten years ago. They won't have time, of course, because Clytemnestra will exact revenge on her daughter's behalf within moments of her husband arriving in their home.

But this does not mean the Furies will leave the halls of the palace, as we see in the second play of the trilogy, *Choephoroi*. Now Orestes has taken on the role of avenger for his dead father, Agamemnon. Orestes and his sister Electra plot to punish Clytemnestra for her actions, as they are sure they have the gods on their side. Surely they must, since Clytemnestra betrayed her husband both sexually and murderously. But perhaps the Furies don't agree, because shortly after killing his mother, Orestes finds himself looking at women who resemble Gorgons, dark-robed, with snakes wrapped closely around them. I cannot stay, he says, panicking.[6] What fantasies could be twirling around you, ask the chorus, when you loved your father more than anyone? Nothing should scare you now.

The Furies apparently care very little for how much someone might love their father if they have also murdered their mother. And Orestes makes it clear in his reply that although the chorus can't see these vengeful beings, he is not imagining them. They're not fantasies, he says. These are the grudge-filled dogs belonging to my (dead) mother.[7] Orestes knows who they are and why they're there: These hateful creatures come in great numbers, he says, and blood drips from their eyes. The chorus cheerfully suggest that Apollo could cleanse Orestes of his crime and thus release him from this awful fate. But Orestes isn't persuaded. You can't see them, he says desperately. But I can. I am driven on, pursued. I cannot stay.

So now we know a little more about what the Furies look like. They loosely resemble Gorgons, at least insofar as both creatures are connected with snakes. Gorgons are usually depicted with these snakes growing from their scalps like hair, whereas the Furies are often depicted with snakes coiling through their hair and around their arms. But the eyes dripping blood, the malevolent dancing, the certainty of the one to whom they are visible that he must move and keep moving? These are qualities we only associate with the Furies. There is something spectacularly nasty about the idea that they sing and dance in Aeschylus's version. They're like the dark sisters of the Muses, taking pleasure in punishing wrongdoers.

The notion that these pursuers are hideous, terrifying, and visible only to the one they are here to punish is an influential one. It is the stuff of nightmares: We run, but they keep gaining on us. We look back, but we haven't lost them. We try to hide, but they always find us. And worst of all is the isolation we experience because no one else can see the creatures that will never, ever leave us alone until we die. Of all the horror movies I saw as a film reviewer (including one rather bleak week watching torture porn for BBC Radio 3), few have stuck in my mind with the same persistence as *It Follows* from 2014. Teen horror often exhibits the morals of a puritan elder, meaning that sexually active teenagers are generally the first to be abducted by vampires/tortured by a masked killer/eaten by zombies. If you hope to survive to the final reel, you had better not get past kissing with any of your classmates. As an aside, I would note that this also extends to thrillers when the film's protagonist is the father of a teenage girl (although this doesn't seem to affect my crush on Liam Neeson).

But *It Follows* intensifies that ethic. Here, the creature that pursues you is sexually transmitted. It will definitely kill you if it catches you: it is following you all the time. If you want to rid yourself of it, you need to have sex with someone else and it will follow them instead. But – and this is crucial – you need to tell them what you have done. Because the creature will keep following you until you give it to someone else.

But if it reaches the next person and kills them, then it returns to follow its previous target. In other words, to rid yourself of it, you need to pass it on to someone who knows what they're up against and is capable of outrunning or outwitting the follower. Otherwise, it will just come back.

The follower takes on the form of a person, perhaps someone you know, sometimes old, unkempt, naked, or wearing white. As you scan an open area, a park or a beach, there it is, walking towards you from the middle distance. It isn't quick, and if you run, you can easily make it to your car, drive as far and fast as you can. But eventually you will run out of gas, and it will soon reappear on the roof, in the parking lot, inside the house. It doesn't have the speed or cunning of a predator – it can be outwitted and outpaced. But it will always be there, wherever you are. It is the horrifying extreme of a sexually transmitted disease, albeit one that offers the tantalizing prospect of a cure if you are willing to risk the lives of others.

Like the Furies, there is a sense in which the follower is an external manifestation of part of the person it follows: something we run away from is not always a monster; it can be an element of our own psyche. In the case of Orestes – their most notorious victim – the Furies are both creatures in their own right and an external representation of the guilt he experiences for the murder of his mother. And in the concluding play of Aeschylus's trilogy, *Eumenides*, they finally get to speak for themselves.

But our first encounter with them is through the eyes of the Pythia, the priestess of Apollo at Delphi. As the play begins, she is heading to the innermost part of the temple to begin her day issuing prophecies. But as she tries to enter, she is turned back by the terrible things she sees inside.[8] Firstly she has seen a man who is *theomusē* – unclean in the eyes of the gods. His hands are dripping blood, his sword has just been wrenched from a wound, and he's holding an olive branch. This certainly sounds like a gory start to her day, but the sight of an armed killer is not what's upset her.

In front of him, she says, is an extraordinary ambush: women, sleeping on chairs. No, definitely not women. Gorgons, I would call them, but they don't look much like Gorgons. They're like a picture I saw of those creatures that snatched food away from Phineus, except I couldn't see any wings.

So the priestess – who occupies a liminal role between mortal and divine, as the spokeswoman for Apollo to those who come seeking oracles and prophecies – can see the Furies, just as Cassandra could in the first play. Although they aren't pursuing the Pythia – and in spite of the fact that she can see Orestes has committed a crime that has earned him the enmity of the gods – she is terrified almost out of her mind. She struggles even to find the words to describe them. She can tell they're female, but they aren't women. She initially compares them to Gorgons (presumably because of the snakes) but then corrects herself: they don't look like images of Gorgons she's seen before. She scrambles for another comparison. They are like the Harpies – winged hybrid bird-woman monsters sent by Zeus to prey on Phineus by stealing his food before he can eat it. The Furies in the temple seem to echo the monstrous ugliness of them in a painting this priestess has seen. Although in the interest of fairness, I should add that according to Hesiod, the Harpies have lovely hair.[9]

The Pythia now tries to give more information. They're the colour of night, she says, completely disgusting, they're snoring with repellent breaths. Some revolting tears drip from their eyes. Their clothing isn't good enough to wear before statues of the gods, or even in the homes of men. I don't know what tribe produced this gang, nor what land could nurture this family without lamenting its efforts afterwards.[10]

I can't deny that part of me feels the Furies are getting a rather rough ride here: lots of us have bad hay-fever and untidy clothes. But the priestess is having none of it. She decides this is now Apollo's problem and leaves. The inner sanctum of the temple is now revealed to the play's audience, and Apollo has appeared there, apparently agreeing with his priestess. He begins speaking to Orestes: I will not betray you. I'll be your guardian whether I'm near to you or far away . . . Look now at these mad, overwhelmed women. These abominations have fallen asleep. The grey-haired old women, ancient children: no god, or man, or beast ever mingles with them. They were created for evil, they live in the gloom of Tartarus beneath the earth, hated by men and by the Olympian gods. Nevertheless, you must flee – don't be weak. For they will drive you on no matter where you go across the wide earth, or on the sea, or to cities surrounded by water. Don't give up, keep going to the city of Pallas (Athens) and take her ancient wooden image in your arms. You'll find your judges there, and with persuasive speeches we'll free you from your toil. Because I'm the one who persuaded you to kill your mother.[11]

So from this speech, we have learned that Apollo – a mighty Olympian god – can subdue the Furies in the short term, in his own temple. But in the longer term, all Apollo can really do is promise Orestes his support and advice: keep moving until you have the chance of a big public showdown in Athens. He has no real authority over these early goddesses of the Underworld, old but childlike, shunned by all. No amount of grandstanding on Apollo's part changes the relevant truth: this lull in their momentum is temporary, and even the fact that Orestes was following divine orders makes no difference to them. The Furies decide who is guilty, and they can't just be overruled by Apollo or anyone else.

Apollo sends Orestes on his way, with Hermes to escort him. We might wonder what chance a man would stand against these Furies without two sons of Zeus to offer him their support. But we scarcely have time to dwell on that thought, because the Furies are about to have an abrupt awakening. The ghost of Clytemnestra rises up to berate them for napping on the job.

I hope you're having a good sleep, she says. Who needs sleepers? It's because of you that I'm dishonoured among the dead. The people I killed never stop rebuking me. I wander around in disgrace. I tell you, they're always accusing me. But I suffered at the hands of my beloveds, yet no deity is raging on my behalf, even though I was murdered by a mother-killer.

She complains as the Furies sleep on, showing them the wounds on her body. She is outraged that Orestes has escaped their clutches, even though she made plenty of offerings to the Furies in the past. His friends are clearly better than mine, she says. The Furies murmur in their sleep and Clytemnestra's ghost keeps haranguing them. Hypnos has overpowered these terrible snake-women, she cries. And finally, the exhausted Furies wake up. They are angry and embarrassed to have been shown up by a younger god. They turn their rage on Apollo, calling him *panaitios* – completely responsible – for Orestes's crime of matricide, which they are now avenging.[12] Apollo hits back: What about when a wife kills her husband?

In his mind, Clytemnestra has waived her rights to be treated well (or at least not murdered) by her son when she killed Agamemnon: one intrafamilial crime deserves another. But for the Furies, there is a crucial distinction between these two killings, because Clytemnestra wasn't murdered by someone *homaimos* – of the same blood.[13] Oh I see, Apollo responds, so you've no respect for the bond between Hera and Zeus? The Furies don't reply to this, but I feel that is because it's beneath them. Nice try, Apollo, but Hera and Zeus are siblings as well as wife and husband, so murder of one by the other actually would be a killing by someone of the same blood. The Furies instead remind Apollo that they are drawn to pursue Orestes by his mother's blood, and they leave the stage to continue their task. Apollo reiterates his commitment to help Orestes, but it's hard to know who you would back in a fight between these opposing forces.

In the way of Greek tragedy – where all the action tends to be squashed into a single day – Orestes now appears at the shrine of Athene in Athens, hugging her statue as instructed by Apollo. The Furies follow close on his heels, out of breath but never far behind their target. They are delighted to have caught up with him, declaring that the smell of human blood makes them smile.[14] They begin taunting Orestes, hurling threats at him for the wrongs he has done. He prays to Athene to come and help him. The Furies don't think Athene or Apollo can do much for him now, and they begin their terrible dance, showing off their *mousan stugeran* – hateful song.[15] They are indeed dark sisters to the Muses, and their song is loathsome, rather than pretty. They remind us that they only persecute those who've committed crimes. If your hands are clean (metaphorically, rather than literally, though I'm sure they'd appreciate both), you have nothing to fear from them. They describe their song as *aphormiktos* – unaccompanied by the lyre.[16] This has a dual meaning: it makes us think of a tuneless piece of music, a dirge. But it also reminds us that the Furies have shunned Apollo and his role in Orestes's matricide. He is the god with the lyre, linked with those Muses from the first chapter. So singing and dancing without such an accompaniment is a rejection, perhaps even a provocation on their part, of all his values. I find myself assuming they are singing off-key, just to spite him and his refined musical sensibilities.

The Furies know no one likes them, they know the other gods shun them, and it makes no difference to them at all. They are monomaniacal, even by the standards of Greek gods: they have their set task – punishing crimes within the family – and they will not waver from it. It's interesting that they are so self-aware about their unpopularity. And yet most of us would surely want to think that if someone we loved was murdered, the killer wouldn't just be able to talk himself out of things by saying a god told him to do it. The Furies are unlikeable, but perhaps they are necessary if we are to maintain a just society: murderers must be punished; good people can walk free.

They begin to close in on Orestes, but they are stopped in their tracks by the arrival of Athene, summoned by Orestes's prayer before the Furies began their song.

She declares herself unafraid of this new gang here on her land, but she isn't rude to them, as Apollo was. Instead, she says her eyes are filled with wonder.[17] Who are you? she asks. I'm speaking to you all here.

The Furies reply as a group: We are the endless children of Night, known as Curses in our home beneath the ground . . . We drive murderers from their homes.

And for the killer, asks Athene, what is the end point of his flight?

This crucial question is at the heart of the play. No one disputes that Orestes killed Clytemnestra. Orestes may want Apollo to take the blame, but he knows that he is the target of the Furies because he himself has done something terrible. And while the Furies have already told Apollo that they consider the god fully responsible for the murder of Clytemnestra, it doesn't at all affect how they treat Orestes. The contentious issue here isn't who did what, but what the fair punishment is for the guilty man. It is typical of Athene to cut straight to it: Okay, you chase him from his home, but then what? What happens when he reaches his limit and can't run any further?

The end point is a place without joy, the Furies respond. They mean this psychologically rather than geographically: they would drive him to a state where he took his own life. And you'd harangue him till he reached this point? Athene offers a fascinating contrast with the other characters who have witnessed the Furies so far in the play: the Pythia, Apollo, Orestes. She doesn't express disgust, she's not afraid, she's simply interested, asking for information in a calm, lawyerly way.

He deserves it, they reply. He murdered his mother.

Was he forced into doing it, she asks, from fear of someone's rage or something else?

What could spur someone on to kill their own mother?

Two sides are here, says Athene. But only one half of the argument.

Then question him, the Furies suggest, and make a fair judgement.

You're willing to turn the decision over to me?

Why not? We honour you.[18]

Athene turns to Orestes and asks if he is also happy for her to decide what should happen to him. Orestes gives a brief summary of his position: that his mother murdered his father, that he therefore murdered his mother in requital for that killing.[19] Apollo is also to blame, he adds, because he threatened me with pain (literally 'a goad to my heart') if I didn't act against the guilty parties. So yes, you can be my judge.

But Athene makes an extraordinary decision. Faced with such a profound ethical dilemma – to ignore the Furies and incur their wrath against all of Athens, or to disregard the pleas of a suppliant – she hands over the decision to a jury of Athenian men. The Furies are somewhat peeved about this change, but they are convinced by the rightness of their argument, which is, in essence, that if you don't murder your parents you won't end up in the state Orestes has found himself in. Be just willingly and without compulsion, they say, and you won't be unhappy.[20]

But the trial is about to begin. It isn't quite the format of a trial we might expect, since Apollo turns up as a witness and the Furies question Orestes directly.

Did you kill your mother?

Yes.

How?

Sword to the throat.

Who persuaded you?

This god (Apollo) is my witness.

He told you to kill your mother?

Yes. And my father will protect me from his grave.

What about your dead mother?

She was doubly polluted – she killed her husband and my father.

Why didn't you chase her?

She didn't murder someone of the same blood.

The Furies are absolutists. But then, Orestes doesn't have to persuade them; he has to persuade the jury of his peers. He calls on Apollo to give evidence in his favour. And Apollo stands up and makes his case: I never lie, I'm the oracular god, and I never say anything Zeus doesn't agree with. And I say that a great warrior was killed by a woman with deceit, and so killing her was nowhere near as bad as what she did when she killed Agamemnon.

Oh, does Zeus prefer fathers? The Furies are astonished. Didn't he bind his own father, aged Kronos? Doesn't that imply the opposite of what you're saying? I hope you're listening, jurors.[21]

Apollo behaves in the time-honoured way of powerful men being contradicted by women to whom they aren't attracted: You all-hateful monsters, loathed by the gods! Zeus could untie his father, but once a mortal man is dead he can't be brought back to life.

But two can play at the game of practicalities. Fine, say the Furies. So having spilled his mother's blood, where do you think this man should live? In his father's house? Is he going to use the public altars?

Their argument is that Orestes is unclean, polluted by his crime, even if Apollo and Athene think otherwise. How will his fellow Argives respond to him if he goes back to the place where he spilled his own mother's blood on the ground? How would he not be profaning their altars when he made his offerings? Apollo can't give them a good answer to this question, so he changes the terms they're debating.

Mothers aren't really parents, anyway; it's fathers that matter. Look at Athene – she doesn't even have a mother, just a father, Zeus. So fathers are more important than mothers, case closed.

Athene now directs the jury to vote. She seems keen again to stress the importance of the role the Furies play and to sympathize with the points they have raised. If clear water is tainted by filth, she tells the jurors, you'll never find a drink.[22] It's advice we might all do well to remember next time someone tells us that, for example, a certain amount of corruption in politics is to be expected. Unlike Apollo, Athene can see that the Furies are necessary in a functioning society. Don't drive fear completely out of the city, she says. Because which mortal is just if he doesn't fear anything?

Apollo and the Furies continue to snipe at one another while the judging takes place. He threatens them; they threaten the city. Only when the jurors have all voted does Athene reveal her position. Her vote goes to Orestes, and for precisely the reason Apollo suggested earlier. She was born without a mother, so in everything except marriage she is on the man's side, and wholeheartedly in favour of the father.[23] She won't value a wife who killed her husband more highly than him, the guardian of the house. So Orestes will win, even if the vote is split equally.

And moments later, the votes are counted and they are indeed equal. Athene has already expressed her preference, so Orestes is free to go. He leaves, as does Apollo. The Furies are devastated.

Oh! You younger gods! You have ridden roughshod over the ancient laws, snatched them from my hands. I am dishonoured, miserable, deeply angered . . . I'll release poison in exchange for this grief . . . They promise to poison the very land itself, to make it barren, to destroy the mortals who live there. I am laughed at by your citizens, one declares. And if we know anything from Greek tragedy, it's that you cannot ignore the pain of a character who feels they have been mocked. They will turn their humiliation outwards (Medea) or inwards (Ajax), but devastation will inevitably follow. The daughters of Night name the emotion they are experiencing: sorrow for their dishonour.[24]

There's a reason why they begin by denouncing the gods who they feel have disparaged them – Apollo and Athene – as younger. The Furies are indeed from an earlier generation of gods, but there's more to their complaint than mere age. It's not just that they have been overruled by younger gods, it's that their values – the values on which society has been predicated until now – are being declared irrelevant. This moment in the play – where Athene swings behind Orestes and the verdict is declared in his favour – is also a profound moment in the development of society, of what it means to live by the law.

In the past, the time the Furies represent, people were expected to obey laws because those laws were immutable and unarguable. Most societies agree that it is wrong, unnatural even, to kill a parent. And there is a universality to some beliefs that exceed other, more culturally specific ones. The Furies are advancing similar values to those we find across other ancient societies, as we can see in the Hebrew Bible: honour your father and mother; don't commit murder. And these are values we expect to see in place in modern societies too. We might think of them as natural laws, in contrast to less universal ones, which we usually think of as customs or mores. So we might expect laws around marriage to be specific to one country's legal system – deciding who you can marry, and where, and from what age. These might change as society changes, as has happened with equal marriage legislation, for example.

Societies struggle to thrive unless a majority of individuals subscribe to the same values. And while customs can and should change, some values – those the Furies defend – are less adjustable. Most of us agree – and have agreed for millennia – that not killing our parents is the right course of action, and that this is the kind of society that we (and perhaps more pertinently, our parents) want.

So how do we police those who don't subscribe to those unchanging values, or who usually do but then suddenly commit an act of great violence, like Orestes? Under the laws that the Furies represent, we deem that person unclean, we hound them out of society with banishment or death, we accept their suicide as the appropriate penalty, the price they must pay for offending the gods who are part of the fabric of our lives. The price for such a transgression is the banishment or death of the transgressor.

And as a way of maintaining social cohesion, this worked reasonably well for a long time. But problems arise when – as happens with the house of Atreus – you have a tiny pool of individuals who cannot help but injure one another with regard to these natural laws. So once Agamemnon has killed Iphigenia – his own daughter – his wife Clytemnestra feels that the gods and the laws support her view of the matter: he is a murderer and so deserves to die. She kills him accordingly. But then her surviving children, Electra and Orestes, are left in an impossible bind. Leave their mother to live her life, and they are betraying their dead father. The values of their society demand that a murdered man's surviving relatives, especially his adult son, take vengeance on his killers. But to do that, Orestes and Electra must break another equally strong law: one which says it is always morally wrong to kill your own mother.

The Furies see no contradiction here: murdering a blood relative is always indefensible and must result in the death of the perpetrator. So by their rationale, Agamemnon is guilty and so is Orestes. Clytemnestra can be viewed as the human embodiment of the values the Furies uphold. If that means that she loses her life to her son, so be it. As we see from her agitated ghost, she believes Orestes should also die and then the problem comes to a belated and bloody end.

But the patriarchal values advanced by Apollo and Athene – that Agamemnon's life is worth more than Clytemnestra's because he was a heroic murderous man and she was a villainous murderous woman – clash with this. Apollo and Athene are advocating the idea that not every murderer is equally guilty, that not all murders are equal because not all people are equal. In order to defend their position – men's lives are worth more than women's – they have to reject a law of nature even more absolute than one that says murdering parents is wrong. Their defence of Orestes rests on the argument that Clytemnestra isn't the true parent of her children. In order to save the young man from the absolutism of the Furies, they don't just ask for clemency in this particular case. They deny that mothers are parents at all. Most of us would find this intellectually suspect, quite aside from its dubious morality. It would certainly raise the eyebrows of a biologist.[25] But still they win.

And while this specific case, and the way in which Apollo defends and Athene decides, might raise our hackles – it certainly does mine – it marks a moment when the world changes for the better. Because even if I don't like their argument, I also don't want to live in a world where the Furies' values aren't even questioned. I don't agree that Orestes was justified and I don't agree that Clytemnestra isn't a true parent. But I can easily imagine a case where I would think killing a parent was morally justifiable: an abused child might kill an abusive parent to prevent them from abusing a younger sibling, for example. I think I'd probably view this as manslaughter rather than murder.

We are better off living in a world in which murderers are tried by a jury than deemed impure and driven to suicide. Divine embodiments of curses called down by the victims of unspeakable crimes offer a kind of justice, but in its bluntest, blindest sense. The survivors of a murdered relative will always be angry and distraught at what they have lost, and how; expecting them to administer justice – rather than vengeance – is not a reasonable request. They deserve us to lift that particular burden from them, and do so within a framework of just laws. We can complain about the times juries decide cases in a way we believe is wrong, but this is what came before that. So though I loathe Agamemnon, and sympathize deeply with Clytemnestra, I abide by the decision of the court: Orestes should go free.

So the Furies are upset not just because they have been overruled by newer gods, but because the very system of laws they defend is being relegated to the past. Society will take on the role of administering justice from now on. But still Athene is quick to try and soothe their wounded feelings. You didn't lose, she says. The votes were equal, you suffered no dishonour. It's just that we had the clear testimony of Zeus (via Apollo) that Orestes shouldn't suffer harm for his deeds. So please don't be angry, and don't punish my land: we'll build you a sanctuary, you'll receive plenty of honour.[26]

The Furies are still angry, still convinced they have been deceived and dishonoured. I have a pain in my ribs, they say, where we might say our heart aches.[27]

I will live with your anger, Athene replies. For you are older than me, and in that you are probably wiser than me. But Zeus gave me no little wisdom myself.[28] She asks them again to stay and be persuaded to let go of their rage.

It seems you have persuaded me. The Furies finally concede that they will let go of their destructive wrath.[29] And then they agree that they will accept a home in Athens, and not drip poison onto the land that they are now making their home. In fact, they will pray earnestly for Athens to have good fortune. They go on to issue prayers that Athens could probably do with today, in these times of extreme weather events: I wish for no trees to come to harm from strong winds, I wish that no buds will be lost to searing heat, I wish that no blight will leave the plants barren, I wish the flocks will thrive and have twins, I wish you an earth that is rich (a reference to the silver mines near Athens).

Athene accepts all these blessings on behalf of her Athenians, and the Furies continue to offer kind prayers for good fortune and curses to ward off bad luck. Athene gives credit to the goddess Persuasion for helping her to craft a successful plea for their goodwill. When she addresses the Furies, Athene now calls them *euphronas* – the kind ones.[30] And so this is how the terrifying creatures called the Erinyes acquire a new reputation for kindness, which gives this play its title: *Eumenides*, or Kindly Ones.

Perhaps they always had the potential for kindness, but didn't have much of an opportunity to demonstrate it. When Orpheus descends to the Underworld, as told by Ovid in the *Metamorphoses*, he sings a lament for his lost Eurydice so beautiful that the torments of those suffering eternal punishment come to a halt: Ixion's wheel stops spinning; Sisyphus is able to pause and sit on the rock he is usually compelled to push uphill. And then – for the first time – overcome by his song, the cheeks of the Eumenides are soaked with tears.[31] I always love this moment in Ovid, the idea that even endless torment can be alleviated by the most beautiful music. And there is something especially lovely about the Furies breaking down in tears at the sound of this man's shattered heart. We think of them as monstrous, certainly at this point in their story, which is earlier than the time of Orestes and their official conversion to kindness. But here they are in the Underworld – terrifying, persecuting daughters of Night – reduced to tears by a sad song.

It's obviously good news for Orestes, and for Athens, that the forces of punishment can be allayed by a smooth-talking goddess and her persuasive charms. But it might be less good news for those who call on the Furies to carry out their vengeance on wrongdoers, not all of whom would find such keen law enforcers in a civic court. The Furies were responsible for more than intrafamilial murder. So let's examine their roles in some other myths before we commit ourselves to the idea that kindly goddesses are always better than terrifying ones.

In addition to their role as avengers, the Furies were guardians of oaths and suppliants. So, for example, Pausanias recounts the story of a place called Helike, a city-state in the northern Peloponnese.[32] The Helikonians are approached by suppliants who make their way to the local temple of Poseidon. The Helikonians disregard the protection that is granted to ritual suppliants, and instead remove them from the temple and murder them. The gods' wrath is swift and lethal. First Helike is hit by a series of earthquakes, and then it is drowned by a tsunami. Pausanias quotes four lines of verse that Zeus apparently sent to Athens reminding them that supplication is holy and pure. He makes a particular mention of the incense burning on the altars of Eumenides so the Athenians remember to treat their suppliants with the respect they deserve. Ancient writers from Homer to Apollonius of Rhodes note that those who swear oaths often include the Furies when they make their pledges.[33] Break your oath and the Erinyes will find a way to punish you. It should scarcely need saying that you would be better off keeping your promises.

As we saw with the ghost of Clytemnestra in the *Eumenides*, the Furies often respond to a curse issued by a mortal being, dead or alive. But not every mortal's curse has quite the same moral weight as Clytemnestra's. Homer also shares the story of Amyntor and Phoinix, in Book Nine of the *Iliad*. Phoinix has come to reason with Achilles and plead with him to come back to fighting in the Trojan War (from which Achilles withdrew eight books earlier, in response to a slight from Agamemnon). He reminisces about the time he first left Hellas – Greece – as a young man. His father Amyntor was having a sexual relationship with a *pallakis*. This word used to be translated as 'concubine', and is now sometimes rendered 'mistress', but either of these implies consent where there may well have been none: someone might become a concubine because she was a slave or a woman captured in war, which rarely afforded her the right of refusal to a Greek king.

Because these sorts of arrangements were commonplace in the ancient world – in both literature and reality – it is easy to assume that the wives of kings and other wealthy men didn't mind. But Amyntor's wife is furious about his behaviour. And, in Phoinix's words, Amyntor dishonours his wife.[34] So obviously some people took exception to men who wanted multiple sexual partners. Phoinix then says that his mother kept begging him on her knees to have sex with the *pallakis* himself so that – having enjoyed a younger lover – the object of Amyntor's affections would soon despise the old man.

There's so much packed into that sentence that it makes me long for a lost Sophoclean tragedy to turn up in a box of Egyptian papyri.

Phoinix and his mother discussing his father's infidelity. His mother on her knees pleading with her son to have sex with the woman in question. The certainty on her part that sex with her son would cause this woman to repudiate the older man. The following line – I obeyed her and did it; my father immediately knew – only adds to the sense we're missing out on quite the drama. Phoinix continues: My father cursed me many times and called on the loathsome Erinyes, praying that he would never put on his knees a beloved son of mine. Did I say one play? It might take a trilogy.

Perhaps you are thinking – as I admit I am – that the Furies must have quite a few more worthy targets to pursue than Phoinix, and indeed that they might not even consider such a petulant request from a man who has dishonoured his own wife (the word in Greek is the same as the one used by the Furies to describe their treatment at the hands of Apollo and Athene in the *Eumenides*). But the gods fulfilled his curse, Phoinix says – both Zeus of the Underworld (a poetic way of saying Hades) and Persephone.

So even though Amyntor has suffered no life-ending trauma – like Clytemnestra – nor even a life-changing one, the gods still hear his cries for vengeance. The Furies don't pursue Phoinix, although he admits to murderous thoughts about his father. But he is forced to flee his homeland anyway, because he knows that if he stays he will kill Amyntor and become precisely the kind of familial murderer they do pursue. And the gods – the Furies, Hades, Persephone – still carry out Amyntor's wish: Phoinix never has a child of his own.

And this is not the only example of a parent cursing their own child that Phoinix cites in this speech to Achilles, where he tries to appeal to the immovable hero by reminding him of their quasi father-son relationship. He continues by telling the story of Meleager, who – you may remember from the chapter on Artemis – was the hero jointly responsible for killing the giant boar sent to ravage the land of Calydon.

Amid his other heroic deeds, Meleager kills the brother of his mother Althaia. She is so devastated by this loss that she prays to Hades and dread Persephone, pounding on the ground over and over again, weeping and asking the gods to send death to her child. The Fury who walks in darkness heard her from the depths of Erebus, and her heart is implacable.[35] Meleager is so angered by his mother's curses that – just like Achilles – he withdraws from fighting, even to save his own besieged city. His people plead with him to rejoin the battle before the city is overrun, offering him huge rewards. At the very last minute he returns to fight and saves the city—though he never receives the promised gifts, so this perhaps isn't the best example Phoinix might have chosen to sway Achilles, a man the Greeks are currently trying to bribe with gifts to return to the battlefield.

Later authors like Pausanias and Hyginus follow this account from Homer.[36] Pausanias says Meleager died because the Fury heard Althaia's curses, and Hyginus includes Althaia in a list of mothers who kill their sons. The message about the Furies seems pretty clear: if one family member curses another – for a variety of intrafamilial wrongdoing – the Furies enact these curses somehow.

But if the narrative sources depict a relentless focus on vengeance by these dread goddesses, vase paintings of the Furies show a more varied picture. The British Museum has a red-figure bell krater from the fourth century BCE, made in Paestum in South Italy. It shows Orestes at Delphi being purified by Apollo as the Furies look on. It is tempting to read this vase as representing all the scenes in the *Eumenides* in a single location. Apollo stands on the right, Athene on the left. Orestes kneels in supplication between them, staring up at Athene. Immediately behind him is an ornate golden tripod – a famous feature of Apollo's shrine at Delphi. The Pythian priestess used to sit on it to deliver her oracular pronouncements, although on this occasion she is absent. She has perhaps been scared away from her usual seat because a Fury has just rushed in at the back of the scene: she almost seems to hover above and behind the tripod, which blocks our view of her lower body. Her expression is calm, but her hair streams out behind her as though she is moving at speed. Snakes are coiling round her right arm and her temples and springing up from her shoulders. Behind her, perhaps urging her on (as in Aeschylus), the ghost of Clytemnestra lurks in the top left corner of the image. No wonder Orestes looks so plaintively at Athene. Is she still his judge here, although we're in Delphi rather than Athens? It certainly looks that way. Her left foot is raised, resting on a small column. It gives the impression of someone adopting a defensive stance, as though she's trying to protect Orestes from the Fury behind them both.

As for Apollo on the right, he is wreathed in laurel leaves, and larger branches of laurel are springing up behind him. He stands with his weight on his right leg, his left leg extended in front of him. Again, it gives the impression of a defensive posture: Orestes is almost imprisoned by these gods. Except they are the ones keeping him safe from the Furies and the ghost of his mother. Apollo is looking away from his sister and Orestes, down and to his left at a second Fury. With his left hand, he fingers a long, slender laurel branch: it looks suspiciously like a club. But the Fury who stands to his left doesn't look nervous at all. She holds his gaze calmly. She has not been rushing around like her sister. She stands quite still, weight on her left foot, right foot lifted, tilting at an awkward angle. Apollo called them all kinds of names in the play, and one of his accusations was that they were both ancient and childlike, a combination he clearly found distasteful. This one – with her turned foot in laced mid-calf boots and her thousand-yard stare – looks every inch the bored teen wearing her Doc Martens. She may be shorter than Apollo, but the feathers on her upright wings tower over him. One small snake slithers along her hairline, and a large snake rears up from her left shoulder; it stares straight into Apollo's eyes. It's hard to imagine anyone could look less impressed or intimidated by an Olympian god in his own place of worship.[37]

And this is not the only vase to depict the Furies looking far from monstrous and indeed far from in a hurry. There is a red-figure vase attributed to the Suessula Painter, held in the Staatliche Museum in Berlin. It's from the mid-fourth century BCE and shows Prometheus bound to a rock (although for some reason the rock looks like the kind of glitzy archway you might find at the side of a cabaret stage, which gives the whole thing quite a disco feel. Perhaps appropriately, since Heracles has arrived to free him from his agonies – there could surely be no better time for the two of them to belt out a show tune). The liver-eating eagle falls away beneath him, while below him and to his right sits a Fury. Her wings are spread wide, and one snake moves in a desultory way across the top of her head. Her expression is mild and quizzical. Perhaps she always looks like this in the Underworld, comfortable and at ease because all the wrongdoers are being punished as they deserve. She has a pair of spears on her lap, the points resting on the ground beneath her. Her hand is only lightly grasping them; her purpose is not to use them but to stop them clattering to the floor. A large white flower has sprung up beside her seat, as though hoping to impress her. I don't suppose Disney will ever make a Furies cartoon, but their princess is right here.[38]

There is a similarly casual pair of Furies on a krater held in the Badisches Landesmuseum in Karlsruhe, again from the mid-fourth century.[39] This painting is also set in the Underworld, so again the Furies are not mid-pursuit. One is sitting on what looks like a stool covered in a sheepskin, leaning back a little, legs stretched out in front of her, crossed below the knee. She is also wearing the lace-up mid-calf boot, as well as a belted knee-length dress and a glittering necklace. A couple of small snakes writhe around her head, and one is twirling around her left forearm and hand. Unusually for a Fury, she doesn't have wings. Her winged sister is standing beside her, same boots, crossed legs: the toes of her left foot are touching the side of her right foot. She's also wearing a knee-length dress, with a simple leafy design around the skirt. Her dress has a more ornate bodice; there are ribbons crossing her chest and a studded belt. She wears a matching necklace, and a snake or two move comfortably through her curly hair, while another encircles her left arm. Her right hand rests on her sister's knee: they look utterly relaxed, sisters putting the world to rights. Or maybe they'll do that in a minute, when they've finished having this chat.

And they are poised for action relative to that of the three Furies we see on a krater in the Louvre from the early fourth century, by the Eumenides painter.[40] This wonderful image depicts Orestes in the act of being purified by Apollo, who dangles a piglet above his head, all ready for sacrifice, we may presume (neither Orestes nor the pig looks delighted about this). Orestes and Apollo are in the foreground, and just behind them, to our left, are the Furies, who have pursued Orestes to this point. One sits with her head resting on her hand, obviously exhausted. The second Fury sits in front of her, lying back onto her, her head resting against her sister's breast, left arm lolling over her sister's left leg. It's hard work pursuing a murderer, it seems.

Intergenerational conflict is a recurring theme in Greek myth, but it's not always as absolute as the case of Orestes and Clytemnestra. In the second book of the *Odyssey*, Telemachus has been trying to persuade his mother's many suitors to leave their house and give up their claims to marry Penelope. Antinous – the most outspoken and obnoxious of these suitors – refuses to leave and threatens only worse behaviour on the part of all the young men if Penelope doesn't do what they want and choose one of them as her next husband. If Telemachus wants them to move out of his house and stop eating and drinking their way through his wealth, he should chuck his mother out, and then her father can let her marry again.

Telemachus offers as an interesting response: Antinous, it's not possible for me to turn my mother out of her own home if she doesn't want to go. She gave birth to me, she raised me. My father is in another country, dead or alive – who knows?

So the opening part of this speech provides the opposite set of familial values to the ones we saw Apollo and Athene espouse. Telemachus may be frustrated with his mother, but he cannot pretend that she is anything but his mother, and indeed his only parent in all practical terms. His father is absent, has always been absent, and may not even be alive. There is no sleight of hand about what constitutes a parent here.

He continues: Penelope's father Icarius would exact a penalty from his grandson if he threw his mother out. But that is only part of the problem he would face. The gods would also punish him, because his mother would pray to the hated Erinyes if she was thrown out of her home. And everyone would say I deserved it.[41]

We know that – thanks to the machinations of Athene – Telemachus will soon set sail for Pylos, and the urgency of dealing with the ever-present suitors will slip away. But it is a fascinating insight into the breadth of the role the Furies played in the Bronze Age society of Greek myth. No one has been murdered (yet) in the palace of Ithaca, and Telemachus is sick of the suitors and exasperated with his mother. But it is fear – not of his mother herself but of the Furies she could summon – that prevents Telemachus behaving badly. He isn't moved by love or kindness to treat his mother with respect, at least not in this moment. He's intimidated into it by the thought of the primeval vengeance goddesses she would rightfully be able to set on his trail. Perhaps an Athenian law court might have found in Penelope's favour, if his mother had brought a case of forcible eviction against him. But by the mere fact of their existence, the Furies prevent a crime – or, at the very least, antisocial behaviour – from occurring.

So while the Furies might incur fear, disgust, hatred, and more – from gods and mortals alike – it is too easy to dismiss them as a negative force, even if Apollo or Orestes might feel that way about them. They serve a crucial role in society before the creation of formalized legal proceedings for ensuring that people maintained a civilized moral code.

Sometimes that was as basic as not committing murder, but it was also a way of protecting oaths and promises in a time before mass literacy. If you swear that you won't harm someone but then later disregard your promise, shouldn't there be someone who can hold you to account? Just because there is no paperwork to prove it doesn't mean that we can – or should – all just forget what was said in the past. We live in a time when it is commonplace to see a politician reverse their position and then simply deny they ever said anything that contradicts their current position. It is a particularly egregious form of lying because it leaves the listener not only uncertain of the truth now, but unsure of whether they had ever grasped it. It's bad enough to be a liar; it is worse to try to persuade people that their memories or understanding are at fault. And although we do now have recorded evidence of their former assertions and their sudden switches in stance, it doesn't always have the effect it once did. Primarily, I think, because too many people have been emboldened to simply lie and keep lying, to deny the truth, to deny the past, to deny the collective memory of those they are supposed to serve. And so I find myself thinking that of all the goddesses in this book, the Furies – not in their role of vengeance goddesses but in the sense of collective, societal shame that they also personify, shame at breaking your word or behaving cruelly and dishonestly – might be the ones I would most like to see restored to a modern pantheon.

ACKNOWLEDGMENTS

THIS BOOK exists because George Morley learned nothing from working with me before, and because Peter Straus never tires of taking care of me. Dream editor, dream agent: never leave me, please. Pan Macmillan is packed with people who work like demons (which is lucky, because that's how I work too). Huge thanks to Elle for her tireless marketing smarts, to Ami for the gorgeous jacket, to Emma for the publicity, and to Lydia for being the ideal audio producer, to everyone who helped make this a book in very little time. I honestly did write it as fast as I could. Additional thanks to Sarah Stein, David Howe, and the whole team at Harper for racing this into production in the US; they have worked so hard to reduce the time lag between publication dates and (given how often I reply to emails) this was a superhuman effort.

A million thanks to Roslynne Bell for checking my art (and so much more – I am sorry about every comma); to Paul Cartledge for his generous knowledge, and for telling me where everything is and how big; to Patrick O'Sullivan for maintaining his 100 percent track record for noticing the mistake everyone had missed. Thank you to Tim Whitmarsh for not saying no, even when he's busy. Never change, Professor.

Thanks to all the classicists and other geeks who told me their favourite versions of these goddesses as I went along – I loved them all, and learned heaps. Among many excellent nerds who helped me formulate my thoughts and arguments, special thanks go to – as often – Adam Rutherford and Andrew Copson. The Cypriot women make me stronger every time we speak – Magdalena Zira took me to Paphos to see Aphrodite's birthplace, Nedie Antoniades organizes us all and gives her voice to my characters as I write them, Athina Kasiou is a warrior like her name-sake.

It always needs saying: without Pauline Lord the wheels would have come off this machine long ago. Thanks, Pauline, for always knowing where I am supposed to be and when, and for only telling me when there is a fighting chance I'll remember it. Christian Hill is still running the website, even while he writes books on subjects I cannot begin to understand: thank you for making time for me for decades (let's not discuss how many decades). Matilda McMorrow is my cheerleader, my partner in crime, my social whirlwind: I'd be lost without you.

Thank you to Mary Ward-Lowery and everyone at Radio 4 who helps us to make *NHSUftC*. It is a vast undertaking (even though it sounds like I'm making it up as I go along) and I couldn't write a book and make a series in fifty-four weeks without a lot of patience and encouragement, not to mention the inverse albatrosses.

Dan Mersh is my first reader, and there is none better. He's a miracle, and I am luckier than I can say that he is still here for me after so long.

Thanks to Helen Bagnall for being a towering mouse of a friend, to Philippa Perry for looking after me always, to Helen and Lottie for taking me out for cake and ice cream when I'm climbing the walls. To Heather, who I know is crying right now, for listening always. To the dojo gang – especially Jo, Carey, Sam, Adam, and of course the Friday night goddesses – your patience is exemplary, and my life is a zillion times better for having you in it. Better again for the fact that even though you could all pummel me, you mostly don't.

Love and thanks to my family – my parents, to whom this is dedicated; to Chris, Gem and the divine and mighty Kez.

NOTES

INTRODUCTION
1. https://www.comics.org/issue/293/
2. https://www.comics.org/issue/442/
3. https://www.dcuniverseinfinite.com/comics/book/all-star-comics-8/41e93b73
   -6471-4828-926b-c07728ab2976
4. https://theamericanscholar.org/wonder-woman/

THE MUSES
1. Hesiod, *Theogony* 1ff
2. Ibid 8
3. Ibid 21
4. Ibid 27–8
5. Pseudo-Apollodorus, *Bibliotheca* 3.5.8
6. Ibid 54
7. Plato, *Phaedrus* 274e ff
8. Hesiod, *Theogony* 60
9. Homer, *Iliad* 2.485
10. Homer, *Odyssey* 24.36ff
11. Hesiod, *Theogony* 77ff
12. Ibid 82, 93
13. Homer, *Iliad* 2.594ff
14. Pseudo-Apollodorus, *Bibliotheca* 1.3.3
15. Homer, *Odyssey* 21.72ff
16. Athenaeus 1.20e–f, Wright, *Lost Plays of Greek Tragedy* Vol. 2, pp. 94–5
17. Eustathius *ad Hom* p. 85
18. Ovid, *Metamorphoses* 5.272
19. Ibid 5.288
20. Ibid 5.300ff
21. Pindar, *Pythian Ode* 1.1
22. Ovid, *Metamorphoses* 5.315

23. Ibid 5.526
24. Ibid 5.664
25. https://www.theparisreview.org/blog/2017/11/09/how-picasso-bled-the -women-in-his-life-for-art/
26. Grace Nichols, *Picasso, I Want My Face Back*, 14
27. Antipater of Sidon, *AP* 9.66

HERA

1. Aelian, *De Natura Animalium* 5.21
2. Aristotle, *Historia Animalium* 6.9
3. Aristophanes, *The Birds* 269
4. Ovid, *Metamorphoses* 1.584
5. Ibid 1.588
6. Ibid 1.599
7. Ibid 1.605
8. Ibid 1.611
9. Ibid 1.624
10. Ibid 1.638
11. Ibid 1.719–20
12. *Suda* A 2735
13. Antiphanes, quoted in Athenaeus, *Deipnosophistae* 655b
14. Homer, *Iliad* 14.201, Ovid, *Metamorphoses* 2.527, Pseudo-Hyginus, *Fabulae* 177
15. Pausanias, *Description of Greece* 2.13
16. Ibid 2.17.4
17. Hesiod, *Theogony* 886
18. Ibid 921
19. Pausanias, *Description of Greece* 2.17.5
20. Scholion of Theocritus, *Idylls* 15.64
21. Homer, *Iliad* 14.296
22. Callimachus, *Aetia* Fragment 48
23. Homer, *Iliad* 14.197, 14.300
24. Ibid 24.28–30
25. Ibid 24.55ff
26. Ibid 24.101–2
27. Ibid 14.315ff
28. Pseudo-Apollodorus, *Bibliotheca* 3.6
29. Hesiod, *Theogony* 925ff
30. Pausanias, *Description of Greece* 1.20.3

31. Pseudo-Apollodorus, *Bibliotheca* 3.9
32. Callimachus, *Hymn* 4.55
33. Pseudo-Apollodorus, *Bibliotheca* 3.4.3
34. Ibid 3.5
35. Ovid, *Metamorphoses* 9.273ff
36. Pseudo-Apollodorus, *Bibliotheca* 2.4
37. Ibid 1.3
38. Homer, *Iliad* 1.593
39. Ibid 1.539
40. Ibid 1.560
41. Ibid 1.568–70
42. Pseudo-Apollodorus, *Epitome* 1.20
43. Pindar, *Pythian Ode* 2.28
44. Ibid 40
45. Rick Riordan, *Percy Jackson and the Battle of the Labyrinth*, UK pb edition p. 99
46. Euripides, *Medea* 242
47. https://web.archive.org/web/20200426125459/https://www.nasa.gov/mission _pages/juno/news/juno20110805.html
48. https://www.nasa.gov/mission_pages/juno/news/lego20110803.html

APHRODITE

1. https://www.uffizi.it/en/artworks/birth-of-venus
2. Pliny the Elder, *Natural History* 36.4
3. *Greek Anthology* 16.160
4. https://www.facebook.com/watch/?v=143250314225629
5. *Homeric Hymn to Aphrodite* 5.70–1
6. Ibid 5.66
7. Homer, *Iliad* 5.370ff
8. Hesiod, *Theogony* 190ff
9. Ibid 196
10. Sappho, 1
11. *Homeric Hymn*, 5.45
12. Ibid 5.65
13. Ibid 5.77
14. Ibid 5.82–3
15. Ibid 5.109
16. Ibid 5.154
17. Ibid 5.167

18. Ibid 5.183
19. Ibid 5.248
20. Sophocles, *Laocoon* F373 (see Wright, Vol. 2, p. 100)
21. Homer, *Iliad* 5.299
22. Ibid 5.330–1
23. Pseudo-Apollodorus, *Epitome* 6
24. Homer, *Odyssey* 8.266ff
25. Ibid 8.302
26. Ibid 8.366
27. Ovid, *Metamorphoses* 10.503–739
28. Ibid 10.515
29. Ibid 10.529
30. Ibid 10.531
31. Ibid 10.565
32. Ibid 10.579
33. Ibid 10.683

ARTEMIS

1. Homer, *Iliad* 24.607
2. Ibid 24.611
3. https://journals.openedition.org/acost/2354
4. https://www.britishmuseum.org/collection/term/BIOG57040
5. *Anth. Pal.* 6, 280. For more, see 'Jointed Dolls in Antiquity', Kate McElderkin, *American Journal of Archaeology*, Vol. 34, No. 4
6. Pausanias, *Description of Greece* 7.18.6/8 ff
7. Ibid 7.13
8. Aeschylus, *Agamemnon* 140–3
9. Pausanias, *Description of Greece* 7.19
10. Stasinus of Cyprus or Hegesias of Aegina, *Cypria* Fragment 1 (from Proclus, *Chrestomathy* 1)
11. Pseudo-Apollodorus, *Bib. Ep* 3.21
12. Euripides, *Iphigenia in Aulis* 308
13. Ibid 360–1
14. Ibid 384
15. Ibid 388–9
16. Ibid 511
17. Ibid 530–1
18. Ibid 533–5

19. Ibid 1465
20. Ibid 1473
21. Euripides, *Iphigenia Among the Taurians* 220
22. Ibid 258–9
23. Ibid 1399ff
24. Pausanias, *Description of Greece* 1.23.7
25. Aristophanes, *Lysistrata* 641–6
26. https://commons.wikimedia.org/wiki/Category:Archaeological_Museum_of _Brauron#/media/File:1δ.jpg
27. Nikita Gill, *Great Goddesses*
28. Callimachus, *Hymn to Artemis* 22–5
29. Pseudo-Apollodorus, *Bibliotheca* 1.4
30. *Homeric Hymn* 9
31. Juvenal, *Satires* X.81
32. Pseudo-Apollodorus, *Epitome* 1.7
33. Pausanias, *Description of Greece* 1.27
34. Suzanne Collins, *The Hunger Games* Chapter 1
35. https://www.theoi.com/Gallery/K6.3.html
36. http://www.perseus.tufts.edu/hopper/artifact?name=Florence+4209&object =Vase
37. https://arthistorians.info/francoisa
38. Homer, *Iliad* 9.537ff
39. Ibid 9.545
40. Ovid, *Metamorphoses* 3.136–7
41. Ibid 3.142
42. Euripides, *Bacchae* 339–40
43. Ovid, *Metamorphoses* 3.155ff
44. Ibid 3.173ff
45. Diodorus Siculus, 4.81.4
46. Pseudo-Apollodorus, *Bibliotheca* 3.4.4
47. Ovid, *Metamorphoses* 3.185
48. Ibid 3.190
49. Ibid 3.198
50. Ibid 3.206
51. Ibid 3.237ff
52. Ibid 3.250
53. https://collections.mfa.org/objects/153654/mixing-bowl-bell-krater-with-the -death-of-aktaion-and-a-pu?ctx=96e19a68-490a-4df3-ae74-eb1ebddf7e15&idx=8
54. *The Death of Actaeon*, National Gallery, London

DEMETER

1. *Homeric Hymn* 2.1ff
2. https://www.jstor.org/stable/3294709, *Cypria* fragment, quoted at *Iliad* 1.5
3. *Homeric Hymn* 2.18
4. https://www.aigai.gr/en
5. http://www.macedonian-heritage.gr/HellenicMacedonia/en/img_C1163a.html
6. https://mymodernmet.com/bernini-the-rape-of-proserpina/
7. *Homeric Hymn* 2.23 If you're wondering if that line might have inspired the olive grove chapters in *Stone Blind*, you'd be correct.
8. Ibid 30
9. Ibid 49–50
10. Ibid 77ff
11. Ibid 159
12. Ibid 189
13. Ibid 203–4
14. Ibid 211
15. Ibid 330
16. Ibid 337–9
17. A. E. Stallings, *This Afterlife*, Carcanet edition p. 4
18. *Homeric Hymn* 2.350
19. Ibid 371
20. Homer, *Odyssey* 11.465ff
21. *Homeric Hymn* 2.375
22. https://www.poetryinternational.com/en/poets-poems/poems/poem/103-23656_Demeter
23. Oliver Thomas, 'Manuscript Readings in *Homeric Hymn to Demeter* 389–479', Ichiro Taida, 'A Chronological Study of the Editions of the *Homeric Hymns*', Zmogus Kalbos Erdveje 8, p. 194
24. *Homeric Hymn* 2.406–33
25. Ibid 410
26. Ibid 4
27. Ibid 434–8
28. Ibid 458–9
29. https://poets.org/poem/pomegranate
30. Hesiod, *Theogony* 969
31. Homer, *Odyssey* 5.119ff
32. https://www.britishmuseum.org/collection/object/G_1816-0610-94
33. *Homeric Hymn* 2.469

34. https://www.britishmuseum.org/collection/object/G_1873-0820-375?fbclid=IwARoz8tCKCrAgN6lZiKAOP8wBuc-b1GzoaAXQWoCxHUYn713Ifs3zxZawkVE

35. https://www.britishmuseum.org/collection/object/G_1859-1226-26

36. Pseudo-Apollodorus, *Bibliotheca* 1.5.3

HESTIA

1. Joan Holub and Suzanne Williams, *Hestia the Invisible*

2. Hesiod, *Theogony* 453ff

3. Ibid 478

4. *The Cambridge Greek Lexicon*, p. 606

5. Homer, *Odyssey* 14.156–9

6. Ibid 18.307

7. Ibid 18.354–5

8. Ibid 19.16–20

9. Ibid 22.481

10. *Homeric Hymn* 29

11. Pergamon Altar, North Frieze, Pergamon Museum, Berlin

12. https://www.britishmuseum.org/collection/object/G_1816-0610-405

13. *Homeric Hymn* 5.7

14. Ibid 21ff

15. Diodorus Siculus, *Library of History* 5.68

16. *Homeric Hymn* 29.7ff

17. Sarah Ruden, *Homeric Hymns*

18. https://www.playmobil.co.uk/hestia/70215.html

19. https://www.theoi.com/Gallery/K13.2.html

20. Callimachus, *Hymn* 6, to Demeter

21. Ibid 6.108

22. https://www.britishmuseum.org/collection/object/G_1971-1101-1

23. Ovid, *Tristia* 2.207

24. Ovid, *Fasti* 4.325ff

25. https://www.theoi.com/Gallery/F39.1.html

26. Ovid, *Fasti* 1.391

27. Propertius, *Elegies* 4.1.21

28. Tacitus, *Annals* 15.44

29. Lactantius, *Divine Institutes* 1.21

30. https://www.pompeiiinpictures.com/pompeiiinpictures/R7/7%2001%2046%2op2.htm

31. https://pompeiiinpictures.com/pompeiiinpictures/R7/7%2012%2011.htm
32. Dionysius of Halicarnassus, *Roman Antiquities* i.54
33. Ibid 57
34. Livy, *Ab Urbe Condita* 1.4
35. Suetonius, *Julius Caesar* 74
36. Cicero, *Pro Murena* 35
37. Pliny the Elder, *Natural History* 28.12
38. https://exhibits.stanford.edu/nash/catalog/pj587fj7368
39. Plato, *Laws* 745b
40. *The Cambridge Greek Lexicon* p. 606
41. Plato, *Cratylus* 400d–401b

ATHENE

1. Pausanias, *Description of Greece* 1.24.4ff
2. https://web.archive.org/web/20160916022900/http://nam.culture.gr/portal/page/portal/deam/virtual_exhibitions/EAMS/EAMG129
3. Pausanias, *Description of Greece* 1.28
4. E.g. Lucian, *Eikones* 4
5. Pausanias, *Description of Greece* 1.14.5
6. Aeschylus, *Eumenides* 736
7. Hesiod, *Theogony* 929
8. Pausanias, *Description of Greece* 1.24.2, 1.24.5, 1.27.1, Pseudo-Apollodorus, *Bibliotheca* 3.14.1
9. Plato, *Phaedo* 109b
10. Plato, Pausanias, *Description of Greece* 1.24.3
11. Ibid 1.27.1
12. *Homeric Hymn 5 to Aphrodite*, 8–11
13. Homer, *Iliad* 1.528
14. Plutarch, *Life of Nicias* 29
15. Homer, *Iliad* 4.21ff
16. Ibid 4.73
17. Ibid 4.130ff
18. Ibid 4.439ff
19. Ibid 5.1–2
20. Ibid 5.908–9
21. Ibid 21.394
22. Ibid 21.408
23. Pseudo-Apollodorus, *Bibliotheca* 2.138

24. Diodorus Siculus, *Library of History* 4.15, 4.27, 5.71
25. Volker Kastner and Huberta Heres, *Der Pergamonaltar* (Philipp von Zabern)
26. Pseudo-Apollodorus, *Bibliotheca* 1.35
27. Homer, *Iliad* 23.754ff
28. Ibid 23.770
29. Ibid 23.782–3
30. E.g. Quintus Smyrnaeus, *Fall of Troy* 13.420–9, Pseudo-Apollodorus, *Epitome* 5
31. Pseudo-Apollodorus, *Epitome* 6, Homer, *Odyssey* 4.499–511
32. Arthur Conan Doyle, *The Sign of Four*
33. Sophocles, *Ajax* 14
34. Ibid 28
35. Ibid 51ff
36. Ibid 79
37. https://www.newyorker.com/culture/culture-desk/theatre-of-war-sophocles
   -message-for-american-veterans
38. Sophocles, *Ajax* 115
39. https://www.uso.org/stories/2664-military-suicide-rates-are-at-an-all-time
   -high-heres-how-were-trying-to-help
40. https://www.npr.org/2021/06/24/1009846329/military-suicides-deaths-mental
   -health-crisis
41. https://theaterofwar.com/projects/theater-of-war
42. Homer, *Odyssey* 1.44-62
43. Ibid 1.63–79
44. Ibid 1.81–95
45. Ibid 1.179–212
46. Ibid 1.214–20
47. Ibid 1.231–51
48. Ibid 1.296–7
49. Ibid 5.21–7
50. Ovid, *Metamorphoses* 6.3–4
51. Ibid 6.9
52. Ibid 6.23
53. Ibid 6.45
54. Ibid 6.101
55. Ibid 6.103–20
56. https://www.nationalgalleries.org/art-and-artists/36168/erigone-deceived
   -bacchus
57. Ovid, *Metamorphoses* 6.122–8

58. Homer, *Odyssey* 15
59. Ovid, *Metamorphoses* 6.129–31
60. Ibid 6.132–45

THE FURIES

1. Virgil, *Aeneid* 4.305
2. Ibid 4.384–7
3. Hesiod, *Theogony* 185
4. Aeschylus, *Eumenides* 321
5. Aeschylus, *Agamemnon* 1189–90
6. Aeschylus, *Choephoroi* 1048–50
7. Ibid 1053–4
8. Aeschylus, *Eumenides* 34
9. Hesiod, *Theogony* 267
10. Aeschylus, *Eumenides* 46–59
11. Ibid 64–84
12. Ibid 200
13. Ibid 212
14. Ibid 253
15. Ibid 308
16. Ibid 333
17. Ibid 407
18. Ibid 415–35
19. Ibid 464
20. Ibid 550–1
21. Ibid 640–3
22. Ibid 694–5
23. Ibid 734–43
24. Ibid 778–92
25. 'I am unaware of any procreation in animals in the last two billion years where a female was not present. Biologists have few rules without exception. This is almost certainly one of them' – Dr Adam Rutherford, WhatsApp conversation with the author.
26. Aeschylus, *Eumenides* 794–807
27. Ibid 842
28. Ibid 848–50
29. Ibid 900
30. Ibid 992
31. Ovid, *Metamorphoses* 10.45–6

32. Pausanias, *Description of Greece* 7.24–5
33. Homer, *Iliad* 19.257, Apollonius, *Argonautica* 4.383
34. Homer, *Iliad* 9.450
35. Ibid 9.565–72
36. Pausanias, *Description of Greece* 10.31, Hyginus 239
37. https://www.britishmuseum.org/collection/object/G_1917-1210-1
38. https://www.theoi.com/Gallery/T21.4.html
39. https://www.theoi.com/Gallery/T40.1.html
40. https://collections.louvre.fr/en/ark:/53355/cl010267176
41. Homer, *Odyssey* 2.130–7

ABOUT THE AUTHOR

NATALIE HAYNES is the author of six books, including the non-fiction work *Pandora's Jar*, which was a *New York Times* bestseller, and the novels *A Thousand Ships*, which was a national bestseller and short-listed for the Women's Prize for Fiction, and *Stone Blind*. She has written and recorded nine series of *Natalie Haynes Stands Up for the Classics* for the BBC. Haynes has written for the *Times*, the *Independent*, *The Guardian*, and the *Observer*. She lives in London.

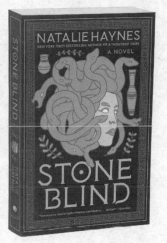
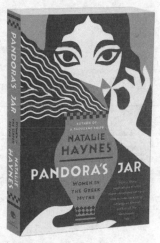
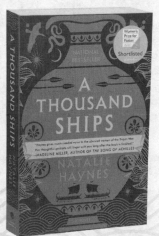